Guide to

SAT®
Writing and Language

by David Lynch

For information, contact StudyLark at info@studylark.com
www.StudyLark.com

Printed in the United States of America

Second edition
ISBN 9798595116251

SAT® is a trademark registered by the College Board, which is not affiliated with, and does not endorse, this publication.

For Hope & Julia

CONTENTS

Introduction 8

How to Improve Your Writing Score 8

The Pillars of Good Preparation 11

Metacognition Questionnaire 18

Verb Form 20

Subject-Verb Agreement 20

Finding the Subject 21

Drill: Ignoring Prepositional Phrases 22

Compound Subjects and Inverted Word Order 22

Drill: Finding Subjects 23

Verb Tense 24

Drill: Using Context to Figure Out Verb Tense 25

Spotting the Question Type 26

Drill: Determining the Question Task 27

Practice Question Set 28

Pronoun & Noun Agreement 32

Pronoun Number Agreement 32

Drill: Finding Antecedents 33

Clear Antecedents 34

Staying Consistent 35

Possessive Pronouns and Contractions 35

Drill: Possessive Pronouns and Contractions 36

Noun Number Agreement 37

Practice Question Set 38

Parallelism & Comparisons..**42**

  Parallelism 42

    Drill: Completing a List 45

  Correlative Conjunctions.. 46

  Comparisons.. 47

    Drill: Demonstrative Pronouns in Comparisons........ 48

    Drill: Using Formal Structures in Comparisons...........51

  Practice Question Set.. 54

Punctuation...**60**

  Semicolons 60

    Drill: Semicolons 60

  Colons 61

    Drill: Colons 62

  Dashes 63

    Drill: Dashes 64

  Apostrophes 65

    Drill: Apostrophes 67

  Quotation Marks... 68

    Drill: Commas with Quotes 69

  Parentheses 70

  Question Marks... 72

  Exclamation Points 72

  Commas 73

    Drill: Coordinate and Cumulative Adjectives.............. 76

    Drill: Names and Titles 78

  Commas Gone Bad... 80

    Drill: Finding Comma Errors.. 82

  Practice Question Set..84

Sentence Structure Part 1: Clauses..**92**

Coordinating Conjunctions 93

Subordinating Conjunctions..94

Relative Pronouns...95

Joining Clauses with Punctuation.....................................101

   Drill: Finding Clauses & Connectors 102

Clauses Gone Bad..103

   Drill: Connecting Clauses 106

Sentence Structure Part 2: Phrases **108**

Prepositional Phrases 108

Appositive Phrases...110

   Drill: Finding Appositive Phrases..............................111

Gerunds 112

Participles 113

Infinitives 114

Distinguishing Verbs from Verbals.................................114

   Drill: Distinguishing Verbs from Verbals..................115

Verbal Phrases 116

   Drill: Introductory Modifiers....................................120

Absolute Phrases...121

Fixing Clause Problems Using Phrases...........................123

Beware of *Being*..124

Combining Sentences...125

   Drill: Combining Sentences......................................129

Practice Question Set...132

Word Choice **146**

Required Words 146

Vocabulary 148

Style and Tone 150

Commonly Confused Words...151

Practice Question Set...152

Redundancy **156**

    Practice Question Set.. 158

Introductions, Transitions & Conclusions **162**

    Transition Words 163

    Introductions, Conclusions & Transition Sentences 167

    Practice Question Set.. 170

Specific Tasks **180**

    Drill: Specific Tasks...181

    Practice Question Set.. 184

Organization **190**

    Drill: Hooking up Sentences... 192

    Practice Question Set.. 196

Adding or Removing Information **206**

    Drill: Evaluating Reasons 210

    Practice Question Set.. 212

Figures & Tables...**222**

    Practice Question Set.. 224

Putting It All Together **234**

    Drill: Identifying Question Types................................... 235

    Final Summary of All the Rules....................................... 239

    Drill: Final Summary of All the Rules 243

Appendix: Grammar Reference Guide **246**

Answers..**250**

❧ Introduction ❧

How to Improve Your Writing Score

This book contains everything you need to know for the SAT Writing and Language section. It's based on years of research, and it provides clear, detailed explanations for all the rules and techniques, along with hundreds of drill and practice questions. We've done our part.

Now it's your turn.

The bad news about the SAT is that it really takes a lot of hard work to achieve mastery. The rules are here in this book, but they won't do you much good unless you put in the many hours it takes to understand, internalize, and master them. You can't cram for the SAT. You have to dedicate yourself to the lengthy process of doing mountains of practice, and you have to make sure you're learning from each question—gaining insights, noticing patterns, and building the skills you need to answer future questions. It takes time and effort. There are no shortcuts. In a nutshell, get ready to work.

But the good news is that, with the right preparation materials, *all* it takes is a lot of hard work to make a big difference in your score. It's not magic. The test is repetitive and predictable, and while it covers a non-trivial amount of material, it's a finite amount of material. After enough practice, you'll start to see the same types of questions over and over, and getting them right will become a matter of reflex. The points are yours for the taking. If you put in the work to master the content, you can improve your score considerably.

The process for getting really good at the SAT writing section looks like this. First you have to achieve **proficiency**:

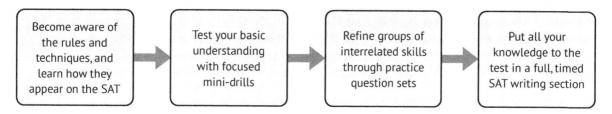

The first three steps are the main concern of this book. This is where you'll learn about everything that shows up on the SAT, and we'll do our best to give you the **knowledge** you need to master it.

But after you've achieved proficiency with that knowledge, you'll have to *keep* working to reach **mastery**. To do that, you need lots of **practice**:

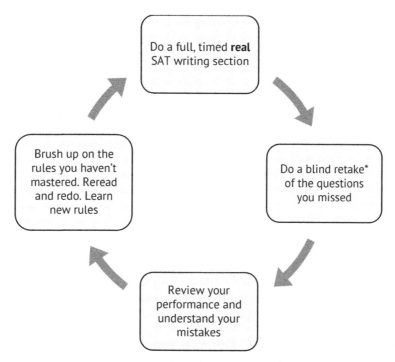

The cornerstone of your practice must be real SAT writing sections. This book has hundreds of practice drills and questions, and they are carefully written to be as realistic as possible. But it does not contain simulated full writing sections, and that is very much on purpose. **There is no substitute for the real thing.** No strategy book or website in the world has questions as good as those on the real SAT. Don't practice on fake tests. To get good, use the good stuff.

---

* Blind retakes are explained on page 15

There are several dozen real SAT and PSAT tests that you can use, which should be enough for even the most thorough study regimen. Some tests are available for free download from the College Board website. Others have been released to the public by the College Board after official test administrations—these are known as "QAS" tests. They can be found online without too much trouble, and any decent tutor will be able to provide copies as well.

> PSATs are just as good as SATs when it comes to practicing for the Writing and Language section.

The SAT has been slowly evolving since its modern format was introduced in 2015. This evolution includes changes to the test content and especially the scoring scales. Thus, the most recent tests are most representative of what you can expect to see on your test day. Use the freshest tests you can get.

If you somehow manage to do every single real test in existence, then what? Should you do the fake tests in commercially available books? We advise against it. It's probably better to just go back and do the same real tests over again. Fake tests can't give you reliable scores anyway, so it's not as if you're missing out on accurate information about how your score is moving.

Students often can't tell the difference, but after years of living and breathing the SAT, we've never seen fake questions that weren't "off" in some subtle (or egregious) way. And there's nothing worse than banging your head against the wall trying to figure out what your mistake is on a question you don't understand, only to find out that the question is poorly written. You don't want to practice using material that isn't representative of what you'll see on test day.

Use the good stuff.

Basic Information

We assume you've got a basic understanding of what the SAT Writing and Language section looks like. So we won't go into detail explaining the mechanics of how the section is structured and how the questions work. If you've never seen a test before, go to the College Board website, download one, and take a look.

We also assume you understand basic grammar terms such as *noun* and *preposition*. But if you're a little rusty, take a look at the appendix on page 246 for a refresher.

The Pillars of Good Preparation

You've got real tests and the right book, and you're ready to work hard. But you also have to make sure you're studying the right way. These are the pillars of good preparation.

Think About the Process Before You Start

All too often, students just jump mindlessly into studying before they have even strategized what to use, without understanding why they are using each resource, and without planning out how they would use the resource to learn effectively. This undermines their own potential to learn well and perform well.

Metacognition is the awareness and understanding of one's own thought processes. Studies have shown that those who reflect on how they want to perform and what they need to do outperform those who do not. The questionnaire on page 18 will help lead you through the metacognitive process.

Establish Good Habits

You're going to do a lot of practice questions, but there is more to preparation than burning through questions. You have to make sure you're getting a good return on your investment each time you sit down to do work. When you understand the pillars listed below, turn them into **habits**. Make sure your study sessions are scheduled, consistent, organized, and deliberate.

Eliminate Distractions

In a recent study, researchers asked subjects to complete a series of tests that required serious concentration to score highly. All the volunteers were told to put their phones in silent, non-vibrating mode or turn them off. Some were asked to put the phone face down on the desk, some kept the phone hidden in a pocket or bag, and others put the phone in another room.

The participants who left their phones in another room **significantly outperformed** those with their phones on the desk, and even outperformed those with their phones in a pocket or a bag. The researchers demonstrated that phones within sight or within easy reach inevitably use up some of our brainpower as we try not to be distracted. In a follow-up survey, the participants themselves didn't feel the location of their phones had any effect on their ability to concentrate on the test. But their cognitive capacity was reduced even without their noticing.

Other research has clearly established that phones, music, television, noise, and other distractions drain energy, decrease performance, and hinder long-term retention and learning. When you study, put yourself in a situation in which the one and only thing available for your attention is the SAT.

Remember: **multitasking is the enemy of accuracy.** The best way to get things done right is through monotasking. This applies to studying and practicing, and even to question and section strategy within the test. Your mantra should be, "Do one thing until it's done."

Know the Purpose of Untimed Practice

This book contains some practice questions sets that are to be completed without time limits. What's the point of doing SAT questions without a timer when the real test has a ticking clock? Your goal is to build accuracy and transferrable skills. That means a big part of what you do must be process-driven. Getting the right answer is meaningless if it came from a wild guess. Instead, you want to make sure you're correctly identifying the issue being tested, correctly recalling the relevant grammar or stylistic rules, and eliminating wrong choices for concrete reasons, not just because they "sound wrong." You want to look for patterns that you can apply to future questions, and notice similarities between the question and others you have seen in the past. When you're down to two choices, you want to keep scrutinizing them until the right answer becomes crystal clear, not just a hunch. If this process takes 10 minutes per question, then so be it. Don't worry about trying to drive speed—speed comes through repetition, not through rushing.

Take Practice Tests as if They Are the Real Thing

It's easy to slack off a little on a practice test and tell yourself that you'll really be locked in when the real thing comes around. For example, you may allow some distractions, be loose with the timing and breaks, eat or drink during the test, not make the extra effort to fully think through a question, or end a section early without using the remaining time to check your work.

It's true that you'll probably get an adrenaline surge when the real test comes, and it's true that such a surge might help your score. But it's a mistake to count on that surge putting you over the top if you haven't been practicing as if each practice test were the real thing.

The hardest thing to control might be your schedule—sometimes you'll be unable to avoid having to do a test late at night or in pieces. That's life. It's better to do a test across several days than to skip it.

But you should definitely carve out as many occasions as you can in which you simulate the real testing experience as closely as possible. Do the test on a Saturday morning when you're well-rested, well-fed, appropriately caffeinated, and undistracted. Get amped up and trick yourself into thinking that you're taking the real test. Imagine that *this is the score* you're going to submit to colleges.

It's a mistake to think you'll do things right for the first time on test day if you haven't been doing them right beforehand. If you skip steps now, you'll skip them later. Cut corners now, you'll cut them later. You get used to what you do most of the time.

Do Concrete Things to Eliminate Careless Errors

Everybody makes careless errors. They're one of the most frustrating parts of the SAT. A careless error is the worst way to lose a point because you really *knew* what you were doing, and you should have gotten credit for the question—but you didn't.

Careless mistakes are probably more common on the math sections of the test, but they happen on the verbal portion as well. When people realize they've made a silly mistake, the first response is frustration and annoyance, of course. That's usually followed closely by one of two responses. Sometimes, people just mentally give themselves "credit" for the question.

"OK, I bubbled C when the answer was B, but I really knew what they were testing! I just overlooked something, or I mis-bubbled. I don't need to study or worry about this because I *would have* gotten it right..."

The second common response is to say, "Well yes, I got it wrong, but that's only because it was practice, so I was rushing or not paying very close attention. When the real test comes, I'll be more locked in, and I'll be more careful." The promise to *be more careful* is such an easy thing to say, and such a hard thing to do. But you can take steps to make it happen.

For one thing, you need to get into the habit of practicing as if it's the real test, as we just discussed. Second, there are actually **concrete things** you can do to help minimize careless mistakes, and you need to make these practices a habit.

- ⊙ **Circle your answer on the page.** This is probably the single most effective thing you can do to eliminate bubbling errors. It gives you a written record of what you were thinking, so if something gets off with your bubbling, you don't have to rethink any questions to get back on track. It also allows you to double-check your bubble sheet.

- ⊙ **Transfer your answers to the bubble sheet in batches.** Do a full page or two facing pages, and then fill in all your answers on the bubble sheet at once.

- ⊙ **Double-check your bubbles and the question numbers.** Once you've filled in a batch of bubbles, double-check right away. Read your answers off the bubble sheet and then make sure they match the test booklet (in other words, transfer your answers "back" from the bubble sheet to the booklet). At the same time, make sure the question numbers match up. Check everything again at the end of the section.

- ⊙ **Articulate a reason for eliminating each wrong choice.** Don't get rid of things because they "sound wrong." Name the grammar, logical, or stylistic rule that the choice violates. If you can't do this for every wrong choice, then you don't know the rules well enough yet, so keep studying!

- ⊙ **Cross out wrong answers.** Don't just cross out the letter; draw a line through the entire choice.

- ⊙ **Don't rush through the easy questions.** And by the time you know all the rules, they should all be easy questions, so this becomes, "don't rush at all." Unless you're scoring perfectly, it's better to finish with no time left over—or even to run out of time before you've answered all the questions—than to finish early. Slow down and focus on accuracy.

- ⊙ **When the question asks you to do something specific, <u>underline</u> what it's asking for.** Don't answer the wrong question or misunderstand what they want you to do.

Know the Rules and Techniques

People who write test preparation books (like this one!) love to categorize things and list seemingly endless rules. It can be easy for a student to dismiss all this labeling as an exercise in pedantry without any practical implications for how to approach the test. Does it *really* matter whether a conjunction is coordinating or subordinating? Is it *worth* caring about whether an action word is a verb or a participle? Is there *really* anything wrong with just going by ear?

In short, YES! The SAT is an incredibly predictable and rule-based test, which is to your advantage—if you know the rules. These rules are not extraneous to the real-time approach. The theory and techniques associated with each question type should be the things running through your mind every time you sit down to do a new set of questions. It's not enough to just pick whatever choice "sounds right."

The easiest way to get a question wrong is to misunderstand what the test writers are asking you to do. Your ultimate goal is to develop a process whereby whenever you see a question on a test, you correctly identify what it's testing, and a summary of all the relevant grammar rules and stylistic techniques immediately pops into your head. When that starts happening, you'll know you're approaching true SAT expertise.

> When we say **stylistic techniques**, we're talking about what the SAT calls **Expression of Ideas**. These questions ask about writing strategy, organization, style, and the flow of ideas within the passage, not grammar.

Think Ahead

Expert SAT takers are always thinking ahead. This means **pausing** as you work to anticipate and predict what will come next.

Did you just read the title of a passage? Before you jump into the reading, think about what the passage is likely to be about.

Did you just finish reading a paragraph? Before you dive into the next one, think about what happened in that paragraph and how it's likely to relate to the next one.

Most importantly, did you just encounter a question? Before you dive into the choices, figure out what issue the question is testing and what rules you'll need to use to answer it. Then **identify the error** in choice A (if there is one) and **predict** how you would fix it. This gives you a target to seek in the choices.

Pausing as you work to think ahead is an investment of time. But that investment will pay off with increased accuracy and speed when you allow your brain to absorb the information you've just read. When you plunge ahead without letting the question content sink in, you create extra work for yourself because each answer choice becomes something you have to consider and think through. If you instead have a target already in mind, right answers jump off the page and wrong ones can be quickly discarded.

Aim for Quantity

Much of the discussion so far has been about good *quality* preparation.

The sad truth about SAT prep is that you're going to need a hefty dose of **quantity** too. Doing 2 or 3 practice tests before the real thing is simply not enough. To achieve real mastery, you need to get through dozens of full, real practice tests and hundreds of drill questions.

The SAT is indeed repetitive, but it covers a non-trivial amount of information. You'll need to do lots of practice before you start noticing the same patterns repeating themselves.

The first few times you work on a skill, you're going to be slow and inaccurate. It's only when you see something for the 100th time that it becomes second nature. When you reach the point where every new SAT question seems eerily familiar, you're getting close. Your ultimate goal is to experience some serious déjà vu when you sit down for the real test: "This stupid question again?! I've seen these all before!" That's when you know you're prepared.

Start to study well in advance of the test administration, and set aside enough time each week for practice. This raises an important question: **what is enough?**

The answer depends on what you need from the SAT. When we first meet students, we always ask what score they're aiming for. The question often surprises people. The obvious answers that spring to mind are "as high as possible" or "1600—what else?" But these answers miss the point of what the SAT is for.

The SAT is simply a tool, and the purpose of that tool is to get you into the college of your choice. If a 1300 would make you a competitive candidate at the college of your choice, then aiming for a 1600 is foolish because there is a serious cost in aiming for a 1600. You would have to put your life on hold and dedicate all your time to studying for the SAT. Why do that if you don't need to? It would be like using a backhoe to plant petunias.

If you're scoring about average and need a 50-point boost to your writing score, a half-dozen practice tests along with some of the low-hanging fruit grammar topics will probably be enough. If you're looking for some quick grammar rules that can easily give you a little boost, check out the first four chapters of this book, along with the chapter on Redundancy.

On the other hand, you might be aiming for a highly competitive school or even one of the top few schools in the country. In that case, you still don't need a 1600, but you might need to be well above 1500. If that's your situation, then you really do need absolute mastery of the writing section, and that calls for maximum quantity. Set a goal of doing 20-30 practice tests and working through this book two or three times. Do as much as possible, up until the point of diminishing returns. When your brain is full, you're bleary-eyed, and the words are just washing over you, then stop, sleep, and get up and do it again.

Practice Blind Retakes

Whenever you complete a practice question set or test, you'll of course need to check how you performed. The whole purpose of practice is to learn from your mistakes. To that end, the first part of your review should be to do **blind retakes** of the questions you missed.

To carry out a blind retake, mark in your book or on your test which questions you got wrong, but **do not indicate the correct answer**. (You'll have to grade your work in chunks, instead of checking each question as you complete it, to avoid letting the right answer stick in your mind and spoil the exercise. You could even recruit a friend to help.)

Then give yourself a chance to come back and work the question again, knowing that your initial response is wrong, but not knowing which of the three remaining choices is right. There will be many occasions in which you will have narrowed the choices down to two, but if the one you picked was wrong, don't automatically assume the other must be right. Begin the question again and work it through fully.

This allows you to consider the question from a different angle and, crucially, to discover your own mistakes. That's an important part of the learning process.

Once you've tried the question a second time, you can check the right answer and continue with your analysis of the question.

Do a Thorough Performance Analysis

It's not enough to just burn through practice questions. You have to extract something from your work that you can apply to future questions.

As we mentioned earlier, counting the number of questions you get right or wrong in each test and homework set is only a small part of the picture. A larger concern is increasing your understanding of every detail of each question. Go back to each question and examine it closely, whether you got it right or wrong. What additional patterns do you notice? Can you articulate how the grammar or the logic works, and can you spot new details that you didn't see the first time? Can you point to the exact reason why each incorrect choice is wrong? Can you see a more efficient path you could have followed to get the right answer?

An important consideration is that you don't want to simply get to the point where you can accept the right answer. Saying to yourself, "Well, I thought it was D but they wanted B— I guess I can buy that B is an OK choice too," is **not good enough**. Instead, you must get to the point at which it becomes **crystal clear** why your choice is absolutely 100% wrong, and the correct choice is utterly and completely right. You have to say to yourself, "Oh. My. God. How could I be so foolish as to pick D?! It is now unmistakably obvious that B is right!"

There are some questions for which you won't be able to reach that level of understanding on your own. That brings us to...

Use Tutoring Sessions Effectively

If you're working with a tutor, it's essential to get the most out of the sessions. This is what I tell my students:

One of the great advantages of personalized individual tutoring is that we can identify your specific weaknesses and address them in an effective way. I can examine your particular methods of reasoning on a question and see where they fell short. I can propose a fix that is aimed at your exact mistake, and if it doesn't click, I can try to present the same idea in a different way that may make better sense to you. We can move at the right pace and give each topic exactly as much time as it needs.

So don't waste that valuable opportunity! When we start each tutoring session, I'll ask if you have any lingering questions from the homework. I'm hoping that you'll have a list of questions that you reviewed thoroughly but still don't feel perfectly clear on. Those represent the most valuable learning opportunities because they identify manifest gaps in your knowledge and abilities, and fixing those gaps will produce a meaningful step forward in your capacity to get a better score.

It's often the highest-scoring students who have the longest lists of questions. When someone scoring near the middle reports that they don't have any questions, it makes me think one of three things is true:

- The person doesn't have any questions because they didn't do the homework at all
- The person doesn't have any questions because they didn't do a thorough review of their work
- The person is pretending that everything in the homework made perfect sense in an effort to please me or make me think that they're progressing beautifully

Impressing me should be the least of your concerns. I'll see that you're progressing beautifully when your score starts going up! My one and only goal is to help you get the score you want, and the best way to do that is to identify your problematic areas so we can work on them together.

> **Looking for a tutor?**
> There are great tutors all over the country. You can even work online with David Lynch, author of this book and founder of StudyLark—go to StudyLark.com for details. We can also provide guidance on how to find a good local tutor or an online study group.

Revisit Old Material

Some people make it through all the real practice tests and wonder what to do next. The best strategy is to do the same tests again! Of course, when you revisit old material, you may remember some of the passages or questions, which would skew your score. So the point of repeating an assignment is not to get a representative or predictive score out of it. Instead, the act of retracing the same familiar pathways reinforces your knowledge and allows you to discover lingering bad habits or areas of weakness. You don't even have to wait until you've done all the tests to start revisiting. You can go back and redo things at any time.

You'd expect to get a higher score when doing the same test a second time—but did you? Were there some questions you got wrong both times? Those are especially important to study. How about something you got right the first time but missed the second time? What changed? Was the first time just luck?

It's a great idea to revisit previous chapters, drills, and practice question sets in this book as well. As the test approaches, go back and take a second look at some of the earliest topics you worked on. That was material you completed when your level of expertise was lowest. So how do you fare on those same crucial questions now that you're more experienced?

You can also pick out individual questions to set aside for later review. Flag anything from a question set or a test that really gave you a lot of trouble. Get an explanation for it, and then look at it a week later. Can you re-create the solution and justification for it yourself? Keep revisiting the question until you can.

Metacognition Questionnaire

Sit down with a pencil and take the time to write out your answers to the following questions.

Which colleges are you targeting? _____

What SAT score do you need in order to be
competitive with other applicants to those schools? _____

How likely do you think it is that you will get that score? _____

How important to you is it that you get that score? _____

What aspects of the SAT do you think will be most challenging for you?

_____

What aspects of SAT *preparation* do you think will be most challenging for you?

_____

How will you address these challenges? What will you do when you encounter a setback?

_____

If you have prepared for a standardized test like this before, how can you do a better job this time around?

_____

What are the first few goals you want to accomplish at the beginning of your preparation?

_____

What habits should you cultivate as you prepare to best support your learning?

_____

What should you *avoid* doing as you prepare?

_____

What strategies will you use to study?

_____

How much time (per week and overall) do you plan to devote to studying?

_____

Where and when will you study?

_____

How are you going to actively monitor your progress?

_____

What information will you seek in order to learn whether your progress is on track or needs adjustment?

_____

What are the different components and steps of your study plan?

_____

What is the purpose or goal of each of those components or steps?

_____

What resources do you need to prepare for the SAT?

_____

How will each resource be useful, and how will you make sure you're getting the most out of it?

_____

๑ Verb Form ๑

Subject-Verb Agreement

Whenever you see a question that gives you several options for an underlined verb, you have to figure out the right **form** of the verb. This means checking for verb **agreement** and for verb **tense**.

What do we mean by verb agreement? This means that the verb has to match the subject's **person** and **number**. On the SAT, you'll really only have to pay attention to number. You have to ensure that singular subjects get singular verbs, and plural subjects get plural verbs.

> Ensuring the right **person** means saying "she is" instead of "she am," for example. This isn't really tested on the SAT.

Sounds easy, right? Well, the test writers have a few tricks to make this task more difficult. Their main trick is to put the subject and verb far apart from each other in the sentence and to stick a bunch of distracting nouns—especially ones with a different number—in between to make you misidentify the subject. Let's take a look:

> ☒ Pollution from cars in cities where people have long commutes <u>worsen</u> on hot days.

The verb in this example is *worsen*. What's the subject for that verb? There are lots of plural nouns floating around, but the actual subject is the singular noun *pollution*. If you put the subject immediately next to the verb, it becomes easy to see that they don't match. Would you say *pollution worsen*? That sounds all kinds of wrong. The correct verb, of course, is *worsens*:

> Throughout this book, we'll use ☒ next to examples sentences that have an error, and ☑ next to those that are completely correct.

> ☑ Pollution from cars in cities where people have long commutes <u>worsens</u> on hot days.

Once you've found the subject, putting it right next to the verb is a great trick. Your ear will always tell you whether they match. (This is easier than asking yourself whether the verb is singular or plural. That's because singular verbs, such as *worsens*, often end in -s, which confuses the heck out of people.)

Finding the Subject

Picking the right verb once you've found the subject is actually the easy part. The hard part is **finding** the subject in the first place. The test writers will insert all sorts of misleading words in an effort to sidetrack you. But your secret weapon is this: **cross out** any prepositional phrases, parenthetical comments, or extra clauses. None of them can contain the subject. Pay extra close attention to prepositional phrases, because it's an unbreakable grammar law that **nothing inside a prepositional phrase can ever be the subject of the sentence**. Get those things out of there!

For example, in our sentence above, how did we know that the subject was *pollution* and not something else, such as *cars*, *cities*, *people*, or *commutes*? The answer is that all those words appear inside prepositional phrases or modifying clauses.

Some Common Prepositions:	
of	by
in	at
to	from
for	as
with	into
on	about
Find a longer list on page 108	

- ⊙ *from cars*   - prepositional phrase
- ⊙ *in cities*   - prepositional phrase
- ⊙ *where people have long commutes* - modifying clause

If you cross out all those sentence elements, the only sensible thing left to be the subject is *pollution*.

That's the grammatical method for finding the subject: use your knowledge of phrases and clauses to eliminate things that can't be the subject. Unfortunately, people don't always have a great command of phrases and clauses, so you may not be able to use this technique with complete accuracy (yet). But there is another technique you can also try: the **logic method**.

To use the logic method, find the verb and then ask yourself, "Which noun is actually *doing* this action?" Use logic and common sense, and if there is only one reasonable possibility, you've found the subject.

In our example, it doesn't make sense to say that *cars* are worsening, or that *cities* are worsening, or that *people* are worsening. Thus, none of those nouns can be the subject. It is, however, possible that *commutes* could worsen, so that's why the logic method isn't foolproof. You'll probably want to use a mixture of grammar and logic to find subjects.

Drill: Ignoring Prepositional Phrases

Find and cross out all the prepositional phrases in the sentences below. If you need more information about recognizing and understanding prepositional phrases, look ahead to the chapter on phrases.

1. The degree program is open to graduates in all fields of engineering.

2. Request–reply is a method whereby a first computer sends a request for data and a second responds to the request.

3. Saraswati remained significant as a goddess from the Vedic period through the modern era of Hindu traditions.

4. He often employs elements from his own life in his work, and he has incorporated representations of himself throughout the series painted for the most recent exhibition.

> Ignoring prepositional phrases is useful when you're looking for a verb's subject. But if a question asks you to complete some different task, then you may need to pay attention to the prepositional phrases.

5. The ruins of Basima Castle, located near the cliffs above a waterfall, were converted to a tourist attraction in 2002.

6. Julia Chandler made her living as a writer, submitting frequent papers on horticultural and agricultural practices to the principal periodicals of the day.

> Answers to all drills are found at the back of the book, starting on page 250.

Compound Subjects and Inverted Word Order

The test writers have some other tricks up their sleeves as well. Something else that can affect verb agreement is a **compound subject**. A compound subject is composed of two or more nouns working together for a single verb. The nouns are typically joined by a conjunction or presented as a list. A compound subject is **always plural**, even if the nouns within it are singular. Here's an example:

❌ Its rising <u>population</u> and confined <u>geography</u> <u>has impacted</u> the city's home prices.

The verb is *has impacted*, and the two nouns associated with it are *population* and *geography*. Use the ear test again, and to make it even more clear, replace *population and geography* with the phrase *two things*. Would you say *two things **has** impacted*? Not unless you were crazy. Saying *two things **have** impacted* makes a lot more sense. The correct version is:

☑ Its rising <u>population</u> and confined <u>geography</u> <u>have impacted</u> the city's home prices.

Another possible trick is the use of **inverted word order**. This occurs when the subject appears **after** the verb. A sentence with inverted word order will often begin with a bunch of prepositional phrases. If you cross them all out, there won't be anything left in front of the verb that could act as the subject. This indicates that the subject must follow the verb.

☑ Around the edge of the bay <u>were</u> the <u>cottages</u> of local fishermen.

☑ There <u>is</u> no <u>reason</u> to buy a robot to mow a lawn the size of yours.

As you can see from the second example above, another situation with inverted word order is a sentence that begins with *there is* or *there are*. The word *there* is an adverb; it can't be the subject. So you have to look after the verb to see whether the subject is singular or plural.

Drill: Finding Subjects

*Each sentence below has one verb marked in **bold** (it may have other verbs as well). Circle the subject of the **marked** verb. In some cases, there is a compound subject, so be sure to circle all parts of it.*

1. The challenges of raising a child without any help from nearby family **have taught** me much about resilience.

2. Margo, like the managers who held the position before her, **came** into the job full of optimism and new ideas.

3. Released earliest in the year **are** the wines made from white grapes.

4. On the album's first track, the bass and the piano **begin** the song, followed by the guitar.

5. In checkers, a move in which a player jumps several opposing pieces to land in one of the back rows **can turn** the tide of the game.

6. Hexagons, triangles, or squares arranged in a repeating pattern **will cover** a surface completely, a phenomenon known as tiling the plane.

7. Into the buckets under the eaves **fell** the rain from the summer storms.

8. The languages spoken in regions as far from each other as southern India and the western part of Europe **derive** from a single common ancestor.

9. There **is** one main area in the region prone to flooding, located to the west of town and inconveniently close to the only highway.

10. Olivia Barber, a chef and entrepreneur with restaurants in several cities across the country, **took** home the top prize.

Verb Tense

There are lots of different verb tenses in the English language, and lots of rules governing them. Luckily, you don't really need to spend a lot of time memorizing all those categories and detailed rules. Questions about verb tense on the SAT are mostly about looking at the **context** of the passage and picking a verb tense that makes **logical sense** with the flow of ideas within the story.

OK, so we must admit—there are in fact a couple of rules that are probably worth knowing. You should know when to use **present perfect** vs. simple past. And you should know when the **past perfect** tense is appropriate.

A perfect tense is one that uses *have*, *has*, or *had* as a helper (auxiliary) verb before the main verb. Present perfect uses *have* or *has*, and past perfect uses *had*.

There are several situations in which present perfect is commonly used, but the most important rule here is that present perfect makes sense when you're talking about an **unspecified** time in the past, but the simple past tense should be used when the time is specified.

Unspecified time – present perfect	Specified time – simple past
☑ The committee <u>has chosen</u> the winner.	☑ The committee <u>chose</u> the winner yesterday.
☑ They <u>have opened</u> the doors to the dining room.	☑ They <u>opened</u> the doors to the dining room at 5 p.m.
☑ She <u>has received</u> an honorary doctorate from her alma mater.	☑ She <u>received</u> an honorary doctorate when she spoke at the commencement.

The past perfect (using the auxiliary verb *had*) is appropriate when you're talking about **two different times** in the past. The past perfect indicates which of the two times occurred in the **more distant past**, while the simple past indicates the more recent past.

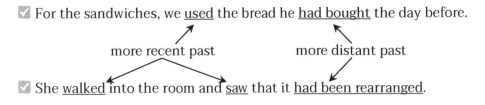

☑ For the sandwiches, we <u>used</u> the bread he <u>had bought</u> the day before.

more recent past   more distant past

☑ She <u>walked</u> into the room and <u>saw</u> that it <u>had been rearranged</u>.

In the first example, he bought the bread **before** we used it. In the second, the room was rearranged **before** she saw it. So the past perfect tense indicates the more distant time in the past.

But for the most part, getting verb tense questions right is more about looking at the nearby verbs and thinking about the story in the passage. You have to **reason** your way to the right answer based on contextual clues. Remember: the choice you pick doesn't necessarily have to use the exact same tense as every verb around it. It's perfectly normal for a story to use a variety of tenses in adjacent sentences. Finding the right answer is more about the logic of the situation than about blindly matching up tenses.

Drill: Using Context to Figure Out Verb Tense

Each question below has a blank and is followed by four options for a verb to fill in the blank. Look at the context of the story and circle the appropriate verb.

1. In 2016, an earthquake opened one of the volcano's long-blocked magma tubes. The chamber filled with molten rock, some of which seeped through an opening to the surface and _____ to flow down the side of the mountain.
   begins / began / will begin / had begun

2. The new study followed 8,375 people over the course of five years, tracking cardiovascular health and overall mortality rate. It found no benefit to using a standing desk, which came as a surprise to researchers, since previous studies _____ that prolonged periods of sitting were associated with negative health outcomes.
   show / showing / had shown / will show

3. The course taught us some of the science behind baking. A longer mixing time builds a stronger network of gluten in the dough. Leavening agents _____ gases that make the dough rise. And sugars are responsible for browning and many other flavors beyond simple sweetness.
   release / released / will release / have released

4. There are many sources of information about great authors, but typically historians _____ primarily on the text of the authors' own papers and the accounts left behind by their contemporaries. New techniques, however, are allowing scientists to pull proteins and other molecules from the documents themselves, adding additional details to our understanding of these figures' lives.
   are relying / have relied / will rely / relying

> A word ending in *-ing* cannot be a verb unless it is preceded by an auxiliary verb— specifically some form of *to be*. For example, *walking* cannot by itself be a verb, but *is walking*, *were walking*, or *will be walking* could all be valid verb phrases.

Spotting the Question Type

You have a different job to do depending on whether a verb-related question is testing agreement or tense. If it's verb agreement, you have to **find the subject** before you can answer. But if it's verb tense, you have to look for surrounding **contextual clues**. So figuring out the question task is an important first step.

Luckily, the test writers often make it easy to determine the question type based on some patterns that show up in the answer choices.

If a question is testing subject-verb agreement, you will almost always see two choices with:

- ⊙ the same verb
- ⊙ in the same tense, with
- ⊙ different number (one singular and the other plural)

If you see that pattern, go find the subject immediately. For example:

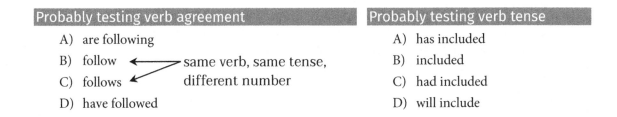

Probably testing verb agreement	Probably testing verb tense
A) are following	A) has included
B) follow	B) included
C) follows	C) had included
D) have followed	D) will include

same verb, same tense, different number

On the other hand, if all the choices use different tenses, then the question is most likely testing verb tense.

There is also another clue to look for in agreement questions. Usually, three of the choices will use one number (plural, for example), and the fourth choice will use a different number (singular). If so, the answer is likely to be the **odd one out**. In the example above, choices A, B, and D (*are following, follow,* and *have followed*) are all plural, while choice C (*follows*) is the only singular verb. So choice C would probably be correct.

> This "odd-one-out" pattern can be helpful, but don't trust it blindly. Ultimately, you can only determine the right answer by finding the subject. You can't get out of doing that.

Drill: Determining the Question Task

Each question below shows a set of four answer choices from an SAT question. Based on the pattern described above, determine whether the question is more likely testing verb agreement or verb tense, and circle the appropriate option.

1. A) changes
   B) has changed   More likely to be testing:
   C) change   Verb agreement / Verb tense
   D) change's

2. A) lose
   B) lost
   C) will lose   Verb agreement / Verb tense
   D) are losing

3. A) has stood
   B) have been standing
   C) are standing   Verb agreement / Verb tense
   D) have stood

4. A) draws
   B) drew
   C) will draw   Verb agreement / Verb tense
   D) has drawn

5. A) returns
   B) reciprocates
   C) yields
   D) replies

   Trick question! Sort of. Question 5 is likely to be testing **word choice** not verb form. That's because you're given a bunch of **different** verbs, all with the same number and tense. Verb form questions will instead give you multiple versions of the **same** verb.

Practice Question Set

The questions in the following practice set test **verb form**. *Work on the set without time limits—focus on accuracy alone.*

The questions are in the style of real SAT questions, but the formatting is slightly different. Instead of presenting the passage on the left side and the question on the right, we include the relevant sentence(s) from the passage immediately above the answer choices. The underlined text works the same as it does on the SAT—you may choose to leave it unchanged, or you may choose to replace it with a different alternative from the answer choices.

We've worked hard to make these practice questions as realistic as possible. Each one is closely modeled after a real, specific test question and addresses the same grammar topics in the same way. With that in mind, however, remember that **there is no substitute for the real thing**. *No strategy book in the world has questions as good as those on the real SAT, so it's vitally important to make sure* **real tests are a central part of your preparation**.

1

Some of the first acts of Congress, including one that regulates the manner of administering an oath of office, <u>remains</u> in effect today.

A) NO CHANGE

B) remaining

C) remain

D) has remained

2

A genetic analysis by a team of molecular anthropologists, led by population geneticist Chuan-Chao Wang of Xiamen University in China, <u>provide</u> the best look yet at the herders' genetic history.

A) NO CHANGE

B) provides

C) are providing

D) have provided

3

Data from the investigation helped Parrish convince the city councilmembers that they could reduce expenditures for the public works department if recycling rules were modernized. Encouraged by these possible savings, officials <u>implemented</u> a new single-stream recycling program.

A) NO CHANGE

B) were implementing

C) had implemented

D) would be implementing

4

Most of the original homemade circuit boards no longer function, as replacement parts have become impossible to find, but others <u>had worked</u> perfectly well.

A) NO CHANGE

B) work

C) worked

D) could have worked

5

Advocates of vitamin D would add that, besides bone strength, <u>their are</u> several additional health benefits conferred by this compound.

A) NO CHANGE

B) there are

C) there is

D) their is

6

People who learn to speak a new language <u>gain</u> new perspectives, improved confidence, better decision-making skills, and deeper connections to other cultures.

A) NO CHANGE

B) to gain

C) gains

D) is gaining

7

The houses, made of a type of cinder block known as cincrete, <u>was unique for its</u> small setback from the street and the placement of the living room at the back of the home.

A) NO CHANGE

B) were unique for their

C) was unique for their

D) were unique for its

8

Friedlieb Ferdinand Runge is widely celebrated as the chemist who first discovered the compound of caffeine in coffee beans. More often overlooked but arguably more important <u>were</u> Runge's isolation of quinine from cinchona bark.

A) NO CHANGE

B) are

C) is

D) had been

9

To a greater degree than many more costly programs, these simple measures can increase employee engagement, which <u>is</u> important for retaining experienced staff.

A) NO CHANGE

B) are

C) is being

D) have been

10

The Deepwater Horizon oil spill in the Gulf of Mexico released a thick plume of oil, some of which flowed along ocean currents and then <u>settled</u> on the seafloor hundreds of miles away.

A) NO CHANGE

B) settles

C) will settle

D) had settled

11

Convinced that many banks had become too accustomed to steadily rising housing prices and <u>was</u> unprepared for a major shock to the economy, the senator called for new financial sector regulations.

A) NO CHANGE

B) were

C) has been

D) will be

12

Geologists who have studied the new lunar survey <u>hypothesizes</u> that a basketball-sized rock hit the moon during the last eclipse.

A) NO CHANGE

B) having hypothesized

C) hypothesizing

D) hypothesize

13

This technology, along with the increasing willingness of people to piece together the separate components of a trip themselves, <u>has</u> led many to declare that travel agents will soon be a thing of the past.

A) NO CHANGE

B) have

C) which have

D) which has

14

The art installation's mirrored outer walls reflected images of the nearby landscape being transformed by developers and <u>allowing</u> visitors to walk through a kaleidoscopic interior.

A) NO CHANGE

B) allowed

C) allows

D) had allowed

15

The fact that chiropractic jobs must be performed in person by practitioners, not computers, <u>make</u> them mostly immune to replacement by AI.

A) NO CHANGE

B) are what makes

C) have made

D) makes

16

In 2009, a Maryland court ruled in favor of two state's attorney's office employees who <u>are supporting</u> their boss in the election and were fired by his opponent after the challenger won.

A) NO CHANGE

B) was supporting

C) had supported

D) will support

17

Researchers now believe that orcas' ability to process sounds at much higher rates than humans <u>arise</u> from physical adaptations related to echolocation.

A) NO CHANGE

B) arises

C) arising

D) have arisen

18

On January 25, 1919, the delegates to the Paris Peace Conference approved a proposal to create the League of Nations. Nearly a year later, on January 16, 1920, the League <u>hold</u> its first meeting with its stated principal mission of maintaining world peace.

A) NO CHANGE

B) held

C) will hold

D) are holding

19

Knitting not only produces practical goods but also has a therapeutic value, and the way in which knitters come together in social groups <u>contribute</u> to this phenomenon.

A) NO CHANGE

B) contributes

C) contributing

D) which contributes

20

Though the building is completely normal, the photographer has rotated the camera to create the illusion that it <u>is</u> sinking into the ground.

A) NO CHANGE

B) was

C) has been

D) had been

Answers on page 252

☙ Pronoun & Noun Agreement ☙

Pronoun Number Agreement

A **pronoun** is a word that stands in for or refers to another noun. That other noun is called the antecedent, and on the SAT, you need to make sure that each pronoun **agrees** with the antecedent's **number**. You also need to make sure that the pronoun has a **single, clear antecedent** somewhere nearby in the passage.

Here are some examples of pronouns, which fall into lots of different categories:

Examples of pronouns			
<u>Subjective</u>	<u>Objective</u>	<u>Possessive</u>	<u>Reflexive</u>
I	*me*	*mine*	*myself*
you		*yours*	*yourself*
she	*her*	*hers*	*herself*
he	*him*	*his*	*himself*
it		*its*	*itself*
we	*us*	*ours*	*ourselves*
			yourselves
they	*them*	*theirs*	*themselves*

<u>Demonstrative</u>	<u>Reciprocal</u>	<u>Interrogative</u>	<u>Relative</u>	<u>Indefinite</u>
this	*each other*	*what*	*that*	*everybody*
that	*one another*	*who*	*which*	*anybody*
these		*which*	*whichever*	*somebody*
those			*who*	*all*
such			*whoever*	*each*
			what	*every*
			whatever	*some*
			whose	*one*
				none

You certainly don't have to memorize these, but you should be able to recognize a pronoun when you see one.

The most basic pronoun task is **number agreement**. When you're given several options for a pronoun, you have to find the antecedent and determine whether it's singular or plural. Then make sure the pronoun matches. Take a look at this example:

☒ By gathering the <u>poems</u> and making <u>it</u> accessible and understandable, Norris refined our understanding of Padilla's artistic evolution.

The underlined pronoun is *it*. What's the antecedent? What does *it* refer to? The answer is whatever Norris made accessible. Looking at the rest of the sentence and using some logic, we can see that the antecedent is *poems*. However, the word *poems* is plural, while *it* is singular, so we have a problem. To fix it, we need to make the pronoun plural.

☑ By gathering the <u>poems</u> and making <u>them</u> accessible and understandable, Norris refined our understanding of Padilla's artistic evolution.

Drill: Finding Antecedents

*Each sentence below has a pronoun marked in **bold**. Circle that pronoun's antecedent.*

1. These attitudes persisted well into the nineteenth century, and aspects of **them** are still active in the present day.

2. As they read and interpret a document, historians consider the historical context within which **it** was created.

3. Many entrepreneurs begin widespread use of a new logo in marketing materials to raise awareness of **their** product.

4. The rebellion started when the government of Massachusetts decided to raise taxes instead of issuing paper money to pay off **its** debts.

5. Increases in ocean acidity may affect shell-forming organisms and the species that depend on **them**.

Because of the way SAT questions are written, an answer choice of *he or she, him or her,* or *his or hers* in a pronoun question is **almost certainly wrong**. Here's how this pattern might typically show up:

☒ <u>Technicians</u> in the field of solar energy will find <u>his or her</u> skills in increasingly high demand.

☒ When <u>artists</u> utilize "found objects," <u>he or she</u> can create art that allows people to see everyday things in a new way.

These sentences are wrong because in both cases, the antecedent is plural. *He* and *she* (and other such pronouns) are singular, so they don't match the number.

To fix this kind of error, use a plural pronoun:

☑ <u>Technicians</u> in the field of solar energy will find <u>their</u> skills in increasingly high demand.

☑ When <u>artists</u> utilize "found objects," <u>they</u> can create art that allows people to see everyday things in a new way.

Clear Antecedents

A pronoun's antecedent doesn't need to be in the same sentence, but there should be a nearby noun (or list of nouns) that the pronoun clearly refers to. If not, the passage becomes ambiguous or confusing, which is a problem that needs to be fixed.

There is a pattern you can look for in the answer choices that indicates the likely presence of a missing or unclear antecedent. If you see **several pronouns** alongside an **actual, specific noun**, then the right answer is probably the noun, not the pronouns.

Here's an example of this pattern:

> Grammarians disagree on how to handle English's lack of a gender-neutral personal pronoun. Some argue we should say "Each student raised **his or her** hand," while others prefer "Each student raised **their** hand." Because there is a lack of consensus on this issue, the SAT stays away from it. That's why an answer choice with *he or she* is typically wrong: the test writers avoid those situations in which it could possibly be correct.

In 2014, New York City converted much of Times Square into a pedestrian-only zone in response to the rising number of people being struck by vehicles in the area. Now more than 355,000 people enter "The Bowtie," as this region is known, each day, and injuries have declined by nearly 60 percent since **32** <u>it</u> was enacted.

32

A) NO CHANGE

B) that

C) one

D) the policy

Choices A, B, and C all contain pronouns. But what could be the antecedent for any of those pronouns? *What* was enacted, exactly? There isn't any clear noun that you can point to. Thus the best choice is D, because it gives you an actual noun. It clears up any ambiguity.

In other cases, there could in fact be some noun that you could point to as the antecedent, but it may be so far back in the passage, or separated from the pronoun by so many other nouns, that it still creates a confusing situation. So it is again best to make the situation more clear by using a specific noun instead of a pronoun.

Staying Consistent

As you saw earlier, there are lots of different categories of pronouns. Sometimes the SAT will create answer choices that are wrong because they cause the passage to improperly switch from one category of pronoun to another.

For example, *you* is a definite pronoun, while *one* is an indefinite pronoun. Once a sentence or passage establishes which it is using, it should remain consistent.

☒ When camping in the Alaskan wilderness, <u>one</u> may go entire days without seeing another person near <u>your</u> campsite.

☑ When camping in the Alaskan wilderness, <u>you</u> may go entire days without seeing another person near <u>your</u> campsite.

☑ When camping in the Alaskan wilderness, <u>one</u> may go entire days without seeing another person near <u>one's</u> campsite.

Another version of this error would be a sentence that mixes up a first-person pronoun, such as *we*, with a third-person pronoun, such as *they*.

☒ The study, published by Swedish scientists in 2013, asked 540 volunteers to record <u>our</u> exercise habits over the course of a year.

☑ The study, published by Swedish scientists in 2013, asked 540 volunteers to record <u>their</u> exercise habits over the course of a year.

> There have been a few questions on the modern SAT that tested the difference between *who* and *whom*, but they are generally quite rare. In a nutshell, the difference is that *who* acts as a subject, while *whom* acts as an object—either a direct object or the object of a preposition.

Possessive Pronouns and Contractions

The following distinctions are not hard, but they appear frequently in test questions, so make sure you've mastered them completely:

Word	Meaning	Example
It's	*It's* is a contraction meaning *it is* or *it has*.	It's pretty cold today.
Its	*Its* is possessive and singular.	The lizard flicked its tail.
Its'	*Its'* is **not a thing**. Don't ever pick this.	☠
They're	*They're* is a contraction meaning *they are*.	They're running a bit late.
Their	*Their* is possessive and plural.	I received their gift.
There	*There* is an adverb indicating a place. *There* can also indicate the existence of something.	I saw her standing there. There is a place for us.

The words *who's* and *whose* also appear, though they are less commonly tested.

Word	Meaning	Example
Who's	*Who's* is a contraction meaning *who is* or *who has*.	Who's on the porch? Who's eaten the last cupcake?
Whose	*Whose* is possessive.	Do you know whose jacket this is? I'm the one whose pencil she borrowed.

Whos' and *who'se* are not words.

Drill: Possessive Pronouns and Contractions

Each sentence below has a blank containing several options for a word to fill it. Circle the appropriate option.

1. Children who study music are better prepared for the future, whether __it's / its / its'__ coping with the challenges they might encounter in school or just having an enjoyable pastime to fall back on.

> **Hint:** Don't pick **its'** for any of these questions. Or on the SAT. Or ever. Because that's not a real English word.

2. Investigative journalists should be careful to ensure the anonymity of __they're / their / there__ sources before publishing sensitive information.

3. As the civil rights movement of the 1960s was reaching __it's / its / its'__ peak, organizers began to look for promising cases to bring before the Supreme Court.

4. Flory Jagoda is a singer and songwriter __who's / whose__ kept the flame of her tradition alive in the face of real adversity.

5. As scientists learn more about how beavers affect ecosystems, __they're / their / there__ beginning to better understand the connections between geography and a diversity of species.

6. When high-speed internet arrives in a remote area, __it's / its / its'__ often expected to improve educational and career opportunities for residents.

7. Some archaeologists believe ancient Egyptians moved heavy stone blocks by sliding them over wet sand, but __they're / their / there__ are several other competing theories.

8. National Hispanic Heritage Month celebrates the histories, cultures, and contributions of American citizens __who's / whose__ ancestors came from Spain, Mexico, the Caribbean, and Central and South America.

Noun Number Agreement

In some cases, there must be number agreement between several **nouns** based on the logic of the sentence. For instance:

- ☒ Hong Kong and London are <u>a good example</u> of cities that have placed a high value on public transportation.
- ☒ Any traveler considering a wintertime visit to South Dakota's Badlands must be <u>meticulous planners and organizers</u>.

Hong Kong and London are two cities, so it doesn't make sense to refer to them as a singular *example*. Instead, we should use the plural *examples*.

In the second sentence, *traveler* is singular. Thus we should refer to the traveler as *a planner*, not *planners*.

- ☑ Hong Kong and London are <u>good examples</u> of cities that have placed a high value on public transportation.
- ☑ Any traveler considering a wintertime visit to South Dakota's Badlands must be <u>a meticulous planner and organizer.</u>

> Need a refresher on parts of speech and basic grammar terms? Check the appendix on page 246.

Practice Question Set

*The questions in the following practice set test **pronoun and noun agreement**. Work on the set without time limits—focus on accuracy alone.*

1

While world travel helps us to understand unfamiliar cultures, <u>they also allow</u> us to create new bonds with the people we meet along the way.

A) NO CHANGE
B) it also allows
C) it also allow
D) these also allow

2

Scientists have long known that dioxin from industrial discharge can adhere to silt and clay, limiting <u>it's</u> ability to filter other pollutants from groundwater.

A) NO CHANGE
B) its
C) there
D) their

3

Anyone contemplating running for statewide office should be <u>skilled debaters and fundraisers.</u>

A) NO CHANGE
B) a skilled debater and fundraiser.
C) skilled both as debaters and fundraisers.
D) both skilled debaters and fundraisers.

4

Certainly, the best sources of feedback on your recipes are the people <u>whom actually try</u> to make them.

A) NO CHANGE
B) whom actually tries
C) who actually tries
D) who actually try

5

While the policy allows businesses to more easily identify promising new markets, it also limits their ability to expand geographically.

A) NO CHANGE
B) there
C) its
D) it's

6

Members of the class, after reading the book, are expected to join the group discussion and share <u>his or her</u> insights.

A) NO CHANGE

B) their

C) our

D) your

7

At the World's Fair, <u>a person</u> could stroll through the exhibition hall and come across countless ideas and inventions you had never seen before.

A) NO CHANGE

B) people

C) one

D) you

8

Study abroad programs, usually run through a university, allow a student to live in a foreign country and attend a foreign university. In many cases, two schools will have an arrangement whereby they can exchange equal numbers of students. <u>It usually grants</u> credit for courses taken at the foreign institution, and some also arrange for a work-study or internship agreement.

A) NO CHANGE

B) They usually grant

C) Such things usually grant

D) Study abroad programs usually grant

9

As I watched the fourth-graders participating in the activity—binoculars glued to their faces and fingers pointing at their discoveries—it occurred to me that <u>one</u> could not possibly be more intensely engaged in the process of observation.

A) NO CHANGE

B) he or she

C) they

D) we

10

The document behind the question, a set of eight colorful pages called the Huexotzinco Codex, was part of a collection donated in the late 1920s. Historians knew that it had been created in 1531 as part of a court case in which the people of Huexotzinco, Mexico, sued representatives of the Spanish colonial government, claiming they were paying excessive taxes, but the historians didn't know the outcome of the trial. <u>For help in interpreting it,</u> researchers called upon Dr. Everette Larson.

A) NO CHANGE

B) For help in interpreting them,

C) For help in interpreting the document,

D) They needed help in the interpretation process, so

11

Such details helped contextualize and place <u>each painting in their</u> specific artistic tradition.

A) NO CHANGE

B) each painting in its

C) each painting in their own

D) all the paintings in its own

12

There is no doubt that Nobel laureates in the natural sciences have made incalculable contributions to society. But no less significant to human progress are the great thinkers, those <u>which help</u> us frame and answer important questions about ourselves as people.

A) NO CHANGE

B) who helps

C) who help

D) whom help

13

In 1885 Wilson Bentley, also known as the Snowflake Man, took the first photomicrographs of snow crystals using a microscope and a camera. Through his work he began to deduce that air temperature may affect the structure of the crystals. He published over 60 articles of his work, along with over 2,400 of his photographs. Starting in the 1930s, Japanese scientist Ukichiro Nakaya, who also took photomicrographs, went a step further and created artificial winter cloud conditions in his laboratory to better understand the meteorological and environmental factors that affect <u>their form.</u>

A) NO CHANGE

B) the form of snow crystals.

C) its form.

D) some of their structures and forms.

14

Researchers asked the subjects to adopt either high-mindfulness or low-mindfulness daily routines and observe those routines for a week. Each participant then switched to a different routine and followed <u>it</u> for another week.

A) NO CHANGE

B) them

C) those

D) those routines

15

Being wasteful with its energy expenditure should interfere with an animal's survival unless the trait proves beneficial in some other manner. So how is it that those small-liver sharks manage to survive even while displaying such energy-intensive behaviors? Looking into the hydrodynamics of swimming animals can provide an answer to <u>those.</u>

A) NO CHANGE

B) them.

C) this question.

D) these objections.

16

Geckos have millions of tiny hairs on each foot that branch off into pad-like objects called spatulae, allowing <u>its</u> feet to create a strong bond to nearly any surface.

A) NO CHANGE

B) it's

C) there

D) their

17

The playground movement accomplished many of its goals, but some of its members' claims—that playgrounds would dramatically reduce crime, for example, or put poolrooms out of business—now seem extreme. Still, it is useful for students today to speculate about why <u>this</u> was so successful and analyze the language and rhetorical strategies its advocates used.

A) NO CHANGE

B) it

C) them

D) this movement

18

David McDermott and Peter McGough both studied at Syracuse University, but their paths never crossed until they both moved to New York City some years later. They started their artistic collaboration in 1980, and <u>it has</u> since become well known for their way of blending art and daily life.

A) NO CHANGE

B) it will

C) they have

D) they had

19

Despite the rise of e-books and the internet, our society's need for librarians <u>as a guide</u> to knowledge and culture is only increasing.

A) NO CHANGE

B) each as guides

C) as guides

D) to be a guide

20

Like <u>their</u> evolutionary ancestors, modern bamboo uses energy from an existing cane to produce more shoots and expand root structures.

A) NO CHANGE

B) they're

C) its

D) it's

❧ Parallelism & Comparisons ❧

Parallelism

Certain situations call for **parallel structure**, which means that the sentence elements must **match**. They must use the same part of speech, or have the same grammatical structure, or be on the same logical footing.

The three main situations on the SAT that require parallelism are:

- ⊙ Lists
- ⊙ Things joined by a conjunction
- ⊙ Comparisons

For example, here's a list of three things, displaying proper parallelism:

> ☑ To prepare for a recording session, an audio engineer <u>positions</u> microphones, <u>runs</u> cables, and <u>labels</u> channels on the mixing board.

The three parallel words on the list are *positions*, *runs*, and *labels*. Those words are all verbs, not a mixture of verbs and other parts of speech (such as gerunds, infinitives, participles, or other things). And they're all in the present tense and singular to correspond with the singular subject *engineer*. So they all match. This is what good parallelism looks like.

So what does bad parallelism look like? An obvious example would be something like this:

> ☒ The old supervisor preferred <u>shouting</u>, <u>micromanaging</u>, and <u>to belittle</u> the employees.

That sounds like a bad boss. But it's also bad parallelism! The first two items on the list are gerunds (nouns ending in *-ing*), while the third item is an infinitive (*to* followed by an action). They don't match.

That example is pretty clear, but the SAT can play games with sentence structure to make mistakes harder to see.

> ☒ Standing just inside the gate, <u>viewing the gardens,</u> the fountain, and the surrounding sculptures in a single glance.

When you first read the sentence, it looks like *standing* and *viewing* will be the first two parallel items on a list, and perhaps *surrounding* will be the third. But there are a couple of problems here. First, this isn't actually a complete sentence. There is no verb. Second, how does *the fountain* fit in? It looks like an item on a list, but how does that work? Where is the rest of the list?

This brings up a couple of important points about parallelism. First, you need to pay attention to punctuation. The SAT's convention is to **use the Oxford comma**—that's the comma after the second-to-last item in a list of three or more things.

Pro Tip:
If you're at a party full of grammarians and want to start a fistfight, bring up the Oxford comma. It's sure to get everyone all riled up.

> ☑ Be sure to bring pencils, tissues, and a snack.

Oxford comma. The SAT uses it.

Using some detective work, we can see that the comma after *fountain* looks like an Oxford comma, which means that *the fountain* must be the second-to-last item on a list.

This gets us to a second important point: it's not always easy to tell how the parallelism will work from looking at the **first item** on a list, but the **second and third items** should make it more clear. That's because, in some cases, parts of the first item can "carry over" to the other items on the list. It's like the distributive property of math.

For example—hey, your phone is lost!

> ☑ <u>You should</u> check in the house, check in the car, and check in the office.

> ☑ <u>You should check</u> in the house, in the car, and in the office.

> ☑ <u>You should check in</u> the house, the car, and the office.

> ☑ <u>You should check in the</u> house, car, and office.

If you simply looked at the first item, "*You should check in the house,*" it wouldn't be clear whether the later items will repeat shared words such as *in* and *the*. But the form of the second item on the list must **match** the form of the third item, and that matching form thus determines what you should consider to be the first item. So your parallel list could be, for example, *in the house, in the car,* and *in the office*—a list of three prepositional phrases. Or it could be *the house, the car,* and *the office*—a list of three nouns.

The rule is that a shared element must be written either in the first list item alone, or in every item—you can't have it, drop it, and then bring it back.

❌ You should check (in) the house, the car, and (in) the office.

So returning to our original funky sentence, it appears that the list is this:

- ⊙ First item: ???
- ⊙ Second item: *the fountain*
- ⊙ Third item: *the surrounding sculptures*

Based on the second and third items, we can tell it's a list of nouns. Thus our first item should be a noun as well. *The gardens* would be a perfect candidate if we could just get it out of that participial phrase and ensure that the sentence has both a subject and a verb. So we can now (finally!) reveal the correct version of this sentence:

☑ Standing just inside the gate, <u>visitors can view</u> the gardens, the fountain, and the surrounding sculptures in a single glance.

That's better. Now it's clear that *standing just inside the gate* is not part of a list. It's just an introductory phrase modifying *visitors*. Sounds like a nice place to visit.

There are just a few last details to mention about lists. First, lists of **three or more** things need the Oxford comma, but lists of **just two** things don't.

☑ He owns a cat, a dog, and a bird.

☑ He owns a dog and a bird.

Finally, a conjunction such as *and*, *but*, or *or* may be used to signal the final item in a list of three or more, but the phrases *as well as* and *in addition to* don't work.

> In a list of prepositional phrases, each list item needs to begin with a preposition, but it doesn't need to be the **same** preposition every time.

☑ I do not like them with a fox, on a train, <u>or</u> in the rain.

❌ The program is driving sales, reducing costs, <u>as well as</u> increasing retention.
❌ The program is driving sales, reducing costs, <u>in addition to</u> increasing retention.
☑ The program is driving sales, reducing costs, <u>and</u> increasing retention.

Drill: Completing a List

Each sentence below has a list of three items. Use the format of the third item on the list to determine the proper choice for the second item.

1. Margaret Flynn was a collector of historical artifacts, _____, and rare animals.
   (A) a collector of books
   (B) of books
   (C) books

2. The new museum has been a boon to the downtown area, bringing additional tax revenue, _____, and focusing national media attention on a formerly run-down neighborhood.
   (A) it has increased tourism
   (B) increasing tourism
   (C) tourism

3. Rescuers use the robots to reach dangerous areas, _____, and relay the details back to authorities.
   (A) to look for people in need of aid
   (B) look for people in need of aid
   (C) people in need of aid

4. In the 18th century, wealthy landowners would employ garden hermits, men who would live in purpose-built hermitages, _____, and provide entertainment for visitors.
   (A) they would dress like druids
   (B) would dress like druids
   (C) dress like druids

5. Most people can tell that the flu is coming on when they begin to feel tired, _____, and feverish.
   (A) start to get congested
   (B) to get congested
   (C) congested

6. When student groups work together to complete an assignment, they may meet in a classroom, _____, or over the internet.
   (A) in a member's home
   (B) a member's home
   (C) over a member's home

Correlative Conjunctions

Many conjunctions are just a single word. For example, *and* is a coordinating conjunction, and *because* is a subordinating conjunction.

Correlative conjunctions, on the other hand, are composed of **several words**. For instance, the pair *neither ... nor* functions as a correlative conjunction. Correlative conjunctions can join two or more things, and when they do so, they create what basically amounts to a list.

Here are some of the more common correlative conjunctions:

- *Not only* X *but also* Y
- *Both* X *and* Y
- *Either* X *or* Y
- *Neither* X *nor* Y
- *Between* X *and* Y

There are two main things to watch out for when you see a correlative conjunction. First, you have to ensure the conjunction itself is **complete and correct**. In other words, if you see *not only*, you need to make sure *but also* shows up somewhere later in the sentence. If a sentence contains *nor*, it should feature *neither* somewhere earlier.

Second, you have to ensure that the two things connected by the conjunction (the X and Y in the list above) have **parallel structure**. For example:

- ❌ Loud noises can cause stress <u>not only</u> in people <u>and also</u> in pets.
- ❌ Loud noises can cause stress not only <u>in people</u> but also <u>pets</u>.

In the first sentence, the conjunction is wrong—it should be *but also*, not *and also*. In the second sentence, the prepositional phrase *in people* is not parallel to the noun *pets*. We would need, for example, two prepositional phrases, or two nouns. The correct version is:

- ✅ Loud noises can cause stress <u>not only in people but also in pets</u>.

Sometimes when the conjunction *not only ... but also* connects full clauses, the word order gets shuffled around a bit:

- ✅ Not only will I come over to visit you, but I will also bring my famous brownies.
- ✅ Not only did he waste all his own money, but he also squandered some of mine.
- ✅ Not only did she write the songs, but she also sang and played all the instruments.

In all three of the examples above, the first auxiliary verb (*will* or *did*) jumps in front of the subject in the first clause. And in the second clause, the *also* splits off from the *but* and moves to the spot immediately before the main verb. While this pattern has appeared on the SAT, the test writers probably won't get into the weeds of testing you on these exact details. Instead, it's more important that you simply read the examples over a few times until the word order sounds natural to you.

Comparisons

Any time you compare or contrast two things, they have to be **logically parallel**. In other words, they have to be the same type of thing, or logically equivalent in some way. For example:

> ☒ The <u>climate</u> in California, like <u>Spain</u>, is characterized by warm, wet winters and hot, dry summers.

The problem with this sentence is that it compares a climate to a place. That's illogical. It would make more sense to compare one place to another place:

> ☑ <u>California</u>, like <u>Spain</u>, has a climate characterized by warm, wet winters and hot, dry summers.

Or to compare one climate to another climate:

> ☑ <u>The climate in California</u>, like <u>the climate in Spain</u>, is characterized by warm, wet winters and hot, dry summers.

This sentence is logically fine, but it is rather wordy because it repeats the phrase *the climate*. A common fix for this redundancy is to replace the second instance of a phrase with a **demonstrative pronoun**. You can use *that* for singular things, and *those* for plural things.

> ☑ The <u>climate</u> in California, like <u>that</u> in Spain, is characterized by warm, wet winters and hot, dry summers.

> ☑ The <u>fingers</u> of a chimpanzee are much stronger than <u>those</u> of a human.

The test writers love to create challenging questions based on illogical comparisons, and demonstrative pronouns are commonly used to solve such problems. If you see an answer choice featuring a phrase like *those of* or *that for*, give it some serious consideration. It's not always right, but it should alert you to look for logical parallelism within a comparison.

A good trick when you're sorting through answer choices is to figure out which noun *that* or *those* refers to and substitute that noun back into the sentence. Would the sentence still make sense? For example:

> ☑ <u>The fingers</u> of a chimpanzee are much stronger than <u>the fingers</u> of a human.

One final way to fix problems with logical parallelism is with possessives:

> ☑ A moth's wings are usually not as brightly colored as a butterfly's.

By using the two possessives *moth's* and *butterfly's*, this sentence makes it clear that the comparison is between *the wings* of one insect and *the wings* of another, even though the word *wings* only appears once.

Drill: Demonstrative Pronouns in Comparisons

*Each sentence below has a demonstrative pronoun marked in **bold**. Find and circle the pronoun's antecedent (the noun that it refers to).*

1. Bauer's testimony stood in marked contrast to **that** of the other witnesses.

2. The forts built near the time of the American Revolution had thicker walls than **those** from later decades.

3. The report showed that the daily output of crude oil in June was about 22,000 barrels less than **that** in April.

4. One reason people disagreed over the words *yanny* and *laurel* is that the acoustic patterns for the syllable *ya* are similar to **those** for *la*.

Each sentence below contains a comparison. Choose which demonstrative pronoun, if any, is needed to ensure that the comparison is logical.

5. Since the debate, the public's support for the challenger has been significantly higher than _____ the incumbent.
    (A) that for
    (B) those for
    (C) Nothing additional is needed.

6. This latest study compares plot lines in fan fiction, written by the novels' enthusiasts, with _____ books by the original author of the series.
    (A) that in
    (B) those in
    (C) Nothing additional is needed.

7. Some consumers prefer non-GMO products because they believe them to be safer and healthier than _____ foods produced with genetic engineering.
    (A) that of
    (B) those of
    (C) Nothing additional is needed.

8. As linguistic research continues to make smart speakers better, their "voices" have started to become indistinguishable from _____ humans.
    (A) that of
    (B) those of
    (C) Nothing additional is needed.

9. You may be surprised to learn that the cola in your refrigerator is more acidic than _____ acid rain.
    (A) that in   (B) those of
    (C) Nothing additional is needed.

10. A person who has traveled extensively through the world's great cities often displays a different outlook on life from _____ a less cosmopolitan individual.
    (A) that displayed by   (B) those displayed by
    (C) Nothing additional is needed.

In addition to displaying logical parallelism, a comparison must also use a **valid grammatical structure**. One very common valid structure is a comparative adjective (*more, better, smaller, less expensive*, etc.) followed by the word *than*.

☑ The new train is <u>quieter</u> <u>than</u> the old one.
☑ The paths near the lake are <u>less treacherous</u> <u>than</u> those in the forest.

Another common pattern is the word *as* followed by another *as*.

☑ The generic version of the drug is <u>as</u> effective <u>as</u> the brand name version.
☑ The school cafeteria is just <u>as</u> busy on weekends <u>as</u> it is during the week.

There are also lots of other possibilities, such as *like, unlike, similar to, different from, the same as*, and more.

These structures probably sound very natural to you. So how could they go wrong? How will the SAT test you on them? By far the most common trick is to try to tempt you to use ***then* instead of *than***.

> Using *then* instead of *than* in a comparison is a common error on the SAT. You're more then likely going to see it on your test.
> What? What's wrong? Something we said?

☒ The situation is even worse <u>then</u> it seems.
☒ An office provides more privacy <u>then</u> a coffee shop.

Another (less common) trick would be to mix and match structures, such as a comparative adjective + *as*, or *as* + *than*:

☒ The president of the gardening company said that her firm sold <u>more</u> ornamental trees in the first five months of this year <u>as</u> it sold in the entire previous year.
☒ By the end of 2018, twice <u>as</u> many inventors had applied for patents at the United States Patent and Trademark Office <u>than</u> had applied in 2008.

A final thing that really messes people up (and is tested regularly) is something that happens with word order. Take a look at this sentence:

☑ Briana <u>has visited</u> more states than Marcus <u>has visited</u>.

It's perfectly correct, but it's a bit redundant to repeat the verb phrase *has visited*. So a common fix is to simply drop the second instance of the word *visited*:

☑ Briana <u>has visited</u> more states than Marcus <u>has</u>.

This is called an **elliptical construction**. Elliptical constructions leave out words that can be guessed from context. These constructions are regarded as both useful and correct, and this sentence probably sounds perfectly normal to you—so far so good.

But there is a more formal version of this type of construction that is highly appealing to the SAT writers because it's not how people usually speak. Thus, it **is correct** but **sounds wrong**—pure catnip to a devious question writer trying to ruin your score. It looks like this:

☑ Briana <u>has visited</u> more states than <u>has Marcus</u>.

The auxiliary verb *has* is now **in front of the subject** *Marcus*. Sounds weird. But it's right.

The general pattern of how this works in comparisons is that, in the clause following the word *than*, the main (repeated) verb drops out, and the auxiliary verb jumps in front of the subject. Here are a couple more examples:

☑ Hard work will produce better results than shortcuts (will) produce.

☑ Hard work will produce better results <u>than will</u> shortcuts.

☑ A head coach should know more about the players than a fan (should) know.

☑ A head coach should know more about the players <u>than should</u> a fan.

The place where this gets especially strange is when there is no helper verb at all, just a main verb. In that case, the main verb transforms into *do*, *does*, or *did*. Then it jumps in front of the subject.

☑ Infants sleep for more hours of the day than older children (sleep.)

☑ Infants sleep for more hours of the day <u>than do</u> older children.

☑ San Antonio grew faster over the last decade than any other large city (grew.)

☑ San Antonio grew faster over the last decade <u>than did</u> any other large city.

☑ Hydropower provides seven times more energy worldwide than wind (provides.)

☑ Hydropower provides seven times more energy worldwide <u>than does</u> wind.

Again, it's a good idea to read over the examples a few times until this structure sounds natural to you. And if you see an answer choice on the test that has a strange-looking *do* or *did* hanging around within a comparison, you can "reverse engineer" it to check whether it's right: figure out what verb the *did* is standing in for, change it back into that verb, and put it after the subject. Sound more normal? Then it's probably right.

> When *do* stands in for another verb, it's called a pro-form. You will never, ever, **ever** have to use that fact. But you like knowing it—we know you do.

Drill: Using Formal Structures in Comparisons

Each question below provides two sentences that describe a comparative situation. Combine the two sentences into one, using the more formal verb structure described on the previous page. You should also use demonstrative pronouns such as that *or* those *when appropriate. The first two questions have been completed for you as examples.*

Ex. 1.   The Ohio River flows.
The Mississippi River flows more quickly.

Combined: <u>The Mississippi River flows more quickly than does the Ohio River.</u>

Ex. 2.   Buildings with dark-colored roofs require air-conditioning.
Buildings with light-colored roofs require less air-conditioning.

Combined: <u>Buildings with light-colored roofs require less air-conditioning than do those with dark-colored roofs.</u>

1.   Italy produces cheese.
France produces more cheese.

Combined: _____

_____

2.   Conventional cars emit carbon dioxide.
Hybrid vehicles emit less carbon dioxide.

Combined: _____

_____

3.   People who speak just one language learn music.
People who speak several languages learn music more easily.

Combined: _____

_____

_____

4.   The wings of a robin produce some power per downstroke.
The wings of a falcon produce more power per downstroke.

Combined: _____

_____

_____

continued ⟶

5. Students who exercised on their own scored high on a fitness test.
    High school student athletes scored 15% higher on a fitness test.

    Combined: _____

    _____

    _____

6. The stomachs of participants in the control group contained bacteria.
    The stomachs of participants in the experimental group contained more diverse bacteria.

    Combined: _____

    _____

    _____

    _____

If you're not making mistakes,
you're not trying

If you're not learning
from your mistakes,
you're not improving

— Jane Elizabeth Brown

Practice Question Set

The questions in the following practice set test **parallelism and comparisons**. *Work on the set without time limits—focus on accuracy alone.*

1

Thanks to subsidies from the federal government, new electric cars can be sold to qualified buyers at prices similar to a conventional vehicle.

A) NO CHANGE

B) that of a conventional vehicle.

C) a conventional vehicle's.

D) those of conventional vehicles.

2

Even after an amphibian has metamorphosed and developed lungs, its respiratory system can still resemble a gilled fish.

A) NO CHANGE

B) the gills of a fish.

C) a fish's respiratory system's gills.

D) that of a gilled fish.

3

For short trips, choosing to walk instead of drive provides a range of environmental benefits, such as improving air quality, reducing consumption of nonrenewable energy sources, and the minimization of noise pollution.

A) NO CHANGE

B) noise-pollution-minimizing benefits.

C) noise pollution minimization.

D) minimizing noise pollution.

4

Kristen Huang, an assistant economics professor at Cornell University, recently co-authored a paper looking at student graduation rates in New York's SMP program and compared them to similar programs in other states.

A) NO CHANGE

B) similar programs'

C) those in similar programs

D) that of similar programs

5

The study demonstrated that those who said they ate fish at least twice per week were 15 percent less likely to develop heart disease after five years than not eating fish.

A) NO CHANGE

B) if saying they ate no

C) when people were not eating

D) those who said they ate no

6

Even for people who are used to its effects, caffeine consumption has been shown to increase people's ability to work at a faster pace, <u>staying</u> mentally focused, and decrease the rate of errors.

A) NO CHANGE

B) in staying

C) stay

D) to stay

7

Those interested in protecting groundwater for use in irrigation must work with local officials to limit contamination from gasoline, road salts, and <u>chemical contamination</u> that can cause it to become unfit for agricultural applications.

A) NO CHANGE

B) contamination from chemicals

C) chemicals

D) that from chemicals

8

The authors found that service programs that put youth in direct contact with people in need lead to more self-awareness, and subsequently to greater civic engagement, than <u>do programs that lack direct contact.</u>

A) NO CHANGE

B) programs that are lacking direct contact.

C) direct-contact-lacking programs can do.

D) it does when programs lack direct contact.

9

Traditional incandescent bulbs have not only illuminated artists' studios for much of the last <u>century and starred</u> in the artworks themselves.

A) NO CHANGE

B) century, also starring

C) century, but starring

D) century but also starred

10

Committing yourself to go for a run after meeting a deadline may seem more like a <u>punishment than</u> a reward, but the strategy can be surprisingly effective.

A) NO CHANGE

B) punishment, than

C) punishment, then

D) punishment then

11

On display at the Rock and Roll Hall of Fame is the guitar of Jimi Hendrix as well as the Beatles' George Harrison.

A) NO CHANGE

B) George Harrison of the Beatles.

C) George Harrison of the Beatles'.

D) that of the Beatles' George Harrison.

12

Personal finance experts agree that certain basic habits such as listing goals, paying off credit card debt, and someone who takes time to create a budget can greatly improve one's financial outlook.

A) NO CHANGE

B) taking time

C) time taken

D) for someone to be taking time

13

Driving through Cougar, Oregon, one can get a sense of the dramatic changes to Mount St. Helens, a peak that was once as tall and symmetrical as what Japan's Mount Fuji is like.

A) NO CHANGE

B) how Japan's Mount Fuji is.

C) those of Japan's Mount Fuji.

D) Japan's Mount Fuji.

14

The extraction of DNA from teeth, especially in an archaeological context, has distinct advantages over other bones when it comes to the extraction of DNA.

A) NO CHANGE

B) the extraction of DNA from other bones.

C) the DNA extracted from other bones.

D) other bones when comparing methods of DNA extraction.

15

Since 2012, the organization has been holding monthly events where members can meet other local businesspeople, connect with potential customers, and can propose initiatives on matters related to the economic health of the community.

A) NO CHANGE

B) initiatives can be proposed

C) they can propose initiatives

D) propose initiatives

Remember—**there's no substitute for the real thing.** Practice questions like these are useful for focusing on a single skill, but completing **full, official practice tests** must be a central component of your preparation.

16

People's memories of the poem are often incomplete and fragmented, little <u>more than a phrase</u> or a line, along with a general sense of the period of life when they read it.

A) NO CHANGE

B) more then a phrase

C) more, than a phrase,

D) more than, a phrase

17

In a 2008 study, French researchers compared the lifespans of baseball players who smiled in their baseball card pictures with <u>players who did not smile</u> and found that the smilers lived longer.

A) NO CHANGE

B) that of players who did not smile

C) players who did not do that

D) those of players who did not smile

18

Lemon laws are statutes designed to protect a consumer who buys a substandard automobile, usually by requiring the manufacturer or dealer either to refund the full purchase price of the vehicle if it meets certain criteria <u>or</u> to replace it.

A) NO CHANGE

B) nor

C) but

D) and

19

Langston Hughes's works helped portray the joys and hardships of working-class African American lives better than <u>did</u> any other poet or writer from the 1920s Harlem Renaissance.

A) NO CHANGE

B) those of

C) was

D) DELETE the underlined portion.

20

On the other hand, younger men who altered their labor force participation to fulfill family duties had self-acceptance levels 12 points higher than <u>following</u> a more conventional path.

A) NO CHANGE

B) their peers who followed

C) they did on

D) DELETE the underlined portion.

StudyLark

21

When it was completed, the statue had intricately painted designs, weighed over seven tons, and <u>a height of twelve feet.</u>

A) NO CHANGE

B) a reach of twelve feet in height.

C) reaching a height of twelve feet.

D) reached twelve feet in height.

22

Despite tremendous advances in video chat technology, most people agree that the experience of conversing in person is superior to <u>that of</u> a screen.

A) NO CHANGE

B) that of conversing through

C) conversing through

D) conversations through

23

Because printing books on demand eliminates the need for a warehouse full of finished product, titles published in this way are typically less expensive than <u>the traditional method.</u>

A) NO CHANGE

B) it was done traditionally.

C) it was done in the past.

D) those published by the traditional method.

24

The company has grown steadily over the last 50 years and now installs its custom sound systems in concert halls, community centers, <u>sports stadiums, also</u> private residences around the country.

A) NO CHANGE

B) as well as sports stadiums and

C) sports stadiums, and places such as

D) sports stadiums, and

25

The experience of a baby elephant raised in a zoo can be lonely, <u>such as</u> a child growing up in a neighborhood with no playmates.

A) NO CHANGE

B) comparing it to

C) as that felt by

D) similar to that of

26

The mass of a dwarf planet is large enough that gravitational forces are more influential than that of mechanical ones in determining the body's shape.

A) NO CHANGE
B) than
C) than those of
D) compared with

27

Not only were these Ghanaian girls engaged in an activity that I had relished in my own girlhood, but also clapped in a pattern identical to one that had been popular on the playgrounds of my own childhood in California.

A) NO CHANGE
B) but also were clapping
C) also clapping
D) but they were also clapping

28

Examining the effectiveness of different approaches, experts from the Institute for Mental Health Research at UT Austin found that meditation tended to reduce stress as well as or better than those of other methods did.

A) NO CHANGE
B) other methods did.
C) they found with other methods.
D) the ones with other methods did.

29

Some architects find themselves duplicating previous building designs because it can be easier to reuse familiar ideas than to rework them into something innovative.

A) NO CHANGE
B) as to rework them
C) than if they are reworked
D) than when they rework them

30

Larisa Miller of Stanford University presented her research on optical character recognition—both its technical evolution and its use as a substitute for the manual processing of archived materials.

A) NO CHANGE
B) it is used
C) for use
D) the use of it

ꙮ Punctuation ꙮ

Semicolons

Semicolons are the easiest points on the entire SAT. That's because there's a very easy way to check whether they are correct:

> On the SAT, a semicolon **is identical to** a period

If you see a semicolon, just **replace it with a period**. That's it.

Could the stuff **before** the semicolon stand alone **as a complete sentence**? Could the stuff **after** the semicolon stand alone? If so, the semicolon is correct.

This fun fact also gives us a pattern to look for. If you see two choices with **exactly the same words**, and one has a **semicolon** while the other has a **period**, then those choices are identical. **Cross them out immediately.** They are guaranteed to be wrong. You don't have to use your brain, not even a little bit. If two choices are the same, then they're either both right, or they're both wrong, and there is no such thing as an SAT question with two right answers.

Drill: Semicolons

Each sentence below includes a semicolon. Decide whether the sentence is correct or incorrect.

1. In an attempt to save the publication, the editors relaunched it under a new name; they wanted to simplify the subject matter and reach a broader audience.
   ☐ Correct   ☐ Incorrect

2. She chooses natural objects for her paintings; a gnarled branch, a speckled stone, or a weathered shell.
   ☐ Correct   ☐ Incorrect

continued ⟶

3. According to industry statistics, the average age of airline pilots has been increasing for the last ten years; raising fears of an impending shortage.
   ☐ Correct   ☐ Incorrect

4. The first product design failed for multiple reasons; the second showed few signs of improvement.
   ☐ Correct   ☐ Incorrect

Which two of the choices below from an SAT question are certainly wrong?

5. A) expressions, they were

   B) expressions; they were

   C) expressions—they were

   D) expressions. They were

> OK, so we admit it: the trick of treating a semicolon as a period is good enough for **99%** of SAT questions, but there is another possible use you might see on rare occasions. A semicolon can also function as a "**super comma**" to separate listed items that themselves already contain commas. For example: *We visited Akron, Ohio; Provo, Utah; and Ames, Iowa.*

Colons

People often associate colons with lists, and sometimes that's true, but it's not the whole story. Not every list needs a colon, and not every colon is followed by a list.

On the test, the best way to check whether a colon is correct is this:

> On the SAT, the stuff **before a colon** needs to be able to stand alone as a **complete sentence**

The stuff **after** the colon can be almost anything. For example, you could indeed have **a list**.

- ✅ She is fluent in three languages: Mandarin, Spanish, and Hindi.
- ✅ He oversaw multiple aspects of the play's production: set design, casting, music direction, and marketing.

You can also follow a colon with **another complete sentence**. Many people don't know about this usage or think it looks wrong, so the SAT writers love to put it on the test.

- ✅ The new constitution had a significant advantage over the old one: it allowed for public servants to be removed from office.
- ✅ The increase in unemployment has had an unexpected result: some men are learning, for the first time, how to cook.

And finally, the stuff after a colon can simply be **a word** or the completion of a thought.

- ✅ The flag of the United Nations features the well-known international symbol for peace: an olive branch.
- ✅ The scholar opened the chest and found what many thought had been lost forever: the original manuscript.

Because the words before a colon need to form a complete sentence, you should **never** use a colon between a verb and its direct object, or between a preposition and its object. The test will often try to tempt you to do this by distracting you with a list.

- ☒ The new software can handle: scheduling, billing, and client communication.
- ☒ The guest speakers included: Ms. Barton, Dr. Hammond, and Professor Mack.
- ☒ Runners often suffer from overuse injuries such as: shin splints, tendonitis, and stress fractures.
- ☒ After two hours of suspense, the play culminated in: a surprise twist.

> A colon after *such as* is **always wrong**.
>
> ~~such as:~~
>
> A colon after *including* is **always wrong**.
>
> ~~including:~~
>
> Other punctuation after those words is typically **wrong** too, except in special rare cases.
>
> ~~such as,~~
>
> ~~such as;~~
>
> ~~such as—~~

The first two incorrect sentences above put a colon between a verb (*handle, included*) and the direct objects of that verb.

The last two are wrong because they put a colon between a preposition (*as, in*) and the object of that preposition. Just because you see a list doesn't mean you need a colon.

The last thing to know about colons is that, while a colon is allowed to connect two complete sentences, they can't be just *any* two sentences. The appropriate place to use a colon is a situation in which the sentence **sets up a thought that needs completion**. The colon indicates that you're about to complete the thought. So a colon between two unrelated ideas is not appropriate.

- ☒ Ruehl's family lives in Cincinnati: he got his degree in chemical engineering.

Look back at all the correct examples on the previous page. Notice how each one sets up a thought that needs completion and then completes the thought after the colon.

Drill: Colons

Each sentence below includes a colon. Decide whether the sentence is correct or incorrect.

1. Several companies in the area manufacture small-scale electrical equipment, such as: motors, storage batteries, and heating systems.
   ☐ Correct   ☐ Incorrect

2. She has made it a habit to attend the conference every year: taking advantage of the opportunity to network.
   ☐ Correct   ☐ Incorrect

3. When a team is poorly conditioned, the effects are apparent: the players become slower and less able to react as the game goes on.
   ☐ Correct   ☐ Incorrect

4. I gazed up as she pointed out the most recognizable winter constellation: Orion.
   ☐ Correct   ☐ Incorrect

Dashes

Dashes are used to indicate nonessential or parenthetical information that could be removed from the sentence.

Sometimes the nonessential information comes in the **middle** of the sentence and interrupts the flow of ideas. In that case, you need **a pair of dashes**. To check whether a pair of dashes is correct, try removing the stuff between the dashes. Would the sentence be logical and grammatical without it? If so, the dashes are correct. You can think of a pair of dashes like a pair of parentheses, or in some cases, a pair of commas. For example:

- ☑ Every part of the brain—and the rest of the body—is densely interconnected with other parts.
- ☑ The civilization is artistically significant—it spawned several important masonry techniques—but little else is known about it.

(If the sentence would require a comma in place of the removed material, that's OK. The dashes can handle the work of the comma.)

Your main task, if you see an answer choice containing a dash, is to check elsewhere in the sentence for another dash. In many cases, you'll need a second dash to "close off" a parenthetical phrase that interrupts the main flow of the sentence.

> Dashes can come alone or in pairs.
>
> A **pair** of dashes acts like **parentheses**.
>
> A **single** dash acts like a **colon**.

Sometimes, on the other hand, the nonessential information comes at the **end** of the sentence. In that case, you need **a single dash**. You can also use the same trick to check for correctness—remove the stuff after the dash and make sure that the sentence is logically and grammatically complete before the dash. You can think of a single dash at the end of a sentence as a colon. For instance:

- ☑ After months of anticipation, the company finally announced the location of its new headquarters—Gurnee, Illinois.
- ☑ Three students in the class were surprised to find that they shared the most common birthday in the US—September 9.

This technique of thinking of dashes as either parentheses or colons raises an interesting point: how do you know which to use? Isn't there some gray area or overlap between the punctuation marks? What should you do if a question offers two valid possibilities? Which one is "more right" or stylistically more appropriate?

The answer is **yes**, there is some overlap between punctuation marks, but **you don't have to worry about it**. The SAT will not test you on the overlap. You will never see two answer choices that could both be right. The SAT will only ever offer one choice that could even possibly be right; the other three will always be straight up wrong.

That's some good news, now isn't it?

Drill: Dashes

Each of the sentences below contains an empty oval into which you could place a dash, a comma, or no punctuation at all. Choose the appropriate option.

1. The American Red Cross, which solicited donations in the wake of Hurricane Floyd in 1999 ◯ raised over $49 million for the relief effort.
   ☐ Use a dash   ☐ Use a comma   ☐ No punctuation needed

2. Using the new telescope, astronomers were able to measure a clear—though still unexplained ◯ signal coming from the nearby star.
   ☐ Use a dash   ☐ Use a comma   ☐ No punctuation needed

3. In an unusual move, officials named the stadium after the current mayor—an honor usually reserved for public figures ◯ who are retired or deceased.
   ☐ Use a dash   ☐ Use a comma   ☐ No punctuation needed

4. It's easy to see why a company might prefer to use contractors ◯ they are less costly and more flexible than full-time employees.
   ☐ Use a dash   ☐ Use a comma   ☐ No punctuation needed

5. Carroll grew up in a small mining town, and she saw how dependence on a single employer ◯ in this case a mine operator, can have a stifling impact on growth.
   ☐ Use a dash   ☐ Use a comma   ☐ No punctuation needed

6. The idea of a dedicated program that could access the internet ◯ referred to variously as an internet viewer, interface, or browser—was still vague at the time.
   ☐ Use a dash   ☐ Use a comma   ☐ No punctuation needed

Apostrophes

' Apostrophes are used to create **contractions** and **possessives**.

Most contractions—such as *I'm*, *don't*, and *you'll*—are not tested on the SAT because they're too easy. Everyone can use these correctly. But there are two important cases—*it's* and *they're*—that do show up frequently. You already saw this chart back in the chapter on pronouns, but it bears repeating:

Word	Meaning	Example
It's	*It's* is a contraction meaning *it is* or *it has*.	It's pretty cold today.
Its	*Its* is possessive and singular.	The lizard flicked its tail.
Its'	*Its'* is **not a thing**. Don't ever pick this.	☢
They're	*They're* is a contraction meaning *they are*.	They're running a bit late.
Their	*Their* is possessive and plural.	I received their gift.
There	*There* is an adverb indicating a place. *There* can also indicate the existence of something.	I saw her standing there. There is a place for us.

The real fun with apostrophes comes with possessives. For the SAT, the thing you need to pay attention to is whether the possessing noun is singular or plural.

For a **singular** noun, make it possessive by adding an **apostrophe + s**.

Singular noun	Possessive version
the land of the <u>farmer</u>	*the farmer's land*
the results of the <u>survey</u>	*the survey's results*
the meeting of this <u>week</u>	*this week's meeting*
the atmosphere of <u>Earth</u>	*Earth's atmosphere*

For a **plural** noun, make it possessive by adding an **apostrophe after the s**.

Plural noun	Possessive version
the workload of the <u>employees</u>	*the employees' workload*
the union of the <u>actors</u>	*the actors' union*
the memories of the <u>siblings</u>	*the siblings' memories*
the feeding habits of the <u>birds</u>	*the birds' feeding habits*

(Some plural nouns, such as *women*, don't end in -*s*. To make them possessive, the rule is to add an apostrophe + *s*. But to our knowledge, this has never been tested on the SAT.)

(Some singular nouns, such as *Thomas*, end in -*s*. Grammarians disagree on what to do with these nouns. Some think "the coat of Thomas" should be *Thomas's coat*, while others argue for *Thomas' coat*. Because there is a lack of consensus, this issue is not tested on the SAT.)

The other important consideration for possessives is to check **whether you even need a possessive at all**. The SAT will often try to tempt you to create a possessive when all you really have is a **plural**.

There is a little test you can do to check whether you really have a possessive that needs an apostrophe. A possessive is correct when:

- There are two nouns in a row
- The apostrophe is on the first noun but not the second
- It would make sense to say "the second noun **of the** first noun"

Check out some of these common errors:

- We sat there enjoying the fresh <u>apple's</u>.

There aren't two nouns in a row here, and you can't say "the apples *of* anything." The word *apples* should simply be plural, not possessive.

- No one knows exactly how Stradivarius made <u>his violin's</u>.

Again, we don't have two nouns in a row. There *is* possession going on here because you could say "the violins *of* Stradivarius," but that's taken care of by the possessive pronoun *his*. You don't need an apostrophe on the plural noun *violins*.

- She tried to visit every one of <u>the city's bookshop's</u>.

Here we do have two nouns in a row—*city* and *bookshops*. Also, it does make sense to say "the bookshops *of the* city," so it is in fact appropriate to use the possessive *city's*. However, there shouldn't be an apostrophe on the second noun. *Bookshops* is, once again, simply plural, not possessive.

In some cases, it is appropriate to have two possessives in a row:

- They spent the holidays at <u>Sandra's parents' house</u>.

You could say "the parents *of* Sandra," so it's correct to use the possessive *Sandra's*. And you could say "the house *of* the parents," so it also makes sense to use the possessive *parents'*. We see the apostrophe after the -*s* in *parents* because that word is both plural and possessive.

Drill: Apostrophes

Fill in each blank below with the appropriate choice.

1. Age affects the _____ to detect nutrient levels in food.
   (A) stomachs' ability
   (B) stomachs ability
   (C) stomach's ability
   (D) stomachs' abilities

2. The new facility has brought an increase in activity among the _____.
   (A) area's competitive swimmer's
   (B) areas' competitive swimmer's
   (C) area's competitive swimmers
   (D) areas' competitive swimmers'

3. The company only promotes _____ to senior management positions.
   (A) it's own employees
   (B) its own employees
   (C) they're own employees
   (D) their own employee's

4. A television producer must consider a _____ tastes when creating a show for international distribution.
   (A) region's residents
   (B) region's residents'
   (C) regions' resident's
   (D) regions' residents

5. The doctor gave a presentation about his _____ on heart disease.
   (A) diets effect's
   (B) diet's effects
   (C) diet's effects'
   (D) diets effects

6. Based on this study, _____ are able to recognize human faces.
   (A) its clear that crows
   (B) its clear that crow's
   (C) it's clear that crows'
   (D) it's clear that crows

7. Artists can create different effects by changing the _____ in a painting.
   (A) lengths of the brushstrokes
   (B) length's of the brushstrokes
   (C) lengths of the brushstroke's
   (D) length's of the brushstrokes'

8. It's best to consult a professional before making updates to _____.
   (A) a houses' electrical system
   (B) a house's electrical system
   (C) a house's electrical systems'
   (D) houses electrical system's

Quotation Marks

 Quotation marks can be used to set off a **direct quotation**, to indicate that a word or phrase is being **discussed** rather than used within the sentence, to show that a word or phrase is regarded as **slang or jargon**, or to **distance** the author from an idea by showing that it contains someone else's words or thoughts, with which the author might not agree.

Quotation marks do show up on the SAT, though less often than things like dashes and apostrophes. The simplest thing to watch for is that quotation marks must **come in pairs**. Remember that a portion of quoted speech can span several sentences.

☒ Neil Armstrong acknowledged the difficulty of looking ahead; science has not yet mastered prophecy. We predict too much for the next year and yet far too little for the next ten."

☑ Neil Armstrong acknowledged the difficulty of looking ahead: "Science has not yet mastered prophecy. We predict too much for the next year and yet far too little for the next ten."

The first example is wrong because we have a closing quotation mark at the very end, but no opening quotation mark. The second example gets it right. That Neil sure was a smart dude.

However, the main thing tested with quotation marks is actually **the punctuation around them**, namely the comma that comes (or doesn't come) before the first quotation mark when the quoted material is embedded within a sentence.

Do you need a comma before quotation marks? You may have learned in school that you always do, but the real answer is... **sometimes**.

If the stuff between the quotes is set up as a **full, separate sentence** of **directly quoted** speech or writing, then you need to do two things:

- ⊙ **Use a comma** before the opening quotation mark
- ⊙ **Capitalize** the first word in the quote

You can spot cases like these because they often start with words such as *said, remarked, commented,* or *declared*. For example:

☑ The lifeguard <u>announced</u>, "Everybody out of the pool!"
☑ Warren Buffett famously <u>said</u>, "Chains of habit are too light to be felt until they are too heavy to be broken."
☑ The piano teacher <u>commented</u>, "You've almost got it," encouraging Paige to continue.

Any punctuation at the end of the quoted material goes **inside** the quotation marks.

On the other hand, if the stuff inside the quotation marks **flows as part of the grammar of the sentence**, then you should:

- ◉ Punctuate the sentence as if the quotes weren't there
- ◉ Follow the rules of capitalization as if the quotes weren't there

This usually means that there **will not be a comma** before the quotes, and that the first word in the quote will **not** be capitalized. For example:

> ☑ The training program is part of the company's ongoing effort to "upskill" its workforce.
> ☑ Charlotte is known as "the Queen City," though many people who live there might struggle to explain why.
> ☑ The Constitution indicates that "the People of the several States" shall choose the members of the House of Representatives.
> ☑ Patel said she created the model because she "wanted people to see what the ancient building really looked like."

> We haven't seen the SAT test people on the rules of capitalization within quotes, but you can use those rules to your advantage. If you see a word capitalized that wouldn't ordinarily be so, then you need a comma before the quotation marks. If the quote doesn't begin with a capital letter, then a comma isn't required.

The last example above may appear to be the kind of direct quote that requires a comma, but it's not, because the quote flows with the grammar of the sentence. The subject *she* is outside the quote, but the verb *wanted* is inside the quote. They work together, so you don't want to separate them with a comma.

Drill: Commas with Quotes

Each sentence below contains quotation marks. Decide whether a comma is needed before the quotation marks, in the position indicated by the circle.

1. I overheard a fellow patron remark◯ "The bread tastes like detergent."
   ☐ Use a comma   ☐ Don't use a comma

2. Foods containing◯ "fake fat" may rob the body of vital nutrients.
   ☐ Use a comma   ☐ Don't use a comma

3. Certain parts of the brain, when measured using fMRI◯ "light up" in response to various cognitive tasks.
   ☐ Use a comma   ☐ Don't use a comma

4. The negotiations were so hostile that one of the participants commented◯ "We're hopeful that one day, grown-ups will take over."
   ☐ Use a comma   ☐ Don't use a comma

5. The library director conceded that the branch would◯ "have to get creative to raise enough funds to remain open."
   ☐ Use a comma   ☐ Don't use a comma

6. Lindsey Cole believes that◯ "Maine is poised for a recovery in its housing market."
   ☐ Use a comma   ☐ Don't use a comma

Parentheses

Parentheses are used to make parenthetical statements (obviously). Those are statements that serve to clarify something in the sentence or insert material that is aside from the main point. If you remove a parenthetical statement, the sentence should still be logical and grammatical without it.

> Parentheses aren't tested all that often. Only around 1 in 4 tests contain a question that asks about parentheses.

The most basic thing to look for with parentheses is that, just like quotation marks, they must **come in pairs**. Thus, if you see an answer choice that offers a parenthesis, check in the passage for another one. Don't let those things be lonely.

It seems as if it would be hard to make a mistake on this issue, but perhaps the reason people occasionally leave parentheses unpaired on the SAT is that other punctuation can be used to create parenthetical statements too. In this regard, parentheses have a lot of overlap with **dashes** and **commas**. For example, the sentences below are all equally valid:

- ☑ The study suggested that curcumin—a compound found in turmeric—may have a positive impact on brain health.
- ☑ The study suggested that curcumin, a compound found in turmeric, may have a positive impact on brain health.
- ☑ The study suggested that curcumin (a compound found in turmeric) may have a positive impact on brain health.

Thus, a trick the test writers sometimes use is to create a long parenthetical statement with a dash or comma at one end and a parenthesis at the other. They're hoping you'll lose track and fail to notice that they don't match. For instance:

- ☒ Some features aimed at safety in cars (such as voice-activated calling or hands-free texting, do little to reduce the core problem of driving while distracted.

To fix this sentence, use parentheses on both sides of the parenthetical. You could also use two commas or two dashes.

The other main issue with parentheses is **the punctuation around them**. Simply put, you should be able to remove a parenthetical and still have a properly punctuated sentence left behind. This means it's not unusual to see a parenthesis and a comma right next to each other. Some people think it looks strange or wrong to have two punctuation marks in a row, but it can be perfectly correct. For instance:

☑ Based on studies of the armadillo (which always gives birth to four genetically identical but physically different offspring) scientists were able to learn that DNA does not completely determine our development.

If you removed the parenthetical, you would need a comma after the introductory phrase *based on studies of the armadillo.*

☑ Based on studies of the armadillo, scientists were able to learn that DNA does not completely determine our development.

Thus you still need the comma in the sentence, even with the parenthetical back in there. And because the parenthetical modifies *armadillo*, the comma should appear **after** the parenthetical so as not to separate them. Here are a few more examples of additional punctuation appearing next to parentheses:

☑ Gordon Bruno—a photographer who helped establish the National Association of Independent Artists (NAIA)—lamented that there was not a single major art festival to serve the East Coast in 1995.

☑ Online retailers have an important advantage over physical stores (which cannot change price tags so easily): the ability to implement surge pricing based on changes in demand.

☑ To gather material for the biography, Monica Griffin visited Tulsa, Oklahoma (where Webb grew up), spoke with relatives, and combed through early recordings.

Question Marks

?

You would think that the proper use of a question mark is pretty obvious, and not the kind of thing that would be tested on the SAT. Who doesn't know how to use a question mark?

For the most part, that's true. But the one issue that does show up and can sometimes be confusing is the **embedded question**. An embedded question is asked indirectly within a statement. For example, here's a regular, direct question:

☑ What time did he arrive?

And here's the same question embedded within a statement:

☑ She asked what time he arrived.

One thing that happens with embedded questions is that the word order gets shuffled around a bit. You have to move the first auxiliary verb so that it's after the subject. If the auxiliary verb is *did*, it disappears and the verb becomes past tense. But the important issue as it pertains to punctuation is that **embedded questions do not use question marks**.

Direct question	Embedded question
When will you wrap the gift?	We'd like to know when you will wrap the gift.
Where was the movie filmed?	He's not sure where the movie was filmed.
Why did the tank overflow?	She asked why the tank overflowed.
Can he ride a unicycle?	I wonder whether he can ride a unicycle.

Most of the time when you see an answer choice that offers the possibility of ending a sentence with a question mark, it will be an embedded question, so you won't need the question mark.

Of course, direct questions **do** use question marks, and they show up sometimes too. So just check carefully.

> Question marks are a rarely tested topic. Only around 15% of tests contain a question about question marks.

Exclamation Points

!

A few very rare (and rather silly-looking) answer choices have offered the option of an exclamation point as a way to end a sentence. But an exclamation point has never been correct! The SAT is not the place to get overly excited!

If you see a correct answer that uses an exclamation point, let us know and we'll give you $100!!!*

*Does not constitute a legally valid offer. Just relax. It's only punctuation.

Commas

This brings us to the grand finale, the Big Kahuna of punctuation marks, the undisputed champion of the punctuation world: **the comma**.

There are dozens of possible uses for commas, so the topic can certainly get complicated. We'll try to keep it simple and stick to the issues you need to know for the SAT. First let's review some of the **valid uses** of commas.

Valid comma use #1: To set off an introductory element

An **introductory element** appears at the beginning of a sentence, before the main subject and verb, and should be followed by a comma. There are several common types of introductory elements:

Introductory element	Example
A phrase indicating time or place	<u>In the early 1980s</u>, Mat Perlot and Curt Lawler founded the Safari Motorcoach Corporation.
A transition word	<u>Surprisingly</u>, the tornado caused little damage.
An appositive	<u>A form of music with roots in Louisiana</u>, Zydeco features guitar, accordion, fiddle, and washboard.
A participial phrase	<u>Cycling through the countryside</u>, Javier realized how out of shape he was.

Valid comma use #2: Before a coordinating conjunction that joins two clauses

Coordinating conjunctions are the FANBOYS conjunctions—*for, and, nor, but, or, yet, so.* When you have such a conjunction **between two complete clauses**, it needs to be preceded by a comma:

- ☑ The inspectors found a number of toxic substances, <u>but</u> the new policy is reducing the risk.
- ☑ I'm going to buy these fuzzy dice, <u>and</u> you can't stop me.

However, you don't need a comma if the conjunction joins two smaller elements, such as two nouns, two verbs, or two adjectives.

- ☑ Kitty O'Neill worked as <u>a stunt woman</u> and <u>a racecar driver</u>.
- ☑ We <u>packed</u> a lunch but <u>forgot</u> to bring it.

Valid comma use #3: Between two clauses when the first clause begins with a subordinating conjunction

There are a lot of **subordinating conjunctions**, but some of the most common are *if*, *because*, *while*, *although*, *before*, *since*, and *unless*. These conjunctions can join two clauses, and if the conjunction appears **before** the first clause, then you need a comma to indicate the end of the first clause and the beginning of the second.

- ☑ <u>Because</u> the nest was hidden in dense bushes◯ it was safe from predators.
- ☑ <u>If</u> families have access to valid medical information◯ they will visit the doctor less often.
- ☑ <u>Unless</u> we can increase revenue◯ we will have to reduce our services.

However, you don't need a comma if the subordinating conjunction appears **between** the two clauses:

- ☑ The nest was safe from predators <u>because</u> it was hidden in dense bushes.
- ☑ We will have to reduce our services <u>unless</u> we can increase revenue.

Valid comma use #4: To set off a nonessential relative clause

A **nonessential relative clause** usually starts with *which* or *who*. For a clause to qualify as nonessential (also known as **nonrestrictive**), you should be able to remove it from the sentence without changing the overall meaning. If such a clause comes in the middle of the sentence, then it needs commas before and after; if it comes at the end of the sentence, then it just needs the one comma before.

- ☑ Wolves◯ <u>which</u> are highly social◯ live in packs.
- ☑ Professor Byrd◯ <u>who</u> twice won the Booker Prize◯ will be retiring next year.
- ☑ Miranda rescheduled the meeting◯ <u>which</u> had been canceled.

(There is another kind of relative clause, the **essential** relative clause, which does not require commas. For complete details on how to tell the two apart, see the chapter on clauses.)

Valid comma use #5: In a list of 3 or more things

In a list of three or more things, each one (except the last) should be followed by a comma.

- ☑ The class studied poetry◯ novels◯ and plays.
- ☑ Cora said she would sand◯ prime◯ and paint the bureau today.

Valid comma use #6: Between coordinate adjectives

It's not unusual to see several adjectives lined up in front of a noun. Sometimes those adjectives need a comma between them, but not always. It depends on whether you've got **coordinate adjective** or **cumulative adjectives**. So what's the difference?

Coordinate adjectives each independently modify the noun. It's like you're learning two separate bits of information about the noun. For example:

☑ The audience suffered through the long, boring lecture.

What do we know about this lecture? First, it's long. Second, it's boring. Those two facts are distinct but on equal footing in terms of how they modify the noun. **Coordinate adjectives should be separated by a comma.**

A little trick to help figure out whether you're looking at coordinate adjectives is this: check whether you could swap the order of the adjectives or insert the word *and* between them. If the sentence still sounds relatively normal, then they're probably coordinate adjectives.

☑ The audience suffered through the long and boring lecture.
☑ The audience suffered through the boring, long lecture.

Cumulative adjectives, on the other hand, modify the noun in differing ways. The adjective closest to the noun creates a single larger unit—it tells you specifically what kind of noun you have. The adjective further away from the noun then modifies that entire unit. For example:

> In either case, be sure **not** to put a comma between the final adjective and the noun.

☑ He showed off his new (electric guitar).

The noun is *guitar*. The closest adjective to the noun is *electric*, which tells you what kind of guitar and creates a single grammatical unit. You can think of the phrase *electric guitar* as one big noun. The more distant adjective is *new*. It modifies the entire unit—it tells you what kind of electric guitar. **Cumulative adjectives do not require a comma.**

To double-check whether these adjectives are really cumulative, try the trick mentioned above. Could you swap the order of the adjectives? Could you insert the word *and* between them? No. The result looks strange and wrong:

☒ He showed off his electric new guitar.
☒ He showed off his new and electric guitar.

Drill: Coordinate and Cumulative Adjectives

Each of the sentences below contains several adjectives lined up in front of a noun. They may be either coordinate or cumulative. Decide whether the sentence displays correct comma usage.

1. He was unnerved by the Ferris wheel's noisy, erratic, lurches.
   ☐ Correct   ☐ Incorrect

2. The new version of the drone comes with highly precise technical specifications.
   ☐ Correct   ☐ Incorrect

3. We set out on the steep twisty path that led to the overlook.
   ☐ Correct   ☐ Incorrect

4. The builders of the first submarine went to great lengths to prepare themselves for the harrowing, dangerous underwater journey.
   ☐ Correct   ☐ Incorrect

5. Jasmin filmed a personal, documentary video to chronicle her experience.
   ☐ Correct   ☐ Incorrect

6. The accountant made a careful, comprehensive review of the year's transactions.
   ☐ Correct   ☐ Incorrect

7. The game show contestant fell through the trap door as a loud buzzing, noise indicated her failure.
   ☐ Correct   ☐ Incorrect

Valid comma use #7: To set off a parenthetical element

A parenthetical element is a word or phrase that interrupts the flow of a sentence and adds additional, nonessential information. You saw previously that dashes and parentheses can create parentheticals. Commas can do so as well.

- ☑ Tortoises⊙ on the other hand⊙ can live for hundreds of years.
- ☑ The performer⊙ after a quick bow⊙ left the stage.
- ☑ Some invertebrates⊙ such as the fruit fly⊙ are known to sleep.
- ☑ Saturn's rings⊙ astronomers say⊙ could disappear within 100 million years.
- ☑ The tribe⊙ therefore⊙ moved into an area with better hunting.

Valid comma use #8: To set off a quotation

See the earlier discussion about quotation marks.

Valid comma use #9: For a nonessential appositive that follows the noun it modifies

An appositive is a big noun phrase that modifies another noun. An appositive can appear either before or after the noun it modifies, and **sometimes** it needs commas. The actual criterion for deciding whether commas are needed has to do with whether the appositive is essential and gives meaning to the sentence (nonessential appositives get commas, essential ones don't). But this gets into some gray area that the SAT doesn't really like to get tangled up in. They don't want angry people calling up after the test to engage in endless philosophical debates about meaningfulness.

The only appositive issues you're likely to be tested on are (1) an introductory appositive to begin a sentence, which needs a comma as discussed above, and (2) the pattern of a **person's name as the noun** and their **title or role as the appositive**. If the title is **before** the name, then it doesn't require any commas, but if it's **after**, then it needs to be set off by commas.

☑ The team chose <u>director of marketing Vivian Parks</u> to lead the project.

☑ The team chose <u>Vivian Parks, director of marketing,</u> to lead the project.

> If you see the pattern of **a title + a name**:
>
> Title first = no commas
>
> Name first = commas around the title

Here are a few more examples. These have the title first, so no commas are needed:

☑ I was accompanied by <u>cultural anthropologist</u> Darren Becker on the tour.

☑ The reporter asked <u>twenty-one-year-old</u> Lydia Norton about the topic.

☑ The study was published by <u>associate professor of musicology</u> Peter Saldo.

These have the name first, and thus use commas:

☑ I was accompanied by Darren Becker, a cultural anthropologist, on the tour.

☑ The reporter asked Lydia Norton, a twenty-one-year-old, about the topic.

☑ The study was published by Peter Saldo, an associate professor of musicology.

If the title both precedes the noun and begins the sentence, it gets a little tricky. But it's safe to say that if the appositive begins with *a*, *an*, *the*, or *one*, then it's an introductory element and needs a comma.

Drill: Names and Titles

Each sentence below includes a title or role used as an appositive. Decide whether the sentence is punctuated correctly.

1. Australia native Priya Cooper won nine Paralympic gold medals in swimming.
   ☐ Correct   ☐ Incorrect

2. When she first moved to New York, Te Ata, a Native American storyteller, hoped to perform in front of audiences with little knowledge of her culture.
   ☐ Correct   ☐ Incorrect

3. Several groundbreaking theories in physics were developed by German mathematician, Emmy Noether.
   ☐ Correct   ☐ Incorrect

4. A leading expert in the field of occupational health Alice Hamilton was the first woman appointed to the faculty of Harvard University.
   ☐ Correct   ☐ Incorrect

5. With fellow arranger Scott Snyder, O'Brien reworked all the music on the album.
   ☐ Correct   ☐ Incorrect

6. The class wrote a report on Walter Gropius, the founder of the Bauhaus Movement and visited one of the buildings inspired by his style.
   ☐ Correct   ☐ Incorrect

7. Later that year, chemist Anthony Mendoza and his son, materials scientist Pedro Mendoza, published their findings.
   ☐ Correct   ☐ Incorrect

8. In 2015, professional surfer, Kelly Slater built a huge artificial wave pool in the middle of a farmer's field.
   ☐ Correct   ☐ Incorrect

Valid comma use #10: To indicate a contrast, a shift, or a distinct pause

- ☑ Incandescent bulbs use most of their electricity to produce heat, not light.
- ☑ The marketplace seemed impossibly chaotic, yet remarkably coherent.
- ☑ He accepted the award in a manner that was humble, almost apologetic.
- ☑ Social structure, not technology, is the focus of most science fiction.
- ☑ Early hominids, like other scavengers, ate primarily fruit.

Valid comma use #11: To set off a participial phrase that acts as an adverb or refers to an earlier part of the sentence

A **participial phrase** begins with a participle—a word that looks like a verb but really acts as a modifier. A participial phrase can either modify an adjacent noun (and thus act as a big adjective) or modify a more distant verb (and thus act as a big adverb).

A participial phrase that comes immediately after the noun it modifies doesn't need a comma:

- ☑ The museum has a log showing each item's origins.

- ☑ The band played a song requested by the audience.

- ☑ The city plans to build a new subway line connecting the two neighborhoods.

But if a participial phrase modifies a distant verb or the entire situation that comes before, then it does need to be set off with commas. This often happens when the participial phrase appears at the end of a sentence.

- ☑ The jet stream changed course over the weekend, increasing the likelihood of tornado formation.

- ☑ Underwater thermal vents discharge chemical nutrients into the surrounding water, sustaining entire ecosystems of unusual creatures.

- ☑ Nationalism and self-indulgence were rampant in the 1920s, leading some historians to blame such attitudes for the Great Depression.
  → modifies the entire preceding situation

For more information about participles, see the chapter on sentence structure.

Valid comma use #12: To separate a city from a state or a date from a year

Don't forget that you need a second comma **following** the state or year.

- ☑ They traveled to Adamstown, Pennsylvania, to shop for antiques.
- ☑ Enthusiasts still talk about the December 31, 1999, concert in the Everglades.

And more!

There are many more valid uses for commas, but this list should cover just about everything you might be tested on.

Commas Gone Bad

Now it's time to talk about common **mistakes** with commas that you'll definitely see in the answer choices. Be sure to avoid these errors.

Comma error #1: The comma splice

The dreaded comma splice occurs when a sentence has **two complete clauses** connected by **nothing but a comma**.

A clause contains both a subject and a verb. In the examples below, the subject and verb of each clause are marked, along with the illegal comma that joins them.

☒ The vacation was wonderful, we saw all the major attractions.

☒ Stinkbugs produce unpleasant chemicals, this strategy discourages predators.

☒ He has been in sales for nine years, he is an expert by now.

For all the rest of the comma errors below, the fix is simply to get rid of the unnecessary comma or move it to the proper position. But to correct a comma splice, you'll have to do something more, such as add a conjunction, rearrange the sentence structure, or break the sentence into two.

Comma error #2: A comma separating a subject from its verb

Unless the comma is there for one of the valid reasons mentioned previously, you should not separate a subject from its verb with a comma.

☒ The most important thing for new gardeners, is good soil nutrition.

☒ Her clever, insightful approach to advertising, made the campaign a success.

☒ A good night's sleep before an important presentation, can have a big effect.

Comma error #3: A comma after a coordinating conjunction instead of before

Commas belong **before** coordinating junctions, not after.

☒ The flood receded after a week but, people talked about it for years afterward.

☒ Regulations are always changing and, professionals must keep up to date.

☒ The bacteria must receive amino acids or, they will begin to die.

Comma error #4: A comma between a preposition and its object

❌ His top economic advisors presented him with, a plan.

❌ The show features several types of dance, such as, ballet and tap.

❌ With her game today, she set a new school record for, goals scored.

Comma error #5: A comma between an adjective and the noun it modifies

This illegal comma often tries to sneak in after coordinate adjectives, but you don't need a comma between an adjective and the noun it modifies.

❌ Cynthia was a calm, forceful, leader in a time of great upheaval.

❌ The tired hikers jumped into the cold, clear, stream.

❌ The sculpture was studded with colorful, eye-catching, buttons.

Comma error #6: A comma between a prepositional phrase and the word it modifies

❌ We left the path and saw a huge bird, in the clearing.

❌ Alejandro knew that someday he would return, to the city.

❌ She was not afraid, of rapid change.

> A comma error that shows up on the ACT is the use of commas surrounding an **intensive pronoun**, which ends in -*self* or -*selves*. For example:
>
> ❌ *The mayor, himself, attended the party.*
>
> These commas are not necessary. We haven't seen this issue yet on the SAT, but they may decide to test it someday.

Drill: Finding Comma Errors

The passage below contains a number of commas. Some are used properly, while others are placed erroneously. Find and mark the comma **errors** *with an X. All the commas in the passage have been circled to make them easier to notice.*

Even from 512 miles above the Earth, holiday lights shine bright and, now we're able to measure just how much. Miguel Román, a research physical scientist and remote sensing specialist at NASA Goddard Space Flight Center, has been looking at daily data, from the Suomi National Polar-orbiting Partnership (Suomi NPP) satellite and has identified how patterns in nighttime light intensity change during major, holiday seasons—Christmas and New Year's in the United States and the holy month of Ramadan in the Middle East. In comparing the six weeks, between Thanksgiving and New Year's in the U.S., he and his team, noticed large areas where night lights were 20-50% brighter than during the rest of the year.

Suomi NPP, which circles the Earth from the North Pole to, the South Pole and back about 14 times a day, carries an instrument that can observe the dark side of the planet and detect the glow of lights in cities and towns across the globe. The analysis of holiday lights uses an innovative, advanced, algorithm that filters out moonlight, clouds, and airborne particles in order to isolate city lights on a daily basis. The data from this algorithm, provides high-quality satellite information on light output across the globe, allowing scientists to track when—and how brightly—people illuminate the night. Holiday light displays have become more affordable, people are pushing them to new limits every year.

Dr. Román believes we need to better understand the driving forces behind energy use, including how dominant social, phenomena, the changing demographics of urban centers, and socio-cultural settings affect energy-use decisions. The satellite data can help cities estimate the timing of their peak energy use, it can also predict how much electricity they will use in a given time period.

The most certain way
to succeed is always
to try just one more time

— Thomas Edison

Practice Question Set

The questions in the following practice set test **punctuation**. *Work on the set without time limits— focus on accuracy alone.*

1

The portrait of businessman Sam Wilson created by James Montgomery Flagg for the July 6, 1916, issue of *Leslie's Weekly* soon became one of the most recognizable symbols of the United <u>States; Uncle</u> Sam.

A) NO CHANGE

B) States. Uncle

C) States, it was Uncle

D) States: Uncle

2

In addition to showcasing dozens of photographs in a vivid <u>narrative. Messenheimer</u> maps the locations of the photographs taken along the routes of the railroad, linking them to the rugged geography of the west.

A) NO CHANGE

B) narrative; Messenheimer

C) narrative: Messenheimer

D) narrative, Messenheimer

3

Given these difficulties, <u>it's obvious that the</u> <u>restoration attempts</u> were far from perfect, but there is hope for improvement.

A) NO CHANGE

B) it's obvious that the restoration attempts'

C) its obvious that the restoration attempt's

D) its obvious that the restoration attempts

4

Those in favor of the effort to change New Zealand's flag cited several <u>reasons, such as,</u> the current flag's similarity to the Australian flag and the idea that it no longer reflects New Zealand's modern status as an independent, multicultural nation.

A) NO CHANGE

B) reasons such as:

C) reasons such as,

D) reasons, such as

5

Astronomers are hoping that the new telescope can help address <u>the issue of why the Milky Way is</u> <u>warped, which is a question that remains</u> <u>unanswered.</u>

A) NO CHANGE

B) why it is that warping is what the Milky Way does.

C) an unanswered question: Why is the Milky Way warped?

D) an unanswered question with regard to the Milky Way: What warped it?

6

Adjusting the recipe in this way turned the unappetizing bricks into warm fluffy, blueberry delights that had the judges asking for more.

A) NO CHANGE

B) warm and fluffy, blueberry

C) warm, fluffy blueberry

D) warm, fluffy, blueberry,

7

Inventor Emile Berliner developed several groundbreaking recording technologies: the microphone, the gramophone player, and the flat recording disc, and is thus responsible for the countless black platters that still populate record stores today.

A) NO CHANGE

B) technologies: the microphone, the gramophone player, and the flat recording disc—

C) technologies—the microphone, the gramophone player, and the flat recording disc—

D) technologies; the microphone, the gramophone player, and the flat recording disc;

8

To be domesticated, a species must have a good disposition and should not panic under pressure, criteria that not all animals meet. Consider zebras, for example, even when they are raised around humans, their unpredictable nature and tendency to attack preclude them from being good candidates for domestication.

A) NO CHANGE

B) zebras, for example:

C) zebras for example,

D) zebras. For example,

9

Once they establish a career, interpreters receive wages that compare favorably with those of many other professions': the median annual salary for translators is $51,790.

A) NO CHANGE

B) professions': the median annual salary for translators'

C) professions; the median annual salary for translator's

D) professions; the median annual salary for translators

10

Telegrams were, of course, employed for official purposes by the military, but servicemen and women also used telegrams to communicate with their family's; they sent the messages to wish people happy holidays, to let them know they had returned to the United States, or simply to convey their love.

A) NO CHANGE

B) families:

C) families'

D) families

11

No one knows for sure why people say "it's raining cats and dogs" to describe a heavy downpour, but etymologists—people who study the origins of words, have suggested a variety of mythological and literal explanations.

A) NO CHANGE
B) words—
C) words;
D) words

12

Haverstraw, a town northeast of New York City, was once nicknamed "brickmaking capital of the world," for supplying the metropolis with materials for many of the city's then-signature brownstone and brick structures.

A) NO CHANGE
B) nicknamed, "brickmaking capital of the world,"
C) nicknamed, "brickmaking capital of the world"
D) nicknamed "brickmaking capital of the world"

13

Solar panel installers know that the amount of insolation, or exposure to the sun's rays; on a surface is largest when the surface faces directly toward the sun.

A) NO CHANGE
B) or exposure to the sun's rays on,
C) or, exposure to the sun's rays on,
D) or exposure to the sun's rays, on

14

Masters initially practiced law, but he eventually realized that his true life's calling was poetry, publishing a collection of poems—titled *A Book of Verses*, in 1898.

A) NO CHANGE
B) poetry; publishing a collection of poems titled *A Book of Verses*, in 1898.
C) poetry, publishing a collection of poems—titled *A Book of Verses*—in 1898.
D) poetry, publishing a collection of poems titled *A Book of Verses*—in 1898.

15

Kruesi's ideal program, the Department of Folklore and Folklife at the University of Pennsylvania eventually accepted her and enabled her to study with a number of prominent folklorists and anthropologists.

A) NO CHANGE
B) program, the Department of Folklore and Folklife at the University of Pennsylvania,
C) program: the Department of Folklore and Folklife at the University of Pennsylvania,
D) program, the Department of Folklore and Folklife (at the University of Pennsylvania)

16

One extreme example of this geography <u>is Death Valley, California; the</u> lowest spot in North America.

A) NO CHANGE
B) is: Death Valley, California, the
C) is Death Valley, California—the
D) is Death Valley, California (the

17

Hundreds of people every day journey to see <u>sculptor, Constantin Brancusi's,</u> *Endless Column,* considered to be one of the great works of 20th-century outdoor sculpture.

A) NO CHANGE
B) sculptor, Constantin Brancusi's
C) sculptor Constantin Brancusi's,
D) sculptor Constantin Brancusi's

18

Allergists have found that children from large <u>families—particularly the younger members—</u> typically have fewer allergies than do children from smaller families.

A) NO CHANGE
B) families, particularly the younger members
C) families particularly the younger members,
D) families—particularly the younger members

19

Before the academic year, teachers usually ask students to acquire standard school <u>supplies, such as</u> pencils, binders, and calculators.

A) NO CHANGE
B) supplies, such as:
C) supplies such as:
D) supplies, such as,

20

These chambers allow the ants to carry out a peculiar <u>activity; "farming"</u> aphids to produce a steady supply of food for the colony.

A) NO CHANGE
B) activity—"farming,"
C) activity: "farming"
D) activity, "farming,"

21

In the next class, the chef discussed three distinctive ingredients used in Cajun cuisine—popcorn rice, cayenne pepper jelly, and fish stock—and helped us incorporate them into a satisfying meal.

A) NO CHANGE

B) popcorn, rice cayenne, pepper,

C) popcorn rice cayenne, pepper

D) popcorn, rice, cayenne, pepper,

22

Given the recent entry into force of the 2013 Marrakesh Treaty to Facilitate Access to Published Works for Persons Who Are Blind, Visually Impaired or Otherwise Print Disabled; there is hope that progress will be made in addressing the book famine that affects visually impaired communities worldwide.

A) NO CHANGE

B) Disabled. There

C) Disabled, there

D) Disabled—there

23

Andres Patrignani and Tyson E. Ochsner developed a Matlab-based tool called Canopeo, which they used to measure fractional green canopy cover—in the Stillwater, Oklahoma, area.

A) NO CHANGE

B) cover, in the Stillwater

C) cover in the Stillwater

D) cover in the Stillwater,

24

Undeterred by the delayed admission, Thorpe, a highly educated woman who had been employed as a social worker before joining the military, quickly caught up with her white counterparts, she graduated on time the following month.

A) NO CHANGE

B) counterparts: she graduated,

C) counterparts; she graduated

D) counterparts, she graduated,

25

What if after 235 years all that was left to tell the story of your life was a single scrap of paper.

A) NO CHANGE

B) single scrap—of paper!

C) single scrap of paper?

D) single, scrap of paper?

26

As a substitute for an eagle's feathers, whose use is legally restricted, the replica Muscogee war bonnet contains twenty <u>hawk feather's.</u>

A) NO CHANGE
B) hawk feathers.
C) hawk feathers'.
D) hawks feathers.

27

The Treasury Department scrapped the $1,000 note shortly after it was released. The Treasury's objection to this design had nothing to do with the font's absurd resemblance to <u>watermelons, however, the</u> true problem was that the design back, which was completely covered with engraving, made it difficult to plainly see the red and blue fibers running through the distinctive new paper.

A) NO CHANGE
B) watermelons, however. The
C) watermelons—however, the
D) watermelons however the

28

Eleanor Perenyi agrees. Her garden, in contrast to those of her Connecticut neighbors, is filled with vibrant colors, sumptuous shapes, and dinner plate dahlias. <u>Perenyi's neighbors</u> tasteful, subdued displays seem uninspiring and dull to her.

A) NO CHANGE
B) Perenyi's neighbors'
C) Perenyis' neighbor's
D) Perenyis' neighbors

29

In the photo, <u>seventy-one-year-old Frank Goss</u> can be seen in front of Hastings's general store and post office, reading his mail.

A) NO CHANGE
B) seventy-one-year-old, Frank Goss
C) seventy-one-year-old, Frank Goss,
D) seventy-one-year-old Frank Goss,

30

"Unfortunately, the courts have been slow in extending the Fourth Amendment to new technology," said James <u>Dempsey vice president for public policy</u> at the Center for Democracy and Technology.

A) NO CHANGE
B) Dempsey; vice president for public policy,
C) Dempsey, vice president for public policy
D) Dempsey: vice president for public policy,

31

It is important to retain the original artifacts for future researchers, for often the <u>precision with which</u> measurements can be made is dependent upon the technology of the time.

A) NO CHANGE

B) precision, with which

C) precision, with which,

D) precision with, which

32

She wrote <u>witty, irreverent poems,</u> similar to limericks to draw attention to the serious issue of unsafe working conditions in the textile factories.

A) NO CHANGE

B) witty, irreverent, poems,

C) witty, irreverent poems

D) witty irreverent poems,

33

According to Plato, there are seven different kinds of love, to which he assigned names. The love between parents and their children <u>is *storge*: for example,</u> while friendship or shared goodwill is *philia*.

A) NO CHANGE

B) is *storge*, for example:

C) is, *storge* for example—

D) is *storge*, for example,

34

Onions produce a chemical irritant known as syn-propanethial-S-oxide, which stimulates the <u>eye's lachrymal gland's</u> and causes them to release tears.

A) NO CHANGE

B) eye's lachrymal gland

C) eyes lachrymal gland's

D) eyes' lachrymal glands

35

Paleontologists have long wondered why <u>dinosaurs went extinct?</u>

A) NO CHANGE

B) did dinosaurs go extinct?

C) dinosaurs went extinct.

D) were dinosaurs caused to go extinct.

36

Contemporary descriptions of Mark Twain's voice describe it as something <u>that,</u> "was an unmistakable and vital part of his humorous presentations."

A) NO CHANGE

B) that—

C) that

D) that:

37

Thanks to improved water <u>quality, catfish, bass, perch, and shad, inhabit</u> the river in increasing numbers.

A) NO CHANGE

B) quality, catfish, bass, perch, and shad inhabit

C) quality catfish bass perch and shad inhabit

D) quality catfish, bass perch and shad inhabit,

38

In an 1893 <u>interview, Russian expressionist painter,</u> Wassily Kandinsky likened painting to composing music.

A) NO CHANGE

B) interview, Russian expressionist painter

C) interview, Russian, expressionist painter

D) interview Russian expressionist painter,

39

The front-page <u>headline in the Chicago Daily Tribune proclaimed,</u> "Dewey Defeats Truman," despite the fact that the polls had not even closed.

A) NO CHANGE

B) headline in the Chicago Daily Tribune, proclaimed

C) headline, in the Chicago Daily Tribune proclaimed,

D) headline, in the Chicago Daily Tribune, proclaimed

40

Likewise, the <u>cheetahs pattern of spots</u> is unique and can be used by wildlife biologists to quickly identify an individual as part of an effort to understand population trends.

A) NO CHANGE

B) cheetahs' pattern of spots'

C) cheetah's pattern of spots

D) cheetah's pattern of spot's

ഒ Sentence Structure ഉ
Part 1: Clauses

Sentence structure is all about how sentences are put together—specifically clauses, phrases, and other large-scale sentence components. There are **a lot** of interlocking rules and moving parts at work, so things can certainly get complicated. Unfortunately, this is also the most commonly tested grammar topic, so there's no escaping it. You have to get a handle on these rules.

We'll divide this discussion into two halves: clauses and phrases.

First, clauses. **A clause contains both a subject and a verb.** A sentence might contain just one clause, or it might have several. When there are several, they have to be joined properly. There are some good ways of joining clauses, and as you can guess, some bad ways.

For the SAT, you need to know about **four valid ways to connect clauses**. They are:

- ⊙ A coordinating conjunction
- ⊙ A subordinating conjunction
- ⊙ A relative pronoun, such as *which, that,* or *who*
- ⊙ A valid punctuation mark, such as a semicolon, a colon, or a dash. But not a comma!

Coordinating Conjunctions

There are exactly seven coordinating conjunctions. You can remember them using the acronym FANBOYS:

F = For
A = And
N = Nor
B = But
O = Or
Y = Yet
S = So

> These words can do other things too. For example, *so* can also be an adverb, and *for* can also be a preposition. So you don't always need to shoehorn them into the coordinating conjunction role.

You use these conjunctions (mostly *and, or, but* & *so*) about a thousand times a day, so they shouldn't come as any big surprise. When you use a coordinating conjunction to join two clauses, put the conjunction **between** the clauses and use **a comma in front** of the conjunction.

In the examples below, the subject and verb of each clause are marked.

- ☑ The instructor gave the signal, (and) we boarded the plane.

- ☑ Parachutes occasionally fail, (so) everyone had a backup chute.

- ☑ Some people were jumping alone, (but) my first jump would be tandem.

- ☑ She reassured me, (for) I appeared quite nervous.

As we mentioned back in the section on commas, coordinating conjunctions can join smaller sentence components too, such as two nouns or two verbs. When that's the case, you don't need a comma before the conjunction. The comma is only required when the conjunction joins two full clauses or a list of three or more things.

- ☑ Fiona snapped a photo of the mother (and) ducklings.
- ☑ Keith spilled the coffee (but) kept his shirt dry.

> No commas necessary

Subordinating Conjunctions

There are a lot of subordinating conjunctions, and some of them are pretty obscure, but some of the most common ones are:

Subordinating Conjunctions		
because	before	once
unless	after	as
if	until	though
although	while	when
so that	since	

These words can connect clauses in two different ways. A subordinating conjunction can appear **between** the clauses, and you **don't need a comma** in that case.

Or the conjunction can appear **before** the first clause. In that situation, you **need a comma** to indicate the end of the first clause and the beginning of the second.

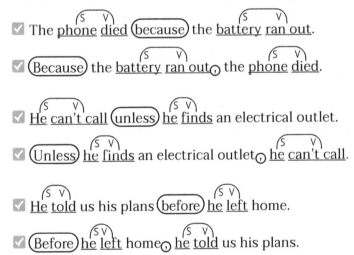

The second example in each pair is not a comma splice, even though there is a comma between two clauses. That's because the subordinating conjunction at the beginning of the sentence serves as the "connective tissue" that properly joins the clauses.

Somehow, the idea that you should not begin a sentence with the word *because* retains a mysterious grip on people's brains. The reason for this might be that a sentence beginning with *because* could end up a fragment if you're not careful to follow up the "because clause" with a second clause. But if the "because clause" is properly connected to another full thought, there is absolutely nothing wrong with it.

Relative Pronouns

Now we start to get complicated! The most common relative pronouns are *which* and *that*. Some others are *who, whose, whom,* and *what*. When a subject-verb pair is connected to the rest of a sentence by a relative pronoun, that clause is called a **relative clause**.

Here's an example of a relative clause:

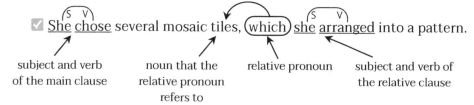

And here's another example, using *that*.

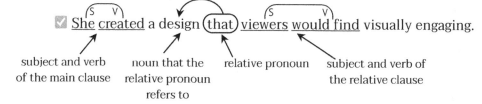

There are a couple important things to notice in these examples. First, each sentence contains two clauses, and the relative pronoun is the "connective tissue" that properly joins the clauses.

Second, relative pronouns are pronouns! So they, just like other pronouns, need an antecedent—a noun to refer to. Typically, it's the noun immediately preceding. Relative clauses are full thoughts, with subjects and verbs, but they're also **modifiers**. They give you further descriptive information about the noun they refer to.

Finally, both of the relative clauses above have a subject separate from the relative pronoun. But it's not always that way. In many cases, **the relative pronoun itself can be the subject of the relative clause**. For example:

☑ Blood contains hemoglobin, <u>which</u> <u>delivers</u> oxygen to the muscles.

The word *which* is doing double duty here. First, it refers to the noun *hemoglobin*, so we know the relative clause is giving us further modifying information about hemoglobin. Second, it acts as the subject for the singular verb *delivers*. Here's another similar example:

☑ The heart secretes hormones <u>that</u> <u>regulate</u> blood pressure.

Here, *that* refers to the noun *hormones*, and it also acts as the subject for the plural verb *regulate*.

> You might see a subject-verb agreement question in which the subject is a relative pronoun. You can't tell just by looking at *which* or *that* whether it's singular or plural. You have to go back and check the number of the antecedent.

Take a look at a few more examples, showing some of the other relative pronouns in action:

☑ The center hosted a lecture by a historian <u>who</u> wrote about Georgia O'Keeffe.
☑ A bean can be any legume <u>whose</u> seeds or pods are eaten.
☑ Corporations should provide appropriate tools for those <u>whom</u> they employ.
☑ He didn't know <u>what</u> he should do about the enormous snowdrift.

But wait, there's more!

- First, there are some issues related to punctuation. Relative clauses come in two flavors—**essential** and **nonessential**—and they are punctuated differently. A nonessential relative clause could be removed from the sentence without substantially changing the meaning. It may also be called a nonrestrictive relative clause because it doesn't restrict or "narrow down" the noun or group of nouns it refers to—it just gives you an extra piece of information about that noun. **A nonessential relative clause should be set off with commas.**

On the other hand, if you removed an essential relative clause from the sentence, the meaning would be altered in some important way. It is sometimes called a restrictive relative clause because it narrows down or further refines the definition of the noun it refers to. **An essential relative clause does not require commas.**

Here's a good example of the difference:

☑ Bats, (which are nocturnal,) have excellent hearing.   - nonessential clause

☑ Bats (that live in cold climates) hibernate during winter.   - essential clause

In the first sentence, the clause is nonessential; if it were removed, the main point of the sentence would still be the same. It is also nonrestrictive because we get some additional information about *all* bats; the clause doesn't restrict the discussion to only certain bats. The nonessential clause is set off with commas.

> The general rule of thumb, good enough for most SAT questions, is:
>
> **which** creates nonessential relative clauses and should be preceded by a comma
>
> **that** creates essential relative clauses and should not be preceded by a comma

But the second sentence refers only to a certain subset of bats. The relative clause is essential because if it were removed, the meaning of the sentence would change—it would suggest that *all* bats, even those in warm climates, hibernate. Keeping the clause restricts the discussion to *only* those bats that live in cold climates. The essential clause does not have commas around it.

The words *which* and *that* are typically pretty easy to sort out. *Which* generally creates nonessential clauses and thus needs a comma. *That* creates essential clauses and doesn't need a comma. Annoyingly, however, the word *who* could go either way.

☑ If you have a question about the printers, find an employee, <u>who</u> can help you.
☑ If you have a question about the printers, find an employee <u>who</u> can help you.

The first sentence, with the comma before *who*, implies that every employee can help you. The second, without the comma, suggests that only certain ones are able to help.

- Next, you should be aware that in an essential relative clause in which the relative pronoun is not the subject, the relative pronoun is allowed to be dropped from the sentence. This creates what is called an **elliptical construction**, which just means that some words that can be guessed from context have been left out. It's perfectly correct, and you probably do it all the time in your speech and writing without thinking about it, but if you're scrutinizing the grammar of a sentence and looking for properly joined-up clauses, an elliptical construction might appear strange or wrong. Here are a couple examples:

> Don't use *which* to refer to a person. Use *who* or *whom* instead.
>
> However, *whose* isn't reserved for people. You can use it for any noun: *They studied the volcano, whose eruption caused a massive earthquake.*

    ☑ This is the time of day I enjoy most.   - elliptical construction
    ☑ This is the time of day <u>that</u> I enjoy most.   - complete construction

    ☑ Have you heard back from the people you invited?   - elliptical construction
    ☑ Have you heard back from the people <u>whom</u> you invited?   - complete construction

The takeaway lesson is this: if you see what looks like two clauses jammed together with no punctuation or any other connecting word, try inserting the word *that* (or *whom* for people) between the clauses. If the sentence works with *that*, then it's OK without it.

- A third issue to notice is **placement**. A relative clause can show up just about anywhere in the sentence. It can be at the end, in the middle, or in special cases, at the beginning. It's also not unusual to see one squeezed between the subject and verb of the main clause:

    ☑ The grammar <u>book</u> that <u>I read</u> <u>was</u> truly thrilling.

But here's the important thing: strictly speaking, a relative clause should always be **next to the noun that it modifies**. So something like the sentence below would be wrong because it doesn't follow that rule:

    ✗ Construction of the monument began in 1914, <u>which</u> lasted eight years.

Logically speaking, the pronoun *which* must refer to the noun *construction*, since that's what lasted eight years. However, the relative clause is too far away from that noun. It creates an unclear sentence.

Another, more subtle problem along the same lines would be a sentence like this:

> ☒ Experts advocate plenty of vitamin C, which they recommend a variety of fruits.

Because *which* is next to *vitamin C*, it must be modifying that noun. The verb in the relative clause is *recommend*, which has the subject *they*. When the relative pronoun is not itself the subject of the relative clause, then it must be the object of the verb. But here's the problem: there is already an object for the verb *recommend*—it's *a variety of fruits*. Thus *vitamin C*, the noun modified by the relative clause, is neither the subject nor the object of the relative clause. That's wrong.

Confused? Don't worry—breaking down a sentence with this level of detail takes a lot of work, so don't feel bad if it seems overwhelming or too much to do in the middle of a test. The good news is that your ear probably alerted you right away that the sentence was wrong. Errors like this do appear on the SAT, but they're not that common, and they'll probably just "seem" wrong to you when you read them, even if you can't articulate the exact grammar reason.

> It may sound obvious, but when you're taking a test, be sure to read the **entire sentence**, not just the underlined bit. An error like this is more likely to sneak past you when it's in the middle of a long sentence and you haven't read the entire thing.

OK, so as we said, **strictly speaking**, a relative clause should always be immediately next to the noun that it modifies. But there are times when the SAT isn't quite so strict. A simple example would be a sentence in which a relative clause modifies the adjacent **noun phrase** (including, for example, prepositional phrases) but not the very last noun in the phrase:

> ☑ Mallory refinished (the new table for the kitchen,) which she'd found at a yard sale.

Even though *which* is immediately next to *kitchen*, we don't interpret this sentence to mean that Mallory found her kitchen at a yard sale. That would be an... unusual yard sale! We understand that *which* refers to the entire noun phrase *the new table for the kitchen*, so this sentence is fine.

A slightly more troublesome example is something like this:

> ⊙ In winter, the sun's rays are oriented more diagonally, which reduces the amount of energy hitting any given spot.

Is this acceptable? Strictly speaking, no. What noun does *which* modify? It can't be *winter*. It can't be *the sun's rays*. There's no good candidate. So, strictly speaking, this is wrong. On the old version of the SAT, it was wrong. On other standardized tests, it's wrong. BUT...

People speak like this all the time. It probably sounds perfectly normal to you, because a little common sense can tell you that the relative clause refers to the **entire situation** of the sun's rays being oriented more diagonally in winter. And here's the annoying thing: a few recent SAT questions have had correct answers that were written in this way. Does this mean the SAT writers made a mistake? Are they getting lazy? Who knows? But if you see an answer choice like this, you'll just have to muzzle your inner grammar police and let it slide.

- The last thing (we promise!) to say about relative clauses is that sometimes a **preposition** appears **before a relative pronoun** when the noun being modified is the object of that preposition within the relative clause. For example:

Full sentence	The relative clause by itself
☑ The panel announced the metrics <u>by which</u> the chefs' submissions would be judged.	☑ The chefs' submissions would be judged <u>by the metrics</u>.
☑ The book details the challenges <u>with which</u> early settlers were confronted.	☑ Early settlers were confronted <u>with the challenges</u>.
☑ Ball lightning is a phenomenon <u>for which</u> no good explanation exists.	☑ No good explanation exists <u>for [the] phenomenon</u>.
☑ The Frisbee's trajectory was governed by principles <u>of which</u> the dog was not aware.	☑ The dog was not aware <u>of [the] principles</u>.

This is a somewhat formal way of speaking or writing. One reason to create a sentence like this would be to avoid ending a sentence with a preposition. In other cases, having the preposition right next to the noun just makes the sentence read more smoothly because words that naturally belong together don't get too far separated. A more conversational way of expressing these same sentences would be:

> You've surely heard the idea that you shouldn't end a sentence with a preposition, but that's **not a real rule**. It's like a grammar urban legend.
>
> Winston Churchill, when told by a speech editor to correct a sentence that ended with a preposition, is said to have replied, "This is the sort of nonsense up with which I will not put."

- ☑ The panel announced the metrics that the chefs' submissions would be judged by.
- ☑ The book details the challenges that early settlers were confronted with.
- ☑ Ball lightning is a phenomenon that no good explanation exists for.
- ☑ The Frisbee's trajectory was governed by principles that the dog was not aware of.

(You'll notice that in these "conversational versions," the relative pronoun is actually *that*, not *which*. The relative clauses are essential and don't use commas. But English doesn't allow us to put a preposition in front of *that* in this particular way, so in the "formal" versions, everything gets converted to *which*. As you'll see on the next page, this type of construction also can be used with nonessential relative clauses, which need commas. So it's similar to the situation with *who*—you'll need to use some logic to determine the proper punctuation.)

Because the SAT doesn't go out of its way to avoid ending sentences with prepositions, you won't see this structure all that frequently on the test. But there is a version of it that the test writers do like and that you should be comfortable with. It uses a relative pronoun after a preposition that modifies the subject of a clause, and it's a great way to avoid a comma splice. It looks like this:

> A comma splice is a grammatical error in which two clauses are joined by nothing but a comma.

Comma splice – wrong	Relative clause – correct
☒ There has been a recent surge of interest in various ballroom dances, <u>some of them</u> are hundreds of years old.	☑ There has been a recent surge of interest in various ballroom dances, <u>some of which</u> are hundreds of years old.
☒ The movie features two famous stars, <u>both of them</u> have won numerous awards for their past films.	☑ The movie features two famous stars, <u>both of whom</u> have won numerous awards for their past films.
☒ The factory has a strong culture of workplace safety, <u>the result of this</u> is a very low number of work-related injuries.	☑ The factory has a strong culture of workplace safety, <u>the result of which</u> is a very low number of work-related injuries.
☒ The football game, <u>the outcome of it</u> was never in doubt, was great fun for all the home fans.	☑ The football game, <u>the outcome of which</u> was never in doubt, was great fun for all the home fans.
☒ Americans older than 65, <u>twenty percent of them</u> still have jobs, are less financially secure than in years past.	☑ Americans older than 65, <u>twenty percent of whom</u> still have jobs, are less financially secure than in years past.

Why is this worth knowing about? Well, you should just be aware that, even when a relative pronoun such as *which* or *whom* appears three or four words deep into a relative clause, it can still be correct and can still provide a valid way of connecting a clause to the rest of the sentence.

> Remember, **who** is for subjects, while **whom** is for objects. So a relative pronoun acting as the object of a preposition will always be *whom*, not *who*.

Joining Clauses with Punctuation

The punctuation marks that are allowed to join full clauses are:

> Semicolons, colons, and dashes are **allowed** to connect clauses, but they **don't have to**. Check out the chapter on punctuation to see what other jobs they can perform.

- ⊙ A semicolon
- ⊙ A colon
- ⊙ A dash

The previous chapter already covered these punctuation marks in all their glory, so we don't need to go through all the details again. But just as a reminder, here are some examples in which clauses are properly joined by punctuation.

Semicolons

☑ In 1637, Dutch tulip bulb prices collapsed; bulbs were selling for less than one tenth of their peak value.

☑ Some chemicals cause cancer in humans but not in rats; thus, we must be careful in evaluating the results of animal studies.

Colons

☑ Dominique showed a deep level of concern for the houseplant: she even hired a botanist for advice.

☑ This newspaper cannot be trusted in its story about the company: it misspelled the president's name.

Dashes

☑ At age four, he already had perfect pitch—he was able to identify the pitch of an isolated musical note.

☑ Some allergies may be alleviated by gradual exposure—a person's immune system can learn not to overreact to certain allergens.

Drill: Finding Clauses and the Words that Connect Them

Each sentence below contains one or more clauses. First, find each clause by underlining the subject and verb and connecting them with a line. Then find and circle each "clause connector" (conjunction, relative pronoun, or punctuation mark). **Note:** *a subject should be just a single noun, so ignore prepositional phrases and other modifiers. But a "verb" may be a longer phrase containing a main verb along with some helper verbs.* **Another note:** *in some cases, a relative pronoun may be* both *the subject of a clause* and *the connector.*

Example: A grass roof on a house is not common, (but) it can be surprisingly practical.

1. This baseball postseason has been a particularly exciting time for baseball fans.

2. On October 13, 1792, the cornerstone of the White House was laid near the banks of the Potomac River.

3. Jade of any kind was revered by the Olmec, the Maya, and other Mesoamerican cultures, and a significant variety of carved jade objects have been found in archaeological contexts.

4. Games are the perfect platform for testing artificial intelligence algorithms because they have very definite outcomes.

5. Everything is related to everything else, but near things are more related than distant things.

6. If we can develop a better way to measure the amount of biomass in a tree, carbon offset programs can be improved.

7. You should be mindful of the rules of respectful civil discourse in everything that you post on a website or on social media.

8. Dacey and Marble's paper, which was widely read at the time, is one of the best treatments of the foundations of geographic information systems.

9. Although Carl Sagan was not himself a poet, the imagery on display in the best of his prose verges on the poetic.

10. In the era before global cable networks, Alistair Cooke's BBC radio feature was one of the primary means by which English-speakers in Africa, Asia, Australia, Latin America, and Europe understood American culture.

11. The puzzling lyrics of "Auld Lang Syne" carry a clear message: no, you should not forget all of your old acquaintances.

12. A coronal mass ejection is invisible, but if you could see its shape, it would cause Earth to resemble a comet with a long magnetic tail behind it.

13. A sneeze is a reflex that is triggered when nerve endings inside the mucous membrane of the nose are stimulated.

14. The city of Oatman, Arizona, hosts an annual Solar Egg Frying Contest on the 4th of July, and the judges allow aids, such as mirrors, aluminum reflectors, or magnifying glasses, which help to focus the sun's energy onto the egg itself.

Clauses Gone Bad

Now that you've seen the proper ways to connect clauses, it's time to talk about the seedy underbelly of clauses—clauses that have turned to a life of crime and broken the laws of grammar. Don't end up like these like these poor, wretched sentences; stay in school and follow the rules!

Clause error #1: A comma splice

A comma alone isn't strong enough to do the heavy lifting of joining clauses. If a comma is the only thing connecting two clauses, you've got the dreaded comma splice.

❌ Computers in modern education are a necessity, every school uses them.

❌ The gold in an artifact contains trace chemical elements, they can identify the relic's source.

❌ Some tarantulas lack venomous fangs, these species make good pets.

Clause error #2: A conjunctive adverb posing as a conjunction

Conjunctive adverbs are transition words. There are dozens of them, but some of the more common ones are:

Conjunctive adverbs			
accordingly	furthermore	moreover	similarly
also	hence	namely	still
anyway	however	nevertheless	then
besides	incidentally	next	thereafter
certainly	indeed	nonetheless	therefore
consequently	instead	now	thus
finally	likewise	otherwise	undoubtedly
further	meanwhile		

These words look a whole lot like conjunctions, and they carry a lot of the same meanings. For example, doesn't *however* seem pretty similar to *although*? But here's the problem: conjunctive adverbs are **adverbs, not conjunctions**. They're **not allowed** to do the work of joining clauses.

The word *however* is the most common offender:

❌ Tarik opened the envelope, however, the letter was missing.

You've surely seen sentences like this (and maybe even written a few), but it's **wrong**! *However* is not a conjunction. It's not allowed to join clauses.

Here are a few more examples of conjunctive adverbs misbehaving:

- ☒ This area has many successful farms, (therefore) it must have good soil.
- ☒ First we'll discuss the budget, (then) we'll move on to the proposed renovations.
- ☒ Purple loosestrife is considered a harmful invasive species, (accordingly) there are efforts in some places to eradicate it.
- ☒ Morris is supposed to be avoiding bacon, (nevertheless) he eats it every morning for breakfast.

This raises two important questions. First, how do you fix such an error? One good option is to swap out the conjunctive adverb for a real, live conjunction:

- ☑ Tarik opened the envelope, (but) the letter was missing.
- ☑ (Because) this area has many successful farms, it must have good soil.

Another possibility is to simply break the sentence into two with a period:

- ☑ First we'll discuss the budget⊙ Then we'll move on to the proposed renovations.
- ☑ Purple loosestrife is considered a harmful invasive species⊙ Accordingly, there are efforts in some places to eradicate it.

The final option is to rearrange the sentence so that something else (punctuation, a relative pronoun, or a conjunction) connects the clauses, with the conjunctive adverb just along for the ride, providing some flavor. A semicolon just before the conjunctive adverb is a popular choice:

> This sentence is correct because the semicolon, not the word *however*, does the work of connecting the clauses.

- ☑ Tarik opened the envelope; however, the letter was missing.
- ☑ Morris is supposed to be avoiding bacon, (which) he nevertheless eats every morning for breakfast.

The second important question is: if conjunctive adverbs aren't allowed to connect clauses, how can they be used correctly? Great question! You're really paying attention. Obviously, these are all real words, so there must be some way of using them. Job #1, as we've discussed, is to make sure they're not connecting clauses. So you can use them in any sentence that has just a single clause, or in any sentence where several clauses are joined by some other, valid method.

After that, you're free to sprinkle in conjunctive adverbs however you like. The only rule is that a conjunctive adverb with more than one syllable must be set off by commas.

- ☑ The new model of vacuum has a much more powerful electric motor. We can be sure, (therefore,) that it is better at picking up dust.
- ☑ Some anthropologists believe human bipedalism developed in open grasslands. Others point to an origin in forest environments, (however.)
- ☑ Our town's landfill is nearly full. (Consequently,) we must find a new solution.

Clause error #3: A run-on sentence

A run-on sentence is even worse than a comma splice. It's got nothing at all connecting the clauses. These are not commonly tested, but just be sure not to create one when deleting the underlined portion of a sentence.

> ☒ Waffles are great they really warm you up.
> ☒ She plays the piano he's on the drums.

Clause error #4: A sentence with too many conjunctions

For each additional clause added to a sentence after the first one, you need exactly one "connector"—a conjunction, a relative pronoun, or a valid punctuation mark. So a sentence with two clauses needs one connector, and a sentence with three clauses needs two connectors, etc.

Sometimes you'll see a sentence with too many connectors. For example, you might see two clauses with two conjunctions. That's an error.

> ☒ <u>Although</u> some experts advise keeping poinsettia plants away from children, <u>but</u> they are in fact not poisonous.
> ☒ <u>Because</u> insects are developing resistance to many common insecticides, <u>so</u> farmers are having to apply it in greater amounts.

Clause error #5: A sentence without a main verb

Sometimes a noun looks like it's trying to be the subject of a sentence, but it gets surrounded by so many modifiers that we never actually get a main verb. This creates a sentence fragment.

> ☒ Understanding that her illness could be serious, <u>Eliana</u>, who decided to see a specialist, with hopes for a quick recovery.
> ☒ An experimental aircraft that took off from the nearby military base, <u>the jet fighter</u>, which startled the townspeople with its sonic boom.

Drill: Connecting Clauses

Each sentence below includes several clauses. Decide whether the way in which the clauses are joined makes the sentence correct or incorrect.

1. People are wonderful engines of chance, and you are more likely to stumble on the unexpected when you engage in the act of discovery with another human, or with a group of humans.
   ☐ Correct   ☐ Incorrect

2. Early next year, the Moon will slip between the Earth and Sun, this has been happening every month or so for more than four billion years as the Moon orbits the Earth.
   ☐ Correct   ☐ Incorrect

3. Emily Greene Balch served on state municipal boards and city commissions, however, she was better known for her involvement in activist movements for racial justice, women's suffrage, and the pursuit of peace.
   ☐ Correct   ☐ Incorrect

4. About 70 percent of the 11,000 silent feature films from cinema's first few decades no longer exist, and many that survived did so in an incomplete form.
   ☐ Correct   ☐ Incorrect

5. At the same time, however, if a piece of writing becomes too edited, sometimes it can lose the spark that made it heartfelt or interesting in the first place.
   ☐ Correct   ☐ Incorrect

6. Excessive milling strips grains of their nutritional benefits, therefore, choosing organic or heirloom whole grains whenever possible is a great way to adhere to the Mediterranean diet.
   ☐ Correct   ☐ Incorrect

7. On November 19, 1863, Abraham Lincoln gave an address in Gettysburg, Pennsylvania, which he delivered—over the course of about two minutes—what has become one of the most widely recognized speeches in the English language.
   ☐ Correct   ☐ Incorrect

8. One of the symptoms of the plague was coughing and sneezing, and it is believed that Pope Gregory suggested saying "God bless you" after a person sneezed in hopes that this prayer would protect them from an otherwise certain death.
   ☐ Correct   ☐ Incorrect

9. Omar Ibn Said, a native of West Africa, was captured in 1807 and brought to North Carolina as a slave; he wrote his unique 1831 autobiography in Arabic while he was still in captivity.
   ☐ Correct   ☐ Incorrect

10. As Americans moved into cities, and pet birds were one of the only ways to enjoy the beauty of birds and feel connected to nature.
    ☐ Correct   ☐ Incorrect

Practice Question Set

Because clause issues and phrase issues are so closely intertwined on SAT questions, we'll hold off on the practice question set until after the next chapter. You're off the hook! For now...

The whole purpose
of education is to turn
mirrors into windows

— Sydney Harris

◈ Sentence Structure ◈
Part 2: Phrases

OK, now it's time for the second half of our big discussion on sentence structure: **phrases**.

A phrase is any group of words that work together for a single purpose. Large phrases can be made up of smaller phrases. For the purposes of this discussion, we'll define a phrase as a group of related words that **does not contain both a subject and a verb**.

So, what do you need to know about phrases for the SAT? Let's review some different types of phrases and discuss how they might be tested.

Prepositional Phrases

A prepositional phrase begins with a preposition and ends with a noun, which is called the **object** of the preposition. It may also contain additional words, such as adjectives describing the object.

We've discussed prepositional phrases already, including back in the section on subject-verb agreement. But here's a refresher on some of the most common prepositions:

Prepositions					
of	on	as	between	before	like
in	at	into	out	under	unlike
to	from	through	against	around	off
for	by	after	during	among	behind
with	about	over	without	within	along

And here are some prepositional phrases in action:

☑ Michigan typically gets a lot **of** snow.
☑ The car is still **in** good condition.
☑ The historic mansion offers tours **to** the public **over** the holidays.
☑ We left **for** the beach **with** our buckets and shovels.

Sometimes there can be more than one object, as in the final example (*buckets* and *shovels*).

If you're trying to figure out where a long prepositional phrase ends—in other words, where the object is—try this trick: ask a question based on the preposition. If the preposition is *of*, ask, "Of *what*?" If it's *to*, ask, "To *where*?" Or "With *what*?" or "For *whom*?" etc. Use some logic to find the **answer** to that question, and then you've found the object.

OK, so why do you need to pay attention to prepositional phrases? There are three issues related to this topic that you may be tested on:

⊙ Subject-verb agreement
⊙ Placement of a prepositional phrase
⊙ Punctuation around a prepositional phrase

As we've already discussed, nothing inside a prepositional phrase can ever be the subject of a sentence. So one good reason to pay attention to prepositional phrases is so that you can ignore them. If you're looking for the subject of a verb in order to pick the proper verb form, find and cross out all prepositional phrases:

☑ The hair **on polar bears** **with algae-filled pools** **at zoos** **in warm climates** turns green in some cases.

See the chapter on subject-verb agreement for more details on this topic.

Second, prepositional phrases must be properly placed. Prepositional phrases are **modifiers**. That means they **act upon** and **give further descriptive information about** some other word in the sentence.

All modifiers should be as close as possible to the words they modify. If you put a modifier too far away, you risk creating an unclear or illogical sentence.

☒ The mother snapped a photo of her son examining a spider <u>in an explorer's hat</u>.

Logically, the prepositional phrase *in an explorer's hat* should modify the noun *son*. However, in this sentence, the phrase is immediately next to the noun *spider*, so it sounds as if the spider is wearing the hat. Bizarre psychedelic hallucinations are **not** considered correct on the SAT. To fix this sentence, rearrange it so that the modifier is next to the noun it modifies.

☑ The mother snapped a photo of her son <u>in an explorer's hat</u> as he examined a spider.

Finally, the SAT will occasionally test you on whether commas are needed around a prepositional phrase. Generally speaking, the answer is no; if a prepositional phrase simply modifies an adjacent word, then there is typically no reason to separate it from that word with commas.

    ❌ Stan Lee was a staunch champion of the power, <u>of comic books</u>, over his nearly 70-year career, <u>in the comics industry</u>.

    ✅ Stan Lee was a staunch champion of the power of comic books over his nearly 70-year career in the comics industry.

However, if a prepositional phrase acts as an introductory element, or creates a distinct pause in or interruption to the sentence, then it may be appropriate to surround it with commas.

    ✅ <u>On January 1, 1892</u>, Ellis Island began welcoming immigrants along its shores at the first federal immigration station.

    ✅ The mayor, <u>along with several other town officials</u>, took part in the festivities.

Appositive Phrases

An appositive is a **noun phrase** that modifies and gives further descriptive information about **another noun**.

    ✅ Web crawling, <u>a highly automated process</u>, allows a data firm to archive a snapshot of the internet.

When it comes to appositives, the SAT wants you to pay attention to two things:

    ⊙ Punctuation around the appositive
    ⊙ Placement of the appositive

We've already covered punctuation in detail; see the section titled "Valid comma use #9" in the previous chapter for lots of information on this topic.

As far as placement, the usual rule for all modifiers applies to appositives too: a modifier should be as close as possible to the word it modifies. Here's an example of a misplaced appositive:

    ❌ <u>Earth's only natural satellite</u>, <u>the orbit</u> of the Moon increases yearly.

The problem in this example is that the appositive *Earth's only natural satellite* should modify the noun *Moon*. But it's next to a different noun—*orbit*.

The following attempt to fix this error is also no good:

❌ Earth's only natural satellite, the Moon's orbit increases yearly.

Even though it may appear that the appositive is now properly next to the noun *Moon*, it turns out that putting an apostrophe + *s* on the noun turns it into a possessive—an **adjective**. So the appositive still modifies the noun *orbit*.

Here's a proper fix:

✅ Earth's only natural satellite, the Moon has an orbit that increases yearly.

If you see an appositive acting as an introductory element at the beginning of a sentence, make sure it's next to the noun it really should be modifying. However, the most common use of appositives on the SAT is at the end of sentences, where they are often used to make sentences more streamlined or to fix errors with improperly joined clauses. More on that topic in a bit.

Drill: Finding Appositive Phrases

Find and underline the appositive phrase in each sentence below. An appositive phrase may include other phrases, such as prepositional phrases, or even entire relative clauses.

1. The artistic development of Kate Chopin, author of *The Awakening*, spanned several phases of nineteenth-century women's fiction.

2. The Parker Solar Probe is the first NASA mission named after a living person, and at 91 years old, Dr. Parker, a University of Chicago Professor Emeritus, was at the launch.

3. A patent medicine heavily advertised in old newspapers, Castoria was designed to alleviate stomach issues in people with weak digestive systems, such as infants, children, and the elderly.

4. Her interest in the photo was captivated not by the central figure, but by a small detail, the words above the door on a building in the background.

5. Music, something we tend to take for granted in the twenty-first century, was much more difficult to produce around the turn of the twentieth century.

6. The most interesting part of Clark's book on the language of cats is the essay by French professor Alphonse Leon Grimaldi.

7. No discussion of United Fruit, Honduras, and the banana trade would be complete without mentioning *banana republic*, a phrase coined by O. Henry in "The Admiral" from his *Cabbages and Kings*.

8. A school that taught skills useful in the business world, Soulé Business College offered classes in typing, shorthand, and bookkeeping, as well as other skills for those looking to work in banks, department stores, and other offices.

Verbals

Verbals are words that come from verbs and look an awful lot like verbs but **are not verbs**. There are three kinds of verbals:

⊙ Gerunds
⊙ Participles
⊙ Infinitives

Verbals are a source of endless confusion for people taking the SAT, but to really excel on this test, you need to get good at spotting verbals and knowing the rules that govern them.

The first reason for this is that you don't want to mistake a verbal for a verb. Verbs are associated with all kinds of rules, such as subject-verb agreement and verb tense. But verbals are not verbs! So you don't want to make the mistake of trying to figure out the "tense" of a verbal or looking for the "subject" of a verbal. Such concepts do not exist.

Second, verbals and the phrases built upon them play an incredibly important role in sentence structure. It's impossible to have a discussion about clauses, phrases, and complex sentences without understanding verbals. So let's take a look.

Gerunds

A **gerund** is a **type of noun**. A gerund looks like the base form of a verb followed by *-ing*. Here's an example of a gerund in action:

☑ <u>Dancing</u> improves your coordination.

The gerund in this sentence is the word *dancing*. It comes from the verb *dance*, and it represents the action of dancing, but it is not a verb. It is a noun, and in this case, it's the subject of the sentence. (The verb of the sentence is *improves*.)

Because a gerund is a noun, it can play any of the typical roles that nouns play:

☑ <u>Painting</u> requires a lot of patience.   *Painting* is the subject. (The verb is *requires*.)

☑ Gordon really enjoys <u>cooking</u>.   *Cooking* is the direct object of the verb *enjoys*. (The subject is *Gordon*.)

☑ Children have a natural affinity for <u>learning</u>.   *Learning* is the object of the preposition *for*. (The subject and verb are *children* and *have*.)

One way you can tell that a gerund is a noun is that you can replace any gerund with the phrase *this thing*. You could say, "*This thing* improves your coordination," or "Gordon really enjoys *this thing*." You can use this trick any time you're looking at an *-ing* word and trying to decide whether it's a gerund. Try it yourself with the other examples on this page.

Participles

A **participle** is a **type of adjective** (or in some cases, adverb). It is a modifier.

There are two common flavors of participles. A **present participle** looks like the base form of a verb followed by *-ing*. That's the same pattern as a gerund, of course, but in this case the *-ing* word acts as an adjective, not a noun.

> ☑ This region has a <u>growing</u> population.

Growing is an adjective that modifies *population*. (The verb is *has*.)

> ☑ She scowled at the <u>squawking</u> parrot.

Squawking is an adjective that modifies *parrot*. (The verb is *scowled*.)

> ☑ The engineers studied the <u>failing</u> dam.

Failing is an adjective that modifies *dam*. (The verb is *studied*.)

The other common flavor, the **past participle**, looks like the base form of a verb followed by *-ed* when it comes from a regular verb. Irregular verbs produce unpredictable past participles.

> ☑ I own all of Walker's <u>published</u> books.

Published is an adjective that modifies *books*. (The verb is *own*.)

> ☑ The restaurant features <u>shared</u> tables.

Shared is an adjective that modifies *tables*. (The verb is *features*.)

> ☑ Some animals can understand <u>spoken</u> English.

Spoken is an adjective that modifies *English*. (The verb is *can understand*.)

We just said on the last page that verbals don't have tense in the way that verbs do. So what's all this about past and present participles? Isn't that tense? Well, no. The difference between a present participle and a past participle doesn't really have anything to do with **time**. Instead, it's more akin to the difference between the active voice and the passive voice. In other words, it's determined by whether the modified noun is **doing** the action represented by the participle or **receiving** that action.

> There is a third, less common flavor of participle called the **perfect participle**. It uses *having* + the participle form of the verb. For example: *The runner, <u>having reached</u> the finish line, stopped*. The SAT isn't likely to test you on this.

For the present participles above, the modified noun is doing the action. The population is *doing* the growing; the parrot is *doing* the squawking; the dam is *doing* the failing.

But that's not the case with the past participles. Walker's books aren't doing the publishing; they *have been published*. The tables aren't sharing anything; they *are shared* by the patrons. English isn't speaking; it *is spoken* by people. The modified noun receives the action.

Infinitives

An infinitive looks like the word *to* followed by the base form of a verb. Some examples:

> *to give, to look, to want, to become, to fly, to ace the SAT writing section*

Treat the two words in an infinitive as a single unit. Don't think of the word *to* as a preposition in this case. Infinitives usually act as nouns, but they can do other things too.

☑ <u>To travel</u> has always been his ambition.	*To travel* is a noun, acting as the subject.
☑ Despite Cassie's pleas, Melvin refused <u>to drive</u>.	*To drive* is a noun, acting as the direct object of the verb *refused*.
☑ Give me a chance <u>to explain</u>.	*To explain* is an adjective that modifies the noun *chance*.
☑ She drank more coffee <u>to stay</u> awake.	*To stay* is an adverb that modifies the verb *drank*.

Distinguishing Verbs from Verbals

It can be easy to mistake a verbal for a verb, and if you start applying verb rules to verbals, you're in trouble. So it's important to be able to tell the difference. Probably the most useful principle is this:

> For an *-ing* word to be a **verb**, it must be preceded by a helper verb, specifically some form of *to be*.
>
> If not, it's a **verbal**—either a gerund or a participle.

-ing word as a verb	-ing word as a verbal
☑ The spacecraft <u>is moving</u> at roughly 430,000 miles per hour.	☑ She wrote several blog posts <u>concerning</u> women in the workforce.
☑ The chimp <u>was studying</u> its reflection.	☑ He thought about <u>starting</u> his own business.
☑ Professor Jiang <u>will be speaking</u> about lithographs.	☑ I noticed a branch <u>obscuring</u> the sign.

To distinguish between a gerund and a present participle, ask yourself, "Is this word *a thing*? Or does it *modify or describe* another word?" Here are some more rules that are generally useful:

- ⊙ If you see a base "verb" following *to*, it's an infinitive.
- ⊙ If you see the participle form of an irregular verb (e.g., *taken, given, found, shown*) without an auxiliary verb (*have, has,* or *had*) in front, it's a participle.
- ⊙ If you see the participle form of a regular verb (*expected, required, contained, trusted*) without a subject before it, it's probably a participle.

Drill: Distinguishing Verbs from Verbals

In the passage below, a number of words have been underlined. Each is either a verb or a verbal. Read the passage and categorize each underlined word appropriately. In some cases, an underlined verb is just the main verb in a larger verb phrase—the auxiliary verbs are not underlined. For infinitives, only the "base verb" (and not the word to*) is underlined, but you should still categorize such cases as infinitives.*

The reign of the pumpkin pie in America began in the 17th century, when the very first cookbook published in the colonies included a recipe for it. Despite some trendy, modern takes on the original—pumpkin chiffon pie, pineapple pumpkin pie, pumpkin ice cream pie—the essential pumpkin pie remains true to its origins: mashed and **1** cooked pumpkin, milk or cream, eggs, sugar and spices, and a pastry crust. But at the same time, almost everything about pumpkin pie has **2** changed radically since the first recipes were published.

One obvious change occurred around the turn of the 20th century, when the rapid expansion of the **3** canning industry brought canned pumpkin to every market. Many cooks were no longer willing or able to **4** stew pumpkin all day and quickly **5** embraced the canned product for its convenience.

Around the same time as commercially canned pumpkin was radically changing home pumpkin-pie **6** making, even more convenient and timesaving options were **7** becoming available. City newspapers of the time described large bakeries or "pie-factories," which turned out thousands of pies for restaurants, hotels, and private families. Finished pies from these bakeries were loaded into pie-wagons, and later, trucks, to **8** be delivered throughout the city.

By the early 1960s, Thanksgiving **9** advertising featured not only canned pumpkin pie mix and bakery pies, but also **10** frozen pies, ready to **11** serve.

1. *cooked* is a(n)
   - ☐ verb   ☐ participle
   - ☐ gerund   ☐ infinitive

2. *changed* is a(n)
   - ☐ verb   ☐ participle
   - ☐ gerund   ☐ infinitive

3. *canning* is a(n)
   - ☐ verb   ☐ participle
   - ☐ gerund   ☐ infinitive

4. *stew* is a(n)
   - ☐ verb   ☐ participle
   - ☐ gerund   ☐ infinitive

5. *embraced* is a(n)
   - ☐ verb   ☐ participle
   - ☐ gerund   ☐ infinitive

6. *making* is a(n)
   - ☐ verb   ☐ participle
   - ☐ gerund   ☐ infinitive

7. *becoming* is a(n)
   - ☐ verb   ☐ participle
   - ☐ gerund   ☐ infinitive

8. *be delivered* is a(n)
   - ☐ verb   ☐ participle
   - ☐ gerund   ☐ infinitive

9. *advertising* is a(n)
   - ☐ verb   ☐ participle
   - ☐ gerund   ☐ infinitive

10. *frozen* is a(n)
    - ☐ verb   ☐ participle
    - ☐ gerund   ☐ infinitive

11. *serve* is a(n)
    - ☐ verb   ☐ participle
    - ☐ gerund   ☐ infinitive

continued ⟶

Convenient and affordable, frozen pies **12** caught on quickly, and they continue to be popular today.

Even with the convenience of frozen and bakery pies, many people continue to **13** bake their own pumpkin pies. For some cooks, that may mean **14** stewing a pie pumpkin, but many baby boomers **15** grew up associating pumpkin pie with the recipe on the back of the pumpkin can, the one with evaporated milk, eggs, canned pumpkin, a prebaked crust—and pumpkin pie spice.

Pumpkin pie spice has become ubiquitous in modern times, and people are **16** putting it to an **17** increasing variety of uses. The mix usually includes some combination of ginger, nutmeg, mace, cloves, cinnamon or allspice—all of which we might recognize as the same spices widely **18** used in colonial American **19** cooking, although they were probably measured out more generously back then than they are today.

12. *caught* is a(n)
    ☐ verb ☐ participle
    ☐ gerund ☐ infinitive

13. *bake* is a(n)
    ☐ verb ☐ participle
    ☐ gerund ☐ infinitive

14. *stewing* is a(n)
    ☐ verb ☐ participle
    ☐ gerund ☐ infinitive

15. *grew* is a(n)
    ☐ verb ☐ participle
    ☐ gerund ☐ infinitive

16. *putting* is a(n)
    ☐ verb ☐ participle
    ☐ gerund ☐ infinitive

17. *increasing* is a(n)
    ☐ verb ☐ participle
    ☐ gerund ☐ infinitive

18. *used* is a(n)
    ☐ verb ☐ participle
    ☐ gerund ☐ infinitive

19. *cooking* is a(n)
    ☐ verb ☐ participle
    ☐ gerund ☐ infinitive

Verbal Phrases

You may have been wondering what this big discussion of verbs and verbals is doing in the middle of a chapter about phrases and sentence construction. The answer is that verbals can serve as the foundation for **verbal phrases**, and those phrases—especially participial phrases—often play a major role in sentence structure. They can often resemble clauses, but they're not clauses, so you have to be able to recognize them and apply the proper rules.

A phrase built upon a gerund is a **gerund phrase**.

> ☑ My father told a story about **working** in a pickle factory as a teenager.
> ☑ **Putting** a pigeon on a treadmill to see whether its head would bob as it walked is just one of the curious experiments performed by avian biologists.

Working in a pickle factory as a teenager is built upon the gerund *working*, and the entire phrase acts as a big noun, the object of the preposition *about*. In the second example, the gerund phrase is built upon the gerund *putting*, and again the whole thing is a big noun, acting in this case as the subject of the sentence.

> The pigeon's head did not bob. Weird, right?

We can have **infinitive phrases** too.

- ☑ Locals are eager **to visit** the neighborhood's new sculpture garden.
- ☑ Tovah called Susannah **to discuss** their plans for the evening.

They're nice.

But by far the most important verbal phrases for the SAT are **participial phrases**.

Participles, as we've discussed, are **modifiers**, and so participial phrases are too. They can modify nouns, thus acting as big **adjectives**. Or they can modify verbs or other parts of speech, thus acting as big **adverbs**. For the SAT, you need to:

- ⊙ not mistake participles for verbs and start trying to apply verb-related rules
- ⊙ make sure any introductory participial phrase is next to the word it properly modifies
- ⊙ be comfortable using adverbial participial phrases, especially at the end of a sentence

Let's check out a few of the different ways in which participial phrases can be used. As you've already seen, **single-word participles** (without any longer phrase attached) are simply adjectives and thus typically appear immediately **in front** of the noun they modify, without any punctuation.

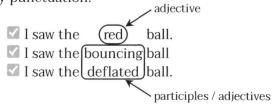

adjective

- ☑ I saw the (red) ball.
- ☑ I saw the [bouncing] ball
- ☑ I saw the [deflated] ball.

participles / adjectives

On the other hand, **longer** participial phrases often appear **after** the noun they modify. They usually don't need any commas unless the phrase gives parenthetical, nonessential information.

> Because the line between essential and nonessential can be a little blurry, the SAT rarely asks about this use of commas.

- ☑ The device has <u>flashing</u> lights.

- ☑ The device has lights <u>flashing in different colors in time to the music</u>.

- ☑ The device has lights <u>arranged in a hexagonal pattern</u>.

- ☑ The device, <u>purchased at a yard sale for a dollar</u>, is starting to give me a headache.

It's also possible for longer participial phrases to appear **before** the noun they modify. This will often occur in the context of an introductory element at the beginning of a sentence. When this happens, the phrase will definitely be set off with a comma, and **you need to make sure the very next noun after the comma is the thing the participial phrase is supposed to be modifying**. This is the kind of thing the SAT loves to test. You've probably seen silly examples of misplaced participial phrases, like these:

> This is basically identical to the issue with appositive placement that we discussed a few pages back.

❌ <u>Squirting water from their trunks</u>, the scientists recorded the elephants' behavior.

❌ <u>Frightened by the puppet show</u>, the father calmed his infant daughter.

These are wrong because they create illogical meanings. It seems unlikely that the scientists have trunks or that the father was frightened by the puppet show, but when the introductory phrases are misplaced next to those nouns, that's what the sentences seem to suggest.

The misplaced participial phrases on the SAT aren't nearly as much fun, but they test the same issue. Here's more of an SAT-style example:

12

Using cues from the Earth's magnetic field, <u>in midsummer the turtles return to their birthplace.</u>

A) NO CHANGE
B) midsummer is when the turtles return to their birthplace.
C) it is in midsummer that the turtles return to their birthplace.
D) the turtles return to their birthplace in midsummer.

The introductory participial phrase is *using cues from the Earth's magnetic field*. Thus, the very next noun after the comma must be whatever is using the cues. Of course, that's the turtles, so choice D must be correct. It's the only choice that begins with *the turtles*.

Keep an eye out for these introductory modifiers. Once you notice that a sentence begins with one, it usually becomes pretty easy to get the question right. Just scan your eye down the answer choices, looking for the choice that begins with the correct noun. There's typically only one choice that does so, and once you've found it, you're done. You don't have to worry about all the jumbled-up nonsense that follows.

Another example:

13

By combining a traditional musical score with modern electronic instruments, <u>an innovative production created by the arrangers</u> left the audience awestruck.

A) NO CHANGE

B) the production was created to be innovative so that it

C) the arrangers created an innovative production that

D) it was an innovative production created by the arrangers that

> The verbal *combining* is actually a gerund here, not a participle. It follows the preposition *by,* and thus the introductory modifier is a prepositional phrase, but the same rule still applies. Put a modifier next to the noun it modifies.

Again, look at the introductory phrase. It's built upon the word *combining,* and it's the arrangers who are doing the combining, so they must come first after the comma. The answer must be C.

Drill: Introductory Modifiers

Each question below shows the introductory modifier that begins a sentence, followed by a comma. The choices that follow show the beginning *of the rest of the sentence. Pick the appropriate choice. For questions like these on the SAT, the important thing is that whatever follows the comma must be the thing that should be modified—the rest of the sentence after that initial noun typically doesn't matter.*

1. In addition to emphasizing ideal behavior in personal relationships, _____
   (A) the posters celebrated...
   (B) it is through the posters that...
   (C) viewers of the posters learned...

2. Though now recognized as the greatest Dutch painter since Rembrandt, _____
   (A) critics considered van Gogh as...
   (B) many considered van Gogh to be...
   (C) van Gogh was considered...

3. A rare type of stringed instrument, _____
   (A) Dawson found the komuz in...
   (B) the komuz is related to...
   (C) musicians play the komuz by...

4. Even with its shortcomings, _____
   (A) the treaty provided...
   (B) the negotiators felt that...
   (C) hundreds of square miles of...

5. Guiding the conversation back on topic, _____
   (A) Luciana pointed out that...
   (B) the discussion returned to...
   (C) there remained the question of...

6. Named for its proximity to the equator, _____
   (A) Ecuador's economy is based on...
   (B) Ecuador is the same size as...
   (C) the residents of Ecuador are...

7. As founder of the Northeast Maritime Institute, _____
   (A) the college provides many...
   (B) he continues to collect...
   (C) it is his work on delivering...

8. While studying an ichthyosaur skull from the museum's collection, _____
   (A) the researcher's hypothesis was...
   (B) a fake bone was found inside...
   (C) the researchers were surprised to find...

Finally, you'll often see participial phrases that don't modify a noun at all, but instead **modify a verb**:

- ☑ Suburban homeowners <u>apply</u> far too much fertilizer to their lawns, <u>contributing to the problem of "dead zones" in waterways</u>.

- ☑ The wet wrench slipped out of Yasuko's hand and <u>fell</u> to the floor, <u>cracking the tile</u>.

In the first example, the participial phrase built on *contributing* modifies the verb *apply*. It doesn't modify the noun *lawns*, since the lawns aren't contributing to anything. In the second example, the participial phrase built on *cracking* modifies the verb *fell*. It doesn't modify the noun *floor*, since the floor didn't crack anything.

Why isn't this wrong? Isn't a modifier supposed to be next to the noun it modifies? The reason these examples are acceptable is that these phrases don't modify nouns at all—they modify verbs and thus act as big **adverbs**. The important thing about adverbial participial phrases is that they ***don't* have to be next to the word they modify**. Mind-blowing. Confusing. But true. Whoever invented English deserves a swift kick in the shins.

In fact, it can be useful to think of such phrases as modifying **the entire situation** that comes before, instead of hunting for the specific verb. For example, what contributes to the problem of dead zones in waterways? It's the *entire situation* of suburban homeowners applying far too much fertilizer to their lawns. And what cracked the tile? It was the *entire situation* of the wet wrench slipping out of Yasuko's hand and falling to the floor.

Ending a sentence with an adverbial participial phrase is more of a written-English kind of thing than a spoken-English kind of thing. If you're in the middle of a test and you try "saying" such sentences to yourself to evaluate them, they might "sound" weird or wrong. But they're perfectly correct, and the SAT especially likes to use them to fix improperly joined clauses. They're also popular in the questions that ask you to combine two sentences into one.

Absolute Phrases

The final type of phrase to know about is the **absolute phrase**. An absolute phrase consists of **a noun plus a modifier** that modifies *that noun*, not some other word in the sentence. An absolute phrase is joined to the sentence with just a comma, not a conjunction. Here's an example:

- ☑ The farmers market was a busy place, each vendor <u>competing for attention</u>.

  absolute phrase
  modifying the entire situation

  participial phrase
  modifying the noun *vendor*

In this example, the noun is *vendor*. The modifier of that noun is the participial phrase *competing for attention*. Unlike an appositive phrase, in which the noun or noun phrase modifies another, adjacent noun, this absolute phrase doesn't modify the adjacent noun or any word in particular. Absolute phrases modify the **entire situation**, not a specific word. The absolute phrase is joined to the sentence with a comma.

Check out another example:

> ☑ Daniel rode his bicycle from Oregon to Chile, <u>a **journey that** took him through some of the most beautiful terrain on the planet</u>.

This one works similarly to the last example. The noun is *journey*. The modifier of that noun is the relative clause *that took him through...* The absolute phrase continues all the way to the end of the sentence, and it modifies the entire situation that comes before.

Absolute phrases can also come at the beginning of a sentence or in the middle:

> ☑ <u>Her voice hoarse from cheering</u>, she left the game overjoyed with the result.
> ☑ The teacher wrapped up the discussion of centrosomes, <u>the class still blinking in confusion</u>, and moved on to talk about pericentriolar material.

What's the point of knowing about absolute phrases for the SAT? The test writers like them because they look very similar to comma splices, especially when the modifier is a participle. After all, the noun could sort of look like a subject, and a participle could easily be confused with a verb. So if you're not careful, you might mistake an absolute phrase for a clause.

The flip side of that issue is that if there is a sentence that really does contain a comma splice, an absolute phrase could be a great way to fix it.

Comma splice (wrong)
> ☒ Fireflies use light to communicate, their flashing <u>patterns</u> <u>convey</u> information to potential mates.

                                                subject   verb

Absolute phrase (correct)
> ☑ Fireflies use light to communicate, their flashing <u>patterns</u> <u>conveying</u> information to potential mates.

                                              noun   participle

Fixing Clause Problems Using Phrases

As you saw in the last chapter, there are all sorts of ways clauses could go wrong. The most common of these problems is the comma splice. And as you also saw, there are several ways to properly join clauses—conjunctions, relative pronouns, and punctuation.

But not every clause problem needs to be fixed by properly joining the clauses. Another possible solution is to **turn a problematic clause into a phrase**. Here are some examples of erroneous sentences fixed in this way:

Problem: comma splice
❌ Some animals contain chlorophyll, it is a chemical that allows them to create energy from sunlight.
Solution: turn the second clause into an appositive
✅ Some animals contain chlorophyll, a chemical that allows them to create energy from sunlight.

Problem: comma splice
❌ At 8:00 the host invites musicians on stage, and the open mic event begins, it often lasts past midnight.
Solution: turn the third clause into a participial phrase that modifies the entire situation
✅ At 8:00 the host invites musicians on stage, and the open mic event begins, often lasting past midnight.

Problem: comma splice
❌ The restaurant industry is known to be quite volatile, the majority of new businesses fail in their first year.
Solution: turn the second clause into an absolute phrase
✅ The restaurant industry is known to be quite volatile, the majority of new businesses failing in their first year.

Problem: comma splice
❌ They were known as *carpas*, these often-satirical shows were performed in tents to mainly working-class audiences.
Solution: turn the first clause into a participial phrase that modifies the noun *shows*
✅ Known as *carpas*, these often-satirical shows were performed in tents to mainly working-class audiences.

Problem: the conjunctive adverb *specifically* is posing as a conjunction
❌ *Archaeopteryx* lived around 150 million years ago, specifically, it was during the late Jurassic period.
Solution: turn the second clause into a prepositional phrase (*during* is a preposition)
✅ *Archaeopteryx* lived around 150 million years ago, during the late Jurassic period.

Beware of *Being*

Being is, of course, a real word. There are some perfectly correct ways of using it. Some acceptable uses include:

- ⊙ As a gerund: *Being on time is important.*
- ⊙ As an auxiliary verb: *The parking lot is being resurfaced.*
- ⊙ To refer to a living creature: *A human is supposedly a rational being.*

However, there are some common ways to misuse this word as well, and broadly speaking, **the vast majority** of SAT answer choices with the word *being* are **wrong**. Of course, you have to use your brain and not just blindly cross out every instance of the word. But in general, beware of *being*.

One possible error occurs when *being* tries to be a main verb, all by itself:

- ☒ Borneo, the world's third-largest island, <u>being</u> located just south of Vietnam.
- ☑ Borneo, the world's third-largest island, <u>is</u> located just south of Vietnam.

But the main problem is when *being* tries to act as the basis of a participial phrase or an absolute phrase. This usually results in an awkward or unnecessarily wordy construction. There is almost always a better way to write the sentence.

Sentence with *being* – awkward or wrong	Better version of the sentence
☒ LED lights are much more energy efficient, being demonstrated by the building's dramatically lowered electric bills.	☑ LED lights are much more energy efficient, as demonstrated by the building's dramatically lowered electric bills.
☒ There are three main phases of matter, those being solid, liquid, and gas.	☑ There are three main phases of matter: solid, liquid, and gas.
☒ There is no single treatment that is best for all cases, patients being advised to consult a physician.	☑ There is no single treatment that is best for all cases, so patients are advised to consult a physician.
☒ Philosopher Emil Cioran, being born and educated in Romania, wrote the majority of his published books in French.	☑ Although philosopher Emil Cioran was born and educated in Romania, he wrote the majority of his published books in French.

Combining Sentences

The questions that ask you to combine two sentences represent the ultimate synthesis of nearly every grammar and stylistic rule. They're the pinnacle of the Writing and Language section! A final cage match showdown in which you battle your greatest foe, the English language, to the death! Only one victor can emerge!

Too much?

OK, so that's a bit overdramatic, but you do have to pay attention to **a lot** of things for these questions:

- **Pronouns.** It's common to see ambiguous or missing-antecedent pronouns lurking in the incorrect answer choices.

- **Punctuation.** Many answer choices will use colons, semicolons, or dashes to link clauses together, so make sure you've mastered those rules. You'll also have to pay close attention to commas and other punctuation marks.

- **Clauses.** The combined sentence will often have multiple clauses, so you'll have to make sure they're properly joined using conjunctions, relative pronouns, or appropriate punctuation.

- **Modifying phrases.** Make sure modifiers are properly placed next to any nouns they modify. Also keep in mind that it's very common to see the last part of a sentence turned into an appositive or a participial phrase. If a participial phrase acts as an adverb, it doesn't need to be adjacent to the verb it modifies (think of it as modifying the entire situation).

- **Transition words.** If there are any transition words used, make sure they're logically appropriate and grammatically suitable. For example, don't use a conjunctive adverb (such as *however*) to connect clauses when you need a full-fledged conjunction. And don't use *therefore* when the sentence logically calls for a word that indicates a contrast.

- **Effective language use.** Make sure to avoid redundancy and overly wordy constructions. And make sure that the choice you pick is clear, logical, and unambiguous.

On the next pages, we'll check out a few examples.

In this first example, the choices deal mostly with grammatical issues. Before you read the explanations on the right-hand side, cover them up and try to answer the question yourself. You should also try to articulate what's wrong with each of the incorrect choices.

1

The typical length of stay for patients at Mansfield Hospital is three days, compared to five days at Bradford Hospital. Readmissions rates at the two hospitals are comparable for patients with similar health issues.

Which choice most effectively combines the sentences at the underlined portion?

A) Hospital with readmissions

A: Incorrect. This sentence has a problem with the grammar of the clauses. The first subject-verb pair is *length ... is*, and the second is *rates ... are*. In this choice, the clauses seem to be connected with the preposition *with*. That's not a valid way to connect clauses.

B) Hospital: readmissions

B: Incorrect. A colon is allowed to connect clauses, but it's an illogical choice in this context. The first clause does not set up a thought that gets completed by the second clause. Instead, the two clauses outline a contrasting situation—different lengths of stay, but comparable readmissions rates.

C) Hospital, but readmissions

C: Correct. This works. The coordinating conjunction *but* is a good grammatical and logical choice to connect the two contrasting clauses.

D) Hospital, whereas

D: Incorrect. The word *whereas* is a subordinating conjunction, so it wouldn't be out of the question as far as connecting the clauses. However, by dropping the word *readmissions*, this choice messes up the logical meaning of the sentence.

In this second example, the choices deal with a mixture of grammatical and stylistic issues. Again, try answering the question yourself first.

2

In the museum's next room are several antique record players, complete with <u>pavillons. Pavillons are</u> horn-shaped tubes mounted on the machines to provide amplification of the sound.

Which choice most effectively combines the sentences at the underlined portion?

A) pavillons,

A: Correct. In this choice, the second sentence gets turned into an appositive that modifies and defines the noun *pavillons*. It works, and that's a common way to deal with multiple clauses—turn one of them into a phrase.

B) pavillons, thus having

B: Incorrect. The participle *having* is grammatically awkward—does it modify a noun? A verb? Which one? Also, *thus* is an illogical word choice because nothing in this situation is a consequence of anything else.

C) pavillons, and pavillons are

C: Incorrect. Although the clauses are properly joined with the coordinating conjunction *and*, this choice is redundant. It unnecessarily repeats the word *pavillons*.

D) pavillons in order to have

D: Incorrect. This version is illogical. Pavillons aren't the *reason* there are horn-shaped tubes on the machine. Pavillons *are* the horn-shaped tubes.

In this third example, the wrong choices all go astray for rhetorical or logical reasons. The correct answer uses good logic and expression of ideas (and grammar).

3

Inventor Harlan Bellamy learned about this technology. Then he began to speculate about its uses in other contexts.

Which choice most effectively combines the underlined sentences?

A) Inventor Harlan Bellamy began to speculate about this technology's uses in other contexts after he learned about it.

A: Incorrect. The logic of this choice seems a bit foolish. Would anyone imagine that he began to speculate about the technology *before* he learned about it? Another problem is the pronoun *it*. Logically, we can assume it refers to the noun *technology*, but that noun never actually appears in the sentence. Instead, we only have the possessive *technology's* (an adjective). The pronoun is missing an antecedent.

B) Inventor Harlan Bellamy learned about this technology, and then Bellamy began to speculate about its uses in other contexts.

B: Incorrect. One problem with this version is that it's redundant. It says *Bellamy* twice, which is enough to make it wrong.

C) Inventor Harlan Bellamy learned about this technology, and its uses in other contexts made him begin to speculate.

C: Incorrect. The logic of this choice is mixed up. The technology's uses in other contexts are what Bellamy was speculating *about*. They're not what *made* him speculate.

D) Upon learning about this technology, inventor Harlan Bellamy began to speculate about its uses in other contexts.

D: Correct. Notice that the first of the underlined sentences got turned into an introductory phrase that modifies *Bellamy*. Again, we've used the common technique of turning a clause into a phrase.

Drill: Combining Sentences

Now it's your turn to write the explanations. Here are two "combining sentences" questions. Write explanations for all the correct and incorrect answer choices.

4

Forty-five nesting sites were built with wooden boxes. These boxes were mounted on posts within the preserve.

Which choice most effectively combines the underlined sentences?

A) Built with wooden boxes, nesting sites, forty-five in total, mounted on posts within the preserve.

A: _____

_____

_____

_____

B) After being built with wooden boxes, forty-five nesting sites were mounted on posts within the preserve.

B: _____

_____

_____

_____

_____

C) Forty-five nesting sites built with wooden boxes were mounted on posts within the preserve.

C: _____

_____

_____

_____

D) Mounted on posts within the preserve there were forty-five nesting sites, and these were built with wooden boxes.

D: _____

_____

_____

_____

_____

continued ⟶

5

> The aim is to create a dramatic painting. It also raises questions about our relationship with nature.

Which choice most effectively combines the underlined sentences?

A) The aim is to create a dramatic painting—it also raises questions about our relationship with nature.

A: _____

_____

_____

_____

_____

B) The aim is to create a dramatic painting that also raises questions about our relationship with nature.

B: _____

_____

_____

_____

_____

C) The aim is to create a dramatic painting; the painting also raises questions about our relationship with nature.

C: _____

_____

_____

_____

_____

D) The aim is to create a painting, and the aim also raises questions about our relationship with nature, dramatically.

D: _____

_____

_____

_____

_____

Where Am I?

Don't lose sight of the overall process of improving your score. It's worth remembering this general outline, as we discussed in the introduction:

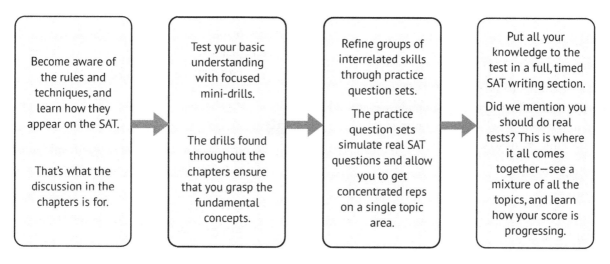

Become aware of the rules and techniques, and learn how they appear on the SAT.

That's what the discussion in the chapters is for.

Test your basic understanding with focused mini-drills.

The drills found throughout the chapters ensure that you grasp the fundamental concepts.

Refine groups of interrelated skills through practice question sets.

The practice question sets simulate real SAT questions and allow you to get concentrated reps on a single topic area.

Put all your knowledge to the test in a full, timed SAT writing section.

Did we mention you should do real tests? This is where it all comes together—see a mixture of all the topics, and learn how your score is progressing.

And here's the general process for practicing in order to reach mastery:

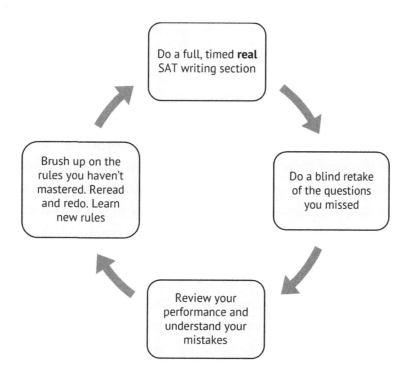

Do a full, timed **real** SAT writing section

Do a blind retake of the questions you missed

Review your performance and understand your mistakes

Brush up on the rules you haven't mastered. Reread and redo. Learn new rules

Practice Question Set

The questions in the following practice set test **sentence structure**. *Work on the set without time limits—focus on accuracy alone.*

1

In a process overseen and guided by the Public Employment Relations Board. State employees are divided into twenty-one bargaining units, plus supervisors and managers.

A) NO CHANGE
B) Board, state
C) Board; thus, state
D) Board, and state

2

After the sugar is removed from the cane fiber, it is sent to a nearby zubron farm, a cross between a cow and a European woods bison.

A) NO CHANGE
B) a cross between a cow and a European woods bison at a nearby farm called zubron.
C) a nearby farm that raises zubron, a cross between a cow and a European woods bison.
D) a nearby farm with a cross between a cow and a European woods bison known as zubron.

3

Estrada looked at the possibility of using proprionate, it is a chemical that can be added to food to make people feel full.

A) NO CHANGE
B) being
C) that is
D) DELETE the underlined portion.

4

Another serious question relates to basic efficacy, some studies show a relationship between sunscreen use and cancer prevention, but others find no evidence of a correlation.

A) NO CHANGE
B) efficacy; some studies showing
C) efficacy: some studies do show
D) efficacy, and some studies that show

5

Ashmole eventually acquired the rare plant specimens, he subsequently donated them to Oxford University as the founding collection of the Ashmolean Museum.

A) NO CHANGE
B) which he subsequently donated
C) subsequently he donated them
D) they were donated subsequently

6

Michael Larson, he gained national recognition by winning an unheard-of amount of money on the game show *Press Your Luck*, had figured out the pattern in the supposedly random flashing of the game squares.

A) NO CHANGE

B) who gained national recognition

C) it was national recognition he gained

D) nationally recognized

7

Rather than being part of a complete mold, which would lead to more consistency in the dimensions of the patterns, but the designs were stamped onto the clay during the construction of the flasks.

A) NO CHANGE

B) yet

C) and

D) DELETE the underlined portion.

8

Students who choose a residential university don't come just for what goes on in the classroom: a substantial part of the learning experience happens in corridors, in houses and dormitories, in between classes, and in debates after class.

A) NO CHANGE

B) classroom, a substantial part of the learning experience happens

C) classroom. A substantial part of the learning experience happening

D) classroom; a substantial part of the learning experience happening

9

Cold food comes in contact with the roof of the mouth, and the headache is triggered, it typically extends from the forehead to the back of the throat.

A) NO CHANGE

B) typically extending

C) which it typically extends

D) DELETE the underlined portion.

10

Because the side chains of amino acids associate with one another and with water to form weak noncovalent bonds, therefore most polypeptide chains fold into only one particular conformation determined by their amino acid sequence.

A) NO CHANGE

B) bonds, most

C) bonds, so most

D) bonds: most

Introductory Modifiers

*The **five questions on this page** all begin with an introductory modifier. Make sure whatever follows the modifier is what really should be modified.*

The questions on the pages after this one return to the full range of sentence structure issues, but there are more questions like these mixed in with the rest of the set.

11

Besides providing services and protection for residents, <u>a stable economic structure is created by government</u> within which people can pursue business activity with confidence.

A) NO CHANGE

B) it is through government that a stable economic structure is created

C) government creates a stable economic structure

D) the creation of a stable economic structure by government

12

Feeling the tension between the worlds of modern dance and Yiddishkeit, <u>and Pearl Lang clearly identified with</u> the play's themes of straddling the realms of the living and the dead, good and evil, and the spiritual and quotidian.

A) NO CHANGE

B) Pearl Lang clearly identified with

C) but Pearl Lang clearly identified with

D) DELETE the underlined portion.

13

After identifying the source of the unwanted vibrations, <u>a new prototype was created by engineers and</u> was able to fly for over three months without the need to land.

A) NO CHANGE

B) a prototype was newly created by engineers so that it

C) engineers created a new prototype that

D) it was a new prototype created by engineers that

14

Although challenging and sometimes stressful, <u>social work</u> is an ideal profession for those who derive satisfaction from helping others.

A) NO CHANGE

B) the choice of social work

C) you should choose social work because it

D) choosing to pursue social work

15

By suggesting that the first and foremost "dodge" is politics, regardless of who the politician may be, <u>staying closest to the song's roots in the theater is Emma Dusenbury's version.</u>

A) NO CHANGE

B) the song's roots in theater are closest to Emma Dusenbury's version.

C) there is a version of the song that has stayed closest to its roots in theater, by Emma Dusenbury.

D) Emma Dusenbury's version has stayed closest to the song's roots in the theater.

16

Good fiction writers try to craft their scenes like a row of dominoes, each one <u>is knocking</u> into the next.

A) NO CHANGE
B) should be knocking
C) knocking
D) knocks

17

The lab's researchers had for years been collecting heavy water as a by-product of their ammonia production <u>process, they supplied</u> samples of the curious liquid to other scientists for basic experiments.

A) NO CHANGE
B) process; whereby they supplied
C) process; supplying
D) process, supplying

18

Inspired by electric eels, researchers have developed a special hydrogel <u>hoping they</u> can one day act as a power source for implantable devices.

A) NO CHANGE
B) hoping that
C) they hope
D) and hope

19

Shortly after winning the first US life insurance charter in 1835, Judge Phillips was told by the Massachusetts state legislature that he had to raise a guaranty fund of $100,000, half <u>of it</u> had to be in cash, before he could begin selling policies.

A) NO CHANGE
B) of the money
C) of which
D) DELETE the underlined portion.

20

The drug discovery process is mostly carried out by new innovative and medium-sized <u>companies, but</u> despite advances in technology and greater understanding of biological systems, new drug discovery is still a difficult, time-consuming undertaking.

A) NO CHANGE
B) companies, and
C) companies; therefore,
D) companies: thus,

21

As a consequence, the group claims, poisoning cases will increase among consumers, that may then lose trust in the food safety system and stop eating fugu altogether.

A) NO CHANGE

B) they

C) which

D) who

22

To demonstrate how the system works, Hicks holds up two flash cards: one that displays musical braille notation, and one that shows traditional print music notation.

A) NO CHANGE

B) cards;

C) cards; being

D) cards—being

23

Watching a movie with subtitles is like learning to ride a bike with training wheels, and many find this method of learning a language to be a technique that is one of the most beneficial ways to practice as they begin their studies.

A) NO CHANGE

B) be, as a technique, one of the most beneficial ways to practice

C) be one of the most beneficial ways to practice

D) be, among all the techniques for practicing, one of the most beneficial

24

There are even "whole body puppets," these are masks or false heads attached to a garment or sheath that covers the whole body of one or more people, like the Dancing Lion of Chinese New Year celebrations.

A) NO CHANGE

B) puppets," which

C) puppets," and which

D) puppets," being those that

25

While investigating the coastal upwelling that nourishes marine wildlife near the coast of Madagascar, a previously unrecognized current was identified by researchers as a rare example of a subtropical surface current flowing in a poleward direction off the western coast of a large landmass.

A) NO CHANGE

B) researchers identified a previously unrecognized current that provides a rare example of a subtropical surface current flowing in a poleward direction

C) an example of a subtropical surface current flowing in a poleward direction, previously unrecognized, was identified by researchers as rare

D) the poleward direction of flow identified by researchers is rare in a subtropical surface current, like the previously unrecognized example

26

She was pleased to find that the photographer had a good eye, she decided to include his works in the exhibition.

A) NO CHANGE

B) eye, thus

C) eye, and

D) eye and so

27

Biologists in Indonesia have had success growing coral through a new process—running a low-voltage charge through a frame of ordinary steel rebar—it was developed by the Global Coral Reef Alliance.

A) NO CHANGE

B) developed

C) its development was

D) development

28

The only problem with this story, it says that a group of jesters convinced Emperor Constantine to make one of them king for a day, is that it's a hoax.

A) NO CHANGE

B) which says

C) it saying

D) saying

29

Decorated with hundreds of sequins, Graham explained the meaning behind the choices of colors and designs in the mask.

A) NO CHANGE

B) Graham explained the meaning, decorated with hundreds of sequins, behind the choices of colors and designs in the mask.

C) Graham, decorated with hundreds of sequins, explained the meaning behind the choices of colors and designs in the mask.

D) Graham explained the meaning behind the choices of colors and designs in the mask, decorated with hundreds of sequins.

30

Actuaries in the region have spent the last few years reassessing the risks of storm damage, they recommend carrying flood insurance even if one's house is not in an area previously prone to flooding.

A) NO CHANGE

B) damage;

C) damage, which

D) damage, therefore,

Find a problem?

Report any issues to curriculum@studylark.com

31

<u>Although</u> the sheets were printed with four images per page and had to be folded and cut correctly, the symbols were included as instructions from the printer to the binder to ensure that proper collation took place.

A) NO CHANGE

B) Because

C) So

D) DELETE the underlined portion and begin the sentence with a capital letter.

32

The organization pioneered several innovative ways of measuring water quality as it conducted the assessment, <u>it was published,</u> as part of the cleanup effort, in a report made available to the public in 2003.

A) NO CHANGE

B) they published it,

C) its publication,

D) published,

33

Over millions of years, the buried organic matter is converted to various hydrocarbon <u>molecules. A</u> transformation that takes place because of the tremendous heat and pressure found at that depth.

A) NO CHANGE

B) molecules, a

C) molecules; a

D) molecules; which is a

34

Working tirelessly to detect and treat students exposed to <u>tuberculosis;</u> Dr. Helen Aird Dickie became a leader in the diagnosis, treatment, and prevention of the disease and succeeded in virtually eradicating it from the campus.

A) NO CHANGE

B) tuberculosis:

C) tuberculosis, and

D) tuberculosis,

35

Seeing that they are approaching a crater about the size of a football field and covered with large rocks, <u>manual control is taken over by Armstrong, who steers the craft to a smoother spot.</u>

A) NO CHANGE

B) Armstrong's takeover of manual control steers the craft to a smoother spot.

C) Armstrong takes over manual control and steers the craft to a smoother spot.

D) a smoother spot becomes the new destination of Armstrong's manual control.

36

When some people complained that the recitations lasted all day and that one should not attend them, Pinarius Natta said, "Surely I cannot be more generous: I am ready to listen to him from sunrise to sunset."

A) NO CHANGE
B) them, therefore
C) them, so
D) them;

37

The women document a diverse range of subjects, some gravitating to war zones or social justice issues, while others focusing on local events and daily life.

A) NO CHANGE
B) issues;
C) issues; while
D) issues,

38

Such choral music remains popular to this day, being demonstrated by the Naselle Finn-Am Choir's many performances at The Finnish American Folk Festival held in Naselle, Washington.

A) NO CHANGE
B) demonstrating this
C) this is demonstrated
D) as demonstrated

39

They now refer to it as Hubble's Law, this relationship allowed astronomers in the late 1920s to calculate the rate of expansion of the universe.

A) NO CHANGE
B) Now referred to as Hubble's
C) It is now referred to as Hubble's
D) Hubble's

40

Lighter and more durable than metal parts, and ceramic components have allowed jet engines to become more reliable than ever.

A) NO CHANGE
B) parts; also,
C) parts,
D) parts;

41

There are fewer languages spoken on Earth with each passing year, <u>with</u> some experts predict that half of existing languages will be gone by the year 2100.

A) NO CHANGE

B) indeed

C) and

D) DELETE the underlined portion.

42

A note of caution was sounded by Charles Emil <u>Bendire, he</u> was aware of the mass market for bird eggs and its detrimental effect on bird populations.

A) NO CHANGE

B) Bendire, who

C) Bendire, which

D) Bendire; he who

43

They were deterred by a ferocious ice <u>storm, it wasn't until later that year that the team was</u> finally able to return to the area.

A) NO CHANGE

B) storm, so it wasn't until later that year that the team was

C) storm. It wasn't until later that year that the team

D) storm. So it wasn't until later that year that the team

44

In its grand finale phase, Cassini made five passes over Saturn, the closest <u>pass</u> was a mere thousand miles above Saturn's cloud tops.

A) NO CHANGE

B) of which

C) of them

D) DELETE the underlined portion.

45

While these programs may provide some workforce development activities, <u>but</u> they do not focus on employment and training as a key program goal.

A) NO CHANGE

B) and

C) for

D) DELETE the underlined portion.

46

In addition to recognizing the benefits of space efforts, Johnson deftly worked to obtain passage of the U.N. Outer Space <u>Treaty, that was</u> based on principles first enunciated by the US during the Kennedy administration.

A) NO CHANGE

B) Treaty. Which was

C) Treaty, which was

D) Treaty; that

47

From indigo snakes to carnivorous pitcher plants to the Florida black bear, whose potential listing as a federally threatened species has been the subject of legal <u>debate. The abundance</u> of plants and animals is one of the defining features of the Okefenokee-Osceola ecosystem.

A) NO CHANGE

B) debate, and the abundance

C) debate; the abundance

D) debate, the abundance

48

After McKeown's appointment to the court in 1998, Judge Beezer helped to hone her writing <u>skills, he was</u> advising her "not to waste words, but also not to mince words."

A) NO CHANGE

B) skills that he was

C) skills also

D) skills,

49

Residents are beginning to understand that the dunes <u>lining the sugar-white sand beaches of the Gulf of Mexico help</u> prevent erosion and should be preserved, even at the expense of their properties' ocean views.

A) NO CHANGE

B) lining the sugar-white sand beaches of the Gulf of Mexico, they help

C) that line the sugar-white sand beaches of the Gulf of Mexico and help to

D) that line the sugar-white sand beaches of the Gulf of Mexico, where they help

50

One of the reasons for that popularity was <u>because of,</u> unlike creamware, which was almost exclusively undecorated, pearlware employed varied forms of ornamentation, including blue and polychrome hand-painted designs.

A) NO CHANGE

B) because that,

C) that,

D) DELETE the underlined portion.

Combining Sentences

The final ten questions in this set ask you to combine two sentences into one. Be sure to consider the full range of grammar and stylistic rules.

51

The 1970s saw <u>Afrobeat musicians winning awards. The award-winning musicians began to enjoy commercial success as well.</u>

Which choice most effectively combines the sentences at the underlined portion?

A) Afrobeat musicians winning awards, and the public bestowed commercial success upon them too.

B) commercial successes being made out of Afrobeat musicians for the awards those musicians won.

C) award-winning Afrobeat musicians begin to enjoy commercial success as well.

D) awards being won by Afrobeat musicians, and they began to enjoy commercial success as well.

52

<u>Tardigrades are active only when surrounded by a film of water. However, they can survive in a latent state for nearly ten years in response to desiccation, temperature extremes, or low oxygen.</u>

Which choice most effectively combines the underlined sentences?

A) Tardigrades can survive in a latent state for nearly ten years in response to desiccation, temperature extremes, or low oxygen, but they mainly do their activities when surrounded by a film of water.

B) Although tardigrades are active only when surrounded by a film of water, they can survive in a latent state for nearly ten years in response to desiccation, temperature extremes, or low oxygen.

C) Tardigrades can survive in a latent state for nearly ten years in response to desiccation, temperature extremes, or low oxygen and are active only when surrounded by a film of water.

D) They can survive in a latent state for nearly ten years, which would be in response to desiccation, temperature extremes, or low oxygen, but tardigrades are active only when surrounded by a film of water.

53

Before nations can effectively explore, use, and manage such resources, they must complete an essential <u>task. That task is</u> mapping the seafloor of these vast undersea regions.

Which choice most effectively combines the sentences at the underlined portion?

A) task that includes

B) task; that is

C) task:

D) task, and that task is

54

There were once gold and iron mining operations in some Virginia Piedmont parks. The operations have since closed down.

Which choice most effectively combines the underlined sentences?

A) Although there were once gold and iron mining operations in some Virginia Piedmont parks, those operations have since closed down.

B) Whereas there were once gold and iron mining operations in some Virginia Piedmont parks, the parks' mining operations for gold and iron have since closed down.

C) The operations in the parks have since closed down, and at one time there were once gold and iron mining operations in some Virginia Piedmont parks.

D) There were once gold and iron mining operations, but they have since closed down in some Virginia Piedmont parks.

55

Claesz often left behind several versions of the same painting. This provides insight into his creative vision and process.

Which choice most effectively combines the two sentences at the underlined portion?

A) painting, providing

B) painting, and such versions provide

C) painting, and these versions are providing

D) painting, being one to provide

56

It was taboo in Stewart's time for a woman to address an audience comprised of both men and women, but she felt absolutely compelled to speak. She also felt a compulsion to work for change and to inspire others to take action.

Which choice most effectively combines the sentences at the underlined portion?

A) speak; while also wanting to work for change and to inspire others

B) speak, to work for change, and besides to inspire others,

C) speak, to work for change, and to inspire others; moreover, she was compelled

D) speak, to work for change, and to inspire others

57

Once the road is built, engineers evaluate the existing speed limit by <u>measuring operating speed. They often do this by measuring, over the course of several days, the speed that 85 percent of drivers are traveling at or below.</u>

Which choice most effectively combines the sentences at the underlined portion?

A) measuring, over the course of several days, operating speed, the speed that 85 percent of drivers are traveling at or below.

B) measuring operating speed, the speed that 85 percent of drivers are traveling at or below, which they measure over the course of several days.

C) measuring operating speed; they do it by measuring, over the course of several days, the speed that 85 percent of drivers are traveling at or below.

D) measuring the speed that 85 percent of drivers are traveling at or below over the course of several days, known as operating speed.

58

<u>Frost was unable to read the text of the poem he'd written for the inauguration because of the sun's glare upon the snow-covered ground. He recited a different poem from memory.</u>

Which choice is the best way to combine the underlined sentences?

A) Frost, reciting a different poem from memory, was unable to read the text of the poem he'd written for the inauguration because of the sun's glare upon the snow-covered ground.

B) Frost would recite a different poem from memory; he was unable to read the text of the poem he'd written for the inauguration because of the sun's glare upon the snow-covered ground.

C) Unable to read the text of the poem he'd written for the inauguration because of the sun's glare upon the snow-covered ground, Frost recited a different poem from memory.

D) Reading the text of the poem he'd written for the inauguration was something he was unable to do because of the sun's glare upon the snow-covered ground, so Frost recited a different poem from memory.

59

Studies show that children who learn to play chess have better problem-solving skills. They also display improved concentration and creativity levels even after just a few months of playing.

Which choice most effectively combines the underlined sentences?

A) Studies show that children who learn to play chess, even after just a few months, have better problem-solving skills, and also with improved concentration and creativity levels.

B) In addition to improved concentration and creativity levels even after just a few months of playing, studies show that children who learn to play chess have better problem-solving skills.

C) Children who learn to play chess have better problem-solving skills, as shown by studies, even after just a few months of playing, with improved concentration and creativity levels.

D) Studies show that children who learn to play chess have better problem-solving skills, concentration, and creativity levels even after just a few months of playing.

60

She leads me into her favorite neighborhood spot. The biscuits are unusually large in comparison to the chicken. People use a shocking amount of hot sauce. Despite all this, the atmosphere feels instantly welcoming, and the food is undeniably good.

Which choice most effectively combines the sentences at the underlined portion?

A) chicken—people use a shocking amount of hot sauce—in light of this,

B) chicken; people use a shocking amount of hot sauce, although

C) chicken; as people use a shocking amount of hot sauce,

D) chicken, and people use a shocking amount of hot sauce, but

✎ Word Choice ✐

Making Effective Use of Language

The SAT has a broad category of questions that it calls **Words in Context**. In the Reading section, WIC questions ask you interpret and analyze the words and phrases an author has used. In the writing section, it will be *your job* to choose the right words. These questions are sometimes said to be testing "diction," but we'll call them **word choice** questions.

Word choice questions are all about—you guessed it—choosing the right word for the job. There are four main things to pay attention to for these questions:

- Some situations call for a **certain specific word** that must be used
- Sometimes you'll have to choose between similar words that have slightly different **definitions** or customary usages
- You may have to decide which choice has the proper **style or tone**
- Sometimes the test will tempt you to mix up **similar-looking words**

Required Words

There are cases in which certain words must go together, not for any logical reason, but because *that's just how English is.*

Many times, those certain specific words are prepositions. For example, which preposition would you use to fill in this blank?

- Nevaeh felt a strong connection   for / around / to / by   the singer's music.

Of course you'd say *to.* You can have a *connection **to*** something, or perhaps a *connection **with*** something, but you can't have a *connection **by*** something. You can have a *preference **for*** something but not a *connection **for*** something. WHY?!? There's no logical reason. That's just how English is. The word *connection* has certain specific prepositions it's allowed to be paired with. That's all.

A similar situation happens with something called a **phrasal verb**. A phrasal verb is group of words—typically a verb plus a preposition—that work together as a unit to refer to a single action. For example:

catch	- verb meaning "to grab a thrown object" (among other things)
catch on	- phrasal verb meaning "to become popular" or "to come to understand"
catch up	- phrasal verb meaning "to reach someone ahead of you"
catch in	- not a thing

As you can see, depending on which preposition is used with *catch* (or whether one is used at all), you have different verbs referring to completely different actions. So if a sentence introduces some particular situation, you may need to pick the correct preposition in order to create the logical phrasal verb for that context:

⊙ He was walking away quickly, so I ran to catch on / up / in .

Of course, *up* is the logical choice here. It's the required word for this situation.

Another case of required words is a **correlative conjunction**. We discussed this back in the chapter on parallelism. Remember this old friend?

⊙ During the Victorian era, dogs were not only beloved family members
  and also / but also / as well as fashionable accessories.

When you see *not only*, you need *but also* later in the sentence. Those words are required to go together. Similarly, if you see *neither*, you have to follow it up with *nor*; other correlative conjunctions work in the same way.

In that same chapter, we saw this issue:

⊙ My sister is twenty months younger than / then me.

As you know, a **comparison** like this uses *than*, not *then*. That's the required word for this construction.

The final place where certain words may be required is in an **idiom** or **figure of speech**—a group of words that *just go together* to create a meaning that is understood from common usage.

⊙ Competitors may go so far / as far / so far as to mimic the layout and look of
  an advertisement in an effort to confuse consumers.

To go so far as to do something is an idiom that means "to do something regarded as extreme." You can't really use logic to figure this out or to know exactly which words make up this standard phrase. Instead, you just have to be familiar with the expression. You need to have encountered it before in conversation or reading. If you have, it will seem normal and easy, and you'll know which specific words are required; if you haven't, you're basically out of luck.

That's the bad news about word choice questions. In many cases, they come down to whether or not you're familiar with the words or phrases in the question. In other words—**it's luck**.

We could easily make a list of all the phrasal verbs and figures of speech that have ever appeared on the SAT, and you could easily memorize that list. Unfortunately, it would be unlikely to raise your score because there are millions of little quirky things like that in the English language, and the SAT doesn't typically repeat them. You're not going to see the same ones on your test.

It's hard to study for word choice questions. It's true that there are a few things you can memorize, such as the correlative conjunctions and some of the commonly confused words we'll discuss in a moment. Those *do* repeat, so you can be ready for them. But for the most part, you're just crossing your fingers and hoping that the word choice questions on your test feature words and phrases you're familiar with.

Well... perhaps there is *one* thing you can do: invent a time machine, go back, and convince your six-year-old self to start reading novels for 3 hours a day for the next ten years. That will definitely help! (If you succeed in doing that, please let us know...)

Vocabulary

When the SAT launched its modern format back in 2015, the College Board put on a big song and dance number about how there would be no more weird vocabulary on the test. Teenagers everywhere rejoiced! People were dancing in the streets!

The only problem: it was lies. All lies.

It's true that there are no more questions like this:

8. The scientist's predictions were so uncannily accurate that his colleagues came to regard them as nearly -------.

   (A) factitious
   (B) ineffable
   (C) circumspect
   (D) discursive
   (E) oracular

> There used to be 19 of these little gems on every SAT before 2015. Aren't you glad you live here in the future? By the way, the answer is E.

But to say that the SAT doesn't test tricky vocabulary anymore is simply not true. For one thing, the authors of the reading comprehension passages (especially the historical passages) may use words that you're simply unfamiliar with, and that unfamiliarity may impact your ability to understand important ideas from the passage.

Furthermore, the SAT writers even admit that they still test people on challenging vocab. According to the Official Guide, "The SAT focuses on high-utility academic words and phrases, the type of vocabulary that you can find in challenging readings across a wide range of subjects." You will certainly see several questions on your test that get into the nuances of obscure or closely related words.

For example, here's a typical question:

30

The power generation industry has come under increasingly <u>scrupulous</u> government regulations in recent years.

A) NO CHANGE

B) disciplinary

C) obstinate

D) strict

The first issue here is that you might not be familiar with all these words. Do you know what *scrupulous* means? How about *obstinate*? Perhaps you do—but not everyone is able to define these words. So right there we have an example of obscure vocabulary. But again, it doesn't make sense to try to study vocabulary for the SAT, since the same words don't show up repeatedly from test to test. You're just hoping to get lucky with words you know.

> **Collocations** are words that frequently occur together. For example, the word *tribulations* is most often accompanied by the word *trials*, as in, "I suffered through the trials and tribulations of studying for the SAT writing section." Even though the phrase *hardships and tribulations* would mean about the same thing, people would look at you funny if you said that, since those words don't customarily go together.

Second, even if you do know the definitions of all those words, you'll notice that they carry somewhat similar meanings.

scrupulous: diligent, thorough, and extremely attentive to details
disciplinary: concerned with enforcing rules or codes of behavior
obstinate: inflexible; difficult to change or overcome
strict: demanding that rules concerning behavior are obeyed

So how do you decide which one is right? Part of it comes down to the nuances of the definitions. *Scrupulous* seems like a poor fit because it would be a bit of stretch to call a regulation *diligent*—that word seems better-suited to describing a person's behavior, not a regulation.

That said, the definitions of *disciplinary* and *strict* do seem very similar. There has to be something more going on. And there is—the central thing to consider is **customary usage**, or which words are **collocations** in certain situations. If you were to check a corpus (that's a huge collection of text and speech that's representative of how people use the English language), you'd find that the phrases "scrupulous regulations" and "obstinate regulations" basically **never occur** in natural English. And while the phrase "disciplinary regulations" does occasionally occur, the phrase "strict regulations" occurs 2145% more often!

In other words, *strict* is correct because that's just what people typically say. The other answer choices aren't really used in that way.

Of course, you're not going to be checking a corpus in the middle of the SAT (or probably any other time). So again, you just have to be familiar with the definitions and typical usage patterns of the words in the question. If you've seen them used before in similar situations, they will seem normal and easy, and you'll know what to pick; if you haven't, you're—again—out of luck.

Style and Tone

Another type of word choice question asks you to pick a word or phrase with the right **style or tone** for the passage.

There is no single style that is always correct. Some passages are first-person, anecdotal, casual, and even funny, while others are more formal and academic. So you need to be paying attention to the entire passage to see what kind of tone the author establishes.

With that said, most passages inhabit a certain region of formality that you've probably gotten used to: **SAT style**. It's academic and precise, displaying a certain degree of curiosity and enthusiasm for the subject matter, without getting too irreverent, creative, or frankly, interesting. You know it when you see it.

> The need to pick up on the author's tone is just one more reason you should **read everything**. Read all parts of the passage, even when there are large gaps between questions. Try to follow the overall story even as you're picking apart the details of the grammar.

Thus, choices with the wrong style usually go wrong by being too casual or slangy. For example:

 ...the company's engineers were asked to <u>think up stuff</u> to address the...
 ...the impact of this loss of legal protection is <u>a pretty big deal</u> for...
 ...specialized gills make it <u>a breeze</u> for basking sharks to live in...
 ...people named game spaces after local streets <u>or whatever</u> and invented...

On the other hand, it's also possible for a choice to go wrong in the other direction. It may be too formal, or "embody a stultifying degree of ponderousness," as the Official Guide says. (That's actually pretty funny on their part, don't you think? No?) For example, there's no need to say *facile protocols* when you could just say *simple directions*.

Here's a sample question:

15

In recent years, several universities in Canada have decided to <u>deep-six</u> public funding for their MBA programs and to greatly raise the tuition rates for students.

A) NO CHANGE
B) ditch
C) forgo
D) disaffirmingly abjure

Some of these choices are too slangy, and choice D is so overinflated that it's just silly. You probably have a good idea as to what the right answer is, but let's imagine you were deciding between choices B and C. If you're ever **truly stuck** between two plausible choices on a style/tone question, a good trick is this: ask yourself which of the two choices you would be **less** likely to say when talking to your friends. That's probably the right answer. You've probably talked with your friends about *ditching* things, but *forgoing* things? Eh, not so much. Thus, you should pick choice C here.

Commonly Confused Words

Some words look or sound very similar to each other, so it could be easy to mix them up. For example, *accept* and *except* sound nearly identical when you say them, and *expanded* and *expended* are spelled almost identically.

Some SAT questions expect you to notice that the choices contain commonly confused words and to know which one is appropriate. Just as with the other word choice topics we've discussed, many of the commonly confused word pairs have shown up only once and aren't repeated from test to test. It's great to know the difference between *perspective* and *prospective*, but since this pair has only appeared on a single test that we know of, you're unlikely to see it again on yours.

There are two main exceptions, however. The following commonly confused words have shown up on **multiple tests**, so you should certainly know them:

Affect vs. Effect

Affect	**Verb** meaning *to influence* A lack of sleep may affect your performance.
Effect	**Noun** meaning *consequence or result* The drought had a harmful effect on the economy.

> *Affect* and *effect* also have some less common, secondary definitions, but you won't need them for the SAT.

Site vs. Cite vs. Sight

Site	**Noun** meaning *a location;* also *a website* Many sites allow people to log in using their Facebook credentials. The professor took us on a tour of the archaeological site.
Cite	**Verb** meaning *to quote or refer to something as evidence for a statement or as an example* She cited the data from Dr. Harper's study to support her argument. He cited *Abbey Road* as the most important album in his musical development.
Sight	**Noun** meaning *vision* The eye operation improved his sight.

There's also one more set of words that might be worth knowing. It has only appeared once on the modern SAT (that we know of), but it was quite common on the previous version:

Assure vs. Ensure vs. Insure

Assure	**Verb** meaning *to reassure someone or to dispel any doubts they may have* The guide assured us that the lions would not attack.
Ensure	**Verb** meaning *to make sure of something* Please ensure that the paperwork is submitted by Friday.
Insure	**Verb** meaning *to arrange for insurance coverage* The museum insured the painting for $2 million.

Practice Question Set

*The questions in the following practice set test **word choice**. Word choice questions are common on the SAT, but as we said in the chapter, there's not a whole lot you can do to effectively study for them. For that reason, we'll keep this practice set relatively short.*

1

The navy, under the direction of Commander Rodgers, decided to convert three side-wheel steamships <u>for</u> what became known informally as "timberclads."

A) NO CHANGE

B) in

C) into

D) by

2

Some argue that culling is needed in certain areas to manage the kangaroo population and to protect the native grassland, which can be adversely <u>effected</u> by kangaroo grazing.

A) NO CHANGE

B) affected

C) effect

D) affect

3

Filamentous algae are a type of green algae that grow in long threads or filaments. <u>When proliferation gets out of hand,</u> large mats can form that stretch from the river bottom to the surface and cover significant portions of a river's length.

A) NO CHANGE

B) On occasions of disproportionate multiplication,

C) If the strand expansion goes haywire,

D) When growth is excessive,

4

In the eighteenth century, odometers were mounted on the wheels of horse-drawn carriages, and the pendulum odometer, the type Jefferson bought from Leslie, was commonly used. The pendulum odometer's triangular shape <u>designated</u> it to be mounted between the spokes of a carriage wheel, where it counted each of the wheel's revolutions.

A) NO CHANGE

B) tolerated

C) entitled

D) allowed

5

The Chicago-based community garden project currently has eight gardens and almost four thousand gardeners <u>engaging in</u> producing their own food, but more importantly, building a stronger community.

A) NO CHANGE
B) filled with
C) being a party to
D) preoccupied by

6

Graphic designers frequently specialize in a particular category or type of client. For example, some <u>forge</u> the graphics used on retail product packaging, while others may work on the visual designs used on book jackets.

Which choice best preserves the overall tone of the passage?

A) NO CHANGE
B) create
C) bring into being
D) churn out

7

At the time the referendum took place, Eritrea was not a state under international law and thus lacked the capacity to confer citizenship <u>for</u> those who took part in the vote.

A) NO CHANGE
B) upon
C) by
D) to

8

The growing popularity of LinkedIn and other <u>sights</u> that enable job seekers and potential employers to more efficiently contact each other is most likely the cause of shorter average jobless periods.

A) NO CHANGE
B) cites
C) cites'
D) sites

StudyLark

9

In 1983, he hiked the Appalachian trail without a tent or stove, having been <u>assured</u> by a friend that he would find shelter and firewood along the way.

A) NO CHANGE
B) ensured
C) ensure
D) insured

10

There was a chill in the air, and the vivid fall colors that once decorated the university campus had given <u>away to</u> a palette of browns and grays.

A) NO CHANGE
B) way to
C) into
D) away into

11

She wanted to see how the climate would be affected by a constant pall of dust, with the amount fluctuating as a result of big impacts, but she was frustrated by the <u>obfuscations</u> of correctly modeling the way the dust would alter the radiation filtering through the atmosphere.

A) NO CHANGE
B) complications
C) nuisances
D) predicaments

12

The size of the control group was small, so a "cage effect" cannot be completely ruled out. However, the mice in the study were reared in a homogenous environment and with a common genetic background, and this may to a certain extent <u>compensate for this defect.</u>

A) NO CHANGE
B) allow this to be swept under the rug.
C) balance out this headache.
D) fix it.

13

Fresh produce tastes best most of the time, but don't diminish the frozen aisle. When fruits and vegetables are flash frozen right after harvesting, there is minimal loss of nutrients, and they can often have great flavor when properly prepared.

A) NO CHANGE
B) discount
C) look right through
D) give the cold shoulder to

14

In a 1921 interview , Marie Curie unveiled that her lab had only a gram of radium to experiment with and that she needed more to continue researching. After learning about Curie's predicament, Mrs. Meloney formed the Marie Curie Radium Fund to raise money to purchase another gram of radium, worth $1.4 million in today's dollars.

A) NO CHANGE
B) uncovered
C) disclosed
D) exhibited

15

Although the novel was respectively received when it was first published, critics today do not regard it as one of his best works.

A) NO CHANGE
B) respectably
C) respectfully
D) responsibly

16

The Raven is approximately the 54th movie or television show to feature the character of Poe, a figure that itself pales by comparison to the 250 or so films and television programs in which Poe is credited as a writer.

A) NO CHANGE
B) pale by
C) pales in
D) pales with

⋄ Redundancy ⋄

Déjà Vu All Over Again

Redundancy is saying the same thing twice for no reason. There's no reason to say the same thing twice for no reason, since then you're just saying the same thing twice—for no reason!

On average, 2 or 3 questions on every test will feature redundancy in the answer choices. The fix is simple: get rid of the unnecessary words. Redundant choices count as grammatically incorrect on the SAT.

How can you spot redundancy questions? The easiest way is to look at the **lengths of the answer choices**. If you see three long choices accompanied by a short choice, the first thing you should check for is redundancy. And remember, an option to **delete** the underlined text is the very shortest choice of all.

> Seeing three long choices and a short one doesn't **guarantee** that you're looking at a redundancy question—it might be testing some other grammar or rhetorical task. But you should certainly check for repeated information whenever you see that pattern.

The most obvious case of redundancy would be something like this in the answer choices:

A) the current road as it is designed at this time
B) the current design of the road

Choice A contains the word *current* and the phrase *at this time*. They mean the same thing, so choice A is wrong.

The reason this case is so easy to spot is that the redundancy occurs right there for you to see in the choices. But it's not always so obvious. Sometimes a choice repeats a concept from the non-underlined part of the sentence, or even from a different part of the paragraph or passage. This is yet another reason to read everything in the passage, even if it's far away from an underlined bit.

Questions that test redundancy test **only redundancy**. In other words, if you notice that some of the choices unnecessarily repeat information, then your one and only task will be to get rid of the unnecessary words. You will **not** have to consider grammar or vocabulary or other stylistic skills. Don't worry about sentence structure or how a choice "sounds." Just trim the fat.

In some cases, a choice might be wrong not because it actually repeats an idea but because it is **unnecessarily wordy**. If you can express an idea in two words instead of eight, it's better to be more concise.

Getting rid of the unnecessary words **almost always** means picking **the shortest choice**. But not every time. Sometimes the shortest choice is so short that it actually cuts out an important piece of information. Check out the following two examples—how would you answer each one?

20

Coca-Cola is made according to a <u>secret, undisclosed</u> recipe that the company keeps in a secure vault.

A) NO CHANGE

B) secret and unknown

C) secret and covert

D) secret

23

The best places to view geothermal features such as geysers and hot springs are in volcanically active areas, including Iceland and New Zealand. Yellowstone National Park offers a popular series of <u>hikes and lectures related to geothermal and geyser attractions in the national park.</u>

A) NO CHANGE

B) geothermal hikes, and geyser lectures are offered.

C) geothermal hikes and lectures.

D) hikes.

What did you choose? In the first example, the shortest choice is indeed correct. The words *undisclosed*, *unknown*, and *covert* don't add anything important that isn't already covered by the word *secret*, so they are unnecessary.

The second example is different. Certainly there is some redundancy going on here. Choice A causes the sentence to say *national park* twice, and it doesn't seem necessary to include both *geothermal* and *geyser*. Choice B has that problem too, and it repeats the word *offer* from earlier in the sentence.

However, if you pick choice D, you lose some important information. First of all, the lectures have disappeared. Second, if you just say *hikes*, it becomes unclear what the nature of the hikes is. Perhaps they're hikes to see wildlife, or mountains, or lakes? It's no longer evident that the hikes have anything to do with geothermal features. Choice C is the best because it gets rid of the unnecessary stuff but keeps what's important.

> We wanted to show you an example in which the shortest choice is wrong because it drops some important information, but keep in mind that the shortest choice will be right on the **vast majority** of redundancy questions.

Practice Question Set

The questions in the following practice set test **redundancy.** *The shortest answer is almost always right. Almost.*

1

Typical bachelor's degree programs in geological engineering include courses in geology, chemistry, fluid mechanics, physics, and mathematics. Relatively few schools, in fact it's a small number, offer geological engineering programs, but a related degree, such as civil or environmental engineering or geoscience, may be acceptable for some positions as a geological engineer.

A) NO CHANGE
B) schools—there aren't that many options—
C) schools, just a handful of programs,
D) schools

2

Cats are carnivores, built to hunt. This was part of their first initial appeal as early farmers encouraged cats to control the rodent populations that threatened their grain supplies.

A) NO CHANGE
B) appeal in the beginning times
C) initial usefulness and appeal
D) initial appeal

3

Recently, the company signed a license to use solar-powered refrigeration systems technology. The goal is to develop and market one of the first battery-free solar-powered refrigerators suitable for safely storing vaccines.

A) NO CHANGE
B) vaccines that provide immunity against disease.
C) vaccines in a protective container.
D) vaccines, which must be kept cold.

4

The man credited with popularizing the idea of saving daylight was an entomologist in New Zealand named George Vernon Hudson, whose shift-work job led him to appreciate extra hours of daylight after work, his time to collect bugs.

A) NO CHANGE
B) appreciate and value
C) be appreciatively grateful for
D) view with a strong measure of appreciation

5

As the vehicle population continues to grow faster than the human population, the challenge of sharing the limited street and intersection space grows increasingly difficult. In some cases, cities have removed lanes intended for cars and other motorized vehicles in favor of bike lanes to accommodate the changing attitude of "pedestrians and bikes first, cars second."

A) NO CHANGE

B) lanes solely for use by vehicles

C) vehicle lanes

D) lanes

6

The report also found that artists are highly entrepreneurial—they are 3.5 times more likely to be self-employed—and they have generally higher levels of education than most other workers who have lower average levels of education.

A) NO CHANGE

B) in addition to their entrepreneurial inclination.

C) according to the report.

D) DELETE the underlined portion and end the sentence with a period.

7

As the irrigation system moves across a field, the sensors determine a crop's water needs based on information from the sensors, triggering the release of water in an amount determined by an algorithm tied to the characteristics of specific crops in specific regions.

A) NO CHANGE

B) needs,

C) needs throughout the field,

D) needs with respect to required hydration,

8

At a time when doing so was uncommon and unusual, Ray's parents provided intellectual opportunities for their daughters as well as their sons. Ray graduated from the University of the City of New York (now New York University) with a master's degree in pedagogy; she was one of only three African-American graduates in her class.

A) NO CHANGE

B) uncommon,

C) unusually uncommon,

D) uncommonly rare,

9

The detection of gravitational waves requires measurements that detect changes in distance less than the size of an atomic nucleus. To carry out this task, scientists use interferometry, which consists of two parts: test masses on either side of a separation gap and lasers to measure that distance.

A) NO CHANGE

B) separated test masses to be used in the measurement

C) test masses separated by a distance

D) test masses

10

Many rural counties grow older because the people moving out over the long term consist overwhelmingly of young adults. Other rural counties grow older as a result of attracting retirees, usually because they are scenic or recreational destinations, which are enticing to those who no longer work.

A) NO CHANGE

B) destinations in areas not overly urbanized.

C) destinations.

D) destinations that offer picturesque landscapes.

11

Dwarf planet Pluto is a member of a group of objects that orbit in a disc-like zone beyond the orbit of Neptune called the Kuiper Belt. This distant realm is populated with thousands of miniature icy worlds, which formed early in the history of our solar system about 4.5 billion years ago.

A) NO CHANGE

B) miniature, small-scale

C) miniature, or minute,

D) miniature frozen-over,

12

Valles recently developed a fire ant test kit for use at truck inspection stations to help keep the ants from spreading and expanding throughout southeastern states. All trucks carrying hay, nursery stock, or soil-moving equipment are inspected for ants when leaving a quarantined area and heading to a location not under quarantine.

A) NO CHANGE

B) enlarging their spread

C) spreading

D) increasing their territory via expansion

No Test Material On This Page

(Good opportunity to draw a funny picture)

☙ Introductions, Transitions ❧ & Conclusions

Follow the Flow of Ideas

We've been talking a lot about the rules of grammar, but about half of the questions in the writing section are concerned with what the SAT calls **Expression of Ideas**. These questions will ask you about writing strategy, organization, style, and the flow of ideas within the passage. You may also hear them referred to as **stylistic** or **rhetorical skills** questions.

Grammar questions are easier to study for because they involve memorizing specific concrete rules that you can carry into the test with you. Expression of Ideas questions are different because there isn't really anything to memorize beforehand. Instead, you'll have to deal with the content of each passage on its own terms.

But you can still get better at these questions. Instead of memorizing rules, your task is to get familiar with the question types and **develop good habits** for how to approach each one. Then practice as much as you can. Repetition builds skill.

So what exactly are these good habits?

The first and most important good habit is to **read everything**, as we've mentioned before. And don't just read it—follow the flow of ideas. Understand the narrative. Treat a writing passage like a reading passage that you really want to grasp, or a heartfelt email from your boringest friend. You want to come away from it with the ability to tell someone else the story of the passage.

> **Good Habit #1**
>
> Read everything and follow the flow of ideas.

This doesn't mean you should read the entire passage before you start on the questions. That would be inefficient and unnecessary. But it does mean that you should, for example, read an entire sentence before dealing with the underlined bit in the middle. Or read a couple sentences before *and after* an underlined transition word. Read the entire paragraph before and after a transition sentence before you answer the question. Even if there is a large gap between grammar-related questions, read everything in between. Pause at the end of each paragraph to let the content sink in. Read the title of the passage. Find a way to trick yourself into thinking that you **actually care** about the topic.

Transition Words

You'll certainly see several questions on your test that ask you to pick the best **transition word** or phrase. You're looking for something to aid the flow of ideas from one sentence to the next.

Context is vitally important here. You won't be able to pick a word that links two ideas unless you know the **relationship** of those ideas. So of course you'll need to have read the sentences **before and after** the transition word before you attempt the question. An important and effective strategy is to ask yourself how the ideas before and after the transition word relate to each other *before* you look too closely at the choices. In other words, **have a prediction in mind**. Do the sentences set up a contrast? Does the second sentence provide an example? Is there a cause-and-effect relationship? A continuation of the same idea? Once you've determined the relationship yourself, you'll be well positioned to pick the right transition word.

> **Good Habit #2**
>
> Examine the ideas before and after a transition and figure out their relationship *yourself—before* you look at the choices.

For example, take a look at these two sentences. How do they fit together?

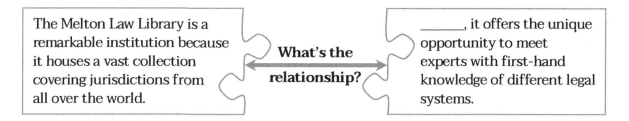

What do you predict? Do you think the second sentence:

- ☐ Sets up a contrast

- ☐ Provides a clarifying example

- ☐ Provides an additional detail along the same general lines

- ☐ Introduces the next chronological step

- ☐ Shows that there is a cause-and-effect relationship

A simplified version of these sentences would be: "The library's great. It has a lot of books. You can meet smart people." Thus the relationship is that the second sentence provides an **additional detail**. It tells us one more reason the library is great. After *first* getting that prediction in mind, you would *then* examine the answer choices, which in this case are:

A) However,

B) Therefore,

C) For example,

D) Furthermore,

Of course, *furthermore* is the best choice here. You could also accept *moreover* or *in addition* or some other word or phrase that indicates an additional detail.

Single-word transitions usually provide a link between the sentence they're in and the previous sentence. Thus, they're usually the first word in the sentence—right at the spot of the transition. But sometimes the test writers stick the transition word in the middle or even at the end of the sentence, and that can occasionally confuse people.

> **Good Habit #3**
>
> Try moving transition words to the beginning of the sentence to help with clarity.

Luckily, there an easy little trick you can try. Just move the transition word to the beginning of the sentence if it isn't already there. This usually makes it easier to figure out what's going on. For example:

Electronics retail stores often allow customers to purchase extended warranties on their products. Because most problems occur during the period covered by the manufacturer's warranty, (however,) consumers are usually better off not purchasing the extended warranty.

With *however* in the middle, you might mistakenly think the contrast is between the two parts of this sentence

Now try moving the transition word to the beginning of the sentence:

Electronics retail stores often allow customers to purchase extended warranties on their products. (However,) because most problems occur during the period covered by the manufacturer's warranty, consumers are usually better off not purchasing the extended warranty.

With *however* at the beginning, it becomes more clear that the contrast is between the two sentences

This trick isn't foolproof, and sometimes the sentence structure gets a little funky with words like *though*. But it's generally helpful.

Another thing to keep in mind is that transition word questions are **only** about the flow of ideas—they don't test you on grammar or sentence structure. However, occasionally a question that *does* test you on grammar can look similar to (and be mistaken for) a transition word question. For example, look at the two sets of answer choices below. Which one is really a transition word question?

> **Good Habit #4**
>
> Be able to recognize true transition word questions and remember that they test only the flow of ideas, not grammar.

Set A

A) indeed,
B) otherwise,
C) nevertheless,
D) moreover,

Set B

A) 1976; therefore,
B) 1976, similarly,
C) 1976: because
D) 1976, but

Set A is the true transition word question. That's because the one and only thing in the choices is a bunch of transition words (or **conjunctive adverbs** if you remember the discussion from "Clauses Gone Bad").

Set B, on the other hand, is likely to be about grammar and sentence structure. There are two tell-tale signs. First, some of the choices contain conjunctive adverbs (*therefore*, *similarly*), but other choices contain full-fledged conjunctions (*because*, *but*). Those two categories of words are meaningfully different when it comes to connecting clauses. Second, look at the punctuation options. You have commas, of course, but also semicolons and colons, which can be used to connect clauses. So for this question, you might have to consider the flow of ideas, but you'd definitely have to consider grammar and sentence structure as well.

Finally, consider going naked. Um... perhaps some clarification is needed on that one. If you see a **true transition word question** that gives you the option to **delete the transition word**, give that choice some serious consideration. It's almost always the right answer. Not every sentence needs a transition word.

> **Good Habit #5**
>
> Strongly consider dropping the transition word, if that's an option.

Know the Words

Some transition words show up all the time on the SAT—you'll see both *however* and *therefore* at least once per test, on average. Others are much less common, but the important thing is to be familiar with what they all mean.

Hopefully we don't need to define *however* for you, but there are some transition words that people are often less sure about. Here are some trickier ones that have appeared recently:

Commonly Misunderstood Transition Words	
Nevertheless/ Nonetheless	Meaning: *in spite of that, even so, however* His statements are technically true. Nevertheless, they are misleading.
Consequently	Meaning: *as a result, as a consequence* On her dentist's advice, Joana cut her consumption of candy. Consequently, she has learned to enjoy fruit more.
Subsequently	Meaning: *later (on), afterward* The band finished the album and subsequently went on tour to promote it.
Moreover	Meaning: *furthermore, in addition* Driving is safer than it used to be because modern cars have better accident avoidance features. Moreover, people are better educated about the dangers of drunk and distracted driving.
Accordingly	Meaning: *appropriately, therefore, consequently* The new walkway served both houses. Accordingly, the neighbors shared the cost.

continued ⟶

Commonly Misunderstood Transition Words

Indeed	Used to reinforce or amplify the previous idea. The new product sold well. Indeed, it was the company's most successful launch ever.
Conversely	Used to introduce an idea that reverses the one just before. Great jazz vocalists often model their singing voices after a horn. Conversely, the best jazz horn players try to emulate the sound of a human voice.
Hence	Meaning: *therefore* I studied the wrong chapter for today's test. Hence, it was something of a disaster.
To that end	Meaning: *in order to achieve that goal* We would like to see a world without advertisements. To that end, we will be removing all the banner ads from our website.
By the same token	Meaning: *in the same way* or *for the same reason* There was little evidence to support the theory. But by the same token, there was little to disprove it either.

Below is a more comprehensive list of the transition words and phrases we've seen on recent tests. You probably know most, if not all, of these, but read through the list carefully. If there are any words or phrases you're not sure about, look them up.

> **Good Habit #6**
>
> Know the words.

Accordingly	Despite this	In other words	On one hand
Afterward	Especially	In particular	On the other hand
Along those lines	Even so	In short	Otherwise
Also	Finally	In spite of	Particularly
Alternatively	For example	Incidentally	Previously
Around the same time	For instance	Indeed	Rather
As a matter of fact	Fortunately	Indubitably	Regardless
As a result	Furthermore	Initially	Similarly
As such	Given this	Instead	Specifically
At any rate	Hence	Likewise	Still
At present	However	Meanwhile	Subsequently
At the same time	In addition	Moreover	That said
Besides	In any case	Nevertheless	Thereafter
By contrast	In broad terms	Next	Therefore
By the same token	In conclusion	Nonetheless	Though
Clearly	In contrast	Notwithstanding	Thus
Consequently	In effect	Of course	To that end
Conversely	In fact	On a similar note	Yet

Introductions, Conclusions & Transition Sentences

Sometimes you'll be asked to create a transition that is not just a single word but an **entire sentence**. The sentence could act as a transition between two paragraphs. Or it could play some other large-scale role, such as an effective introduction or conclusion to a paragraph or even to the whole passage.

Many of the things we said about transition *word* questions remain true here. It's still vitally important to consider context and the flow of ideas. So if you need an introduction to a paragraph or a transition between two paragraphs, it's essential that you read the **entire paragraph** following the transition before you answer the question. Sounds obvious, but people don't always do this. And you should again have a prediction in mind before you look at the options. What is the main topic of the paragraph? Or what is the relationship between the two paragraphs? Figure that out yourself first before you examine the choices.

> **Good Habit #7**
>
> Fully read the paragraphs before and after a transition sentence and decide how they're related.

Furthermore, remember that transition sentence questions are only about the flow of ideas— just as with the transition word questions, **they don't test grammar** or sentence structure. So even though you may be tempted to examine the clauses and modifiers or check whether a sentence "sounds right," that stuff doesn't matter. All the choices are grammatically correct. You just need the one that sets up the proper flow of ideas.

> **Good Habit #8**
>
> Don't pay attention to grammar on transition sentence questions.

For all transition sentence questions, remember that the sentence that initially occupies that spot in the passage isn't necessarily the one that belongs there. If the right answer is B, C, or D, then you're going to remove that sentence and replace it with a different one. The underlined sentence is suspect. So when you're checking out the entire paragraph to see what it's all about, it's better to **read it without the underlined sentence**. Just pretend that the sentence isn't there in the paragraph but instead that it's written as choice A alongside the other choices. It's better not to let that sentence pollute your mind, because then you might start to get the idea that the underlined bit plays some necessary role in the paragraph.

> **Good Habit #9**
>
> Read the paragraph *without* the underlined sentence to avoid being swayed by what might be irrelevant info.

If a question near the beginning asks for a good introduction to the passage, you may wonder how you're supposed to introduce the passage when you don't know what it's going to be about. The answer is—you shouldn't. You need to read the entire passage before you're ready to answer such a question, but you shouldn't immediately go read the whole thing just for the sake of that one question. Instead, you should **postpone the question**. Skip it, go do the rest of the questions as normal (which will involve reading and comprehending the whole passage, of course), and come back to that question once you know what the passage is about. It's important that you don't forget to come back, so write yourself a little note. As soon as you decide to postpone question #13, for example, immediately turn to #22 (the last question in the passage) and write after it, "Go do #13."

Good Habit #10

Postpone questions that ask about the whole passage until after you've read the whole passage.

If a question near the end asks for a good conclusion to the passage, you should be pretty well prepared, since you will have read and followed the entire story. Right? But you might want to give the passage another quick skim just to remind yourself of all the ideas it discussed. And another nice trick is to go back and **read the title of the passage**. Sometimes the SAT tries to get clever or punny with the title, but it usually also gives you a nice summary of what the passage is about.

Good Habit #11

Use the title of the passage to help you summarize the overall topic.

Start where you are

Use what you have

Do what you can

— Arthur Ashe

Practice Question Set

*The questions in the first half of this practice set test **transition words and phrases**.*

*The second half of the set contains longer questions that ask about **introductions, transitions, and conclusion sentences**.*

1

Although larger metropolitan areas tend to attract jobseekers because of robust job markets, some occupations have higher employment levels in smaller areas. Conversely, Midland, Texas, is among the areas with the highest employment of wellhead pumpers, and Fort Collins, Colorado, is among the areas with the highest employment of conservation scientists.

A) NO CHANGE
B) However,
C) For example,
D) Moreover,

2

Food-borne illnesses cause thousands of hospitalizations each year, but not all bacteria present in food products are harmful. However, bacterial species are essential in the production of delicious and safe yogurt and cheese products.

A) NO CHANGE
B) In fact,
C) Even so,
D) Despite this problem,

3

The risks from forest fires are growing. Over the last three decades, fire season lengths have increased by 60-80 days, and annual area burned has more than doubled to over 7 million acres. Nonetheless, growing housing development in forests has put more people and houses in harm's way, also making firefighting efforts more expensive.

A) NO CHANGE
B) However,
C) Conversely,
D) In addition,

4

Ask someone to name a classical musician, and they'll likely reel off names such as Mozart, Chopin, Beethoven, Bach, or Tchaikovsky. Ask them to name a classical musician from the 21st century, especially, and the task might become a little more difficult.

A) NO CHANGE
B) therefore,
C) though,
D) furthermore,

5

When the orchestra attempted to play through the composition, the unconventional notation and dependence only on density of textures with no linear material or change of dynamics presented difficulty. With this problem in mind, however, Knussen worked with the musicians to create a modified version of the piece that was better suited to live performance.

A) NO CHANGE
B) for example,
C) subsequently,
D) DELETE the underlined portion.

ITC Introductions, Transitions & Conclusions ITC

6

Looking through the atmosphere is like looking through a piece of old stained glass. The glass has defects that distort the image. The atmosphere too has such distorting defects, but the defects in the atmosphere also move, thus blurring the image as well. The glass is colored, so only some colors get through, and the same is true for the atmosphere. For one thing, astronomers had been eager for decades to put a telescope above the atmosphere.

A) NO CHANGE,
B) For these reasons,
C) In the same manner,
D) In light of these advantages,

7

After her appointment ended, Lansing did not resign herself to obscurity. For example, she set herself to writing.

A) NO CHANGE
B) Likewise,
C) Instead,
D) In spite of this,

8

From 2000 to 2006, the price of residential housing in the New York City area doubled. Driving this price increase were gains in employment and income in both the financial and legal services industries. Furthermore, low interest rates and wider availability of loans and mortgages contributed to increased demand and thus higher prices for residential housing.

A) NO CHANGE
B) However,
C) That said,
D) Accordingly,

9

Today's readers owe a debt of gratitude to the early printers whose efforts made reading materials increasingly available, and thus furthered the spread of literacy and learning. Because of his innovative moveable type, Johannes Gutenberg is the best known of those printers, but there were many other printers in the 15th and 16th centuries who are still remembered today.

A) NO CHANGE
B) Regardless of
C) In contrast to
D) In addition to

10

In the Arctic, the rate at which ocean plants create organic material has increased over the past decade. Like plants on land, however, plants in the ocean use chlorophyll to convert carbon dioxide to sugar and oxygen through photosynthesis.

A) NO CHANGE
B) for instance,
C) on the other hand,
D) DELETE the underlined portion.

11

When, still in her early thirties, Boyd inherited her family's fortune, she continued on as a philanthropist and a society woman. Behind the scenes, for instance, she started to build a second life—as a rugged polar explorer.

A) NO CHANGE
B) therefore,
C) likewise,
D) however,

StudyLark

12

The practice, known as "biological control," is one that has already found its way onto some golf courses. In other words, a 2018 survey by the Environmental Institute for Golf found that 42 percent of 27-plus-hole golf facilities sometimes or frequently use biocontrol in their pest management practices.

A) NO CHANGE

B) Indeed,

C) Nonetheless,

D) However,

13

April Fools' Day pranks are usually fairly short term: an entire class simultaneously falls asleep or a teacher assigns a forty-page essay due the next day, and everyone laughs once the trick is revealed. Hoaxes, particularly, have a different intent, as they are engineered to deceive over the long term, and often on a large scale.

A) NO CHANGE

B) consequently,

C) on the other hand,

D) as a result,

14

After that success, Marian Anderson began to tour the country, but because of racial intolerance, Anderson was unable to have an active career in the US at that time. She decided, therefore, to use scholarship money from the Julius Rosenwald fund to build a career in Europe instead.

A) NO CHANGE

B) otherwise,

C) for example,

D) moreover,

15

Pollution is a real concern not just on our planet but in space as well. Earth's outer atmosphere is littered with human-generated debris. As a result, spacecraft and satellites are vulnerable to collision with this debris. The moon and other planets, moreover, retain abandoned human-generated equipment.

A) NO CHANGE

B) however,

C) for example,

D) in particular,

16

{The passage is about celebrated jazz singer Ella Fitzgerald}

Throughout these troubled years, Fitzgerald and Gulliver often rode a trolley and subway to 125th Street to watch performing artists like Earl "Snake Hips" Tucker. They took the newest dance moves back to their neighborhood to practice with their friends. By the age of 16, Fitzgerald was dancing on the streets of Harlem to earn money to survive.

The Apollo theater grew to prominence during the Harlem Renaissance, billing itself as a place "where stars are born and legends are made." After the main show every Wednesday, amateurs competed for the honor of appearing onstage the following week. On November 21, 1934, the Edwards Sisters, a dancing team, were the main attraction. Although Fitzgerald originally planned to dance, she changed her mind because the Edwards Sisters had danced so well. Instead, she sang two songs, "The Object of My Affection" and "Judy." The audience loved her voice so much that she won first prize.

Which choice provides the best transition from the previous paragraph?

A) NO CHANGE

B) Harlem attracted many musicians and dancers, who often appeared at the Apollo Theater.

C) Everything changed dramatically when Fitzgerald entered the Amateur Night competition at the Apollo Theater in Harlem.

D) One unique feature of the Apollo during Amateur Nights was "the executioner," a man with a broom who would sweep performers off the stage if audiences expressed disapproval.

17

17 Esther cut the basic design for the individual valentines, and the assembled group carefully copied each card. Each young lady was assigned a special task; one cut out pictures and kept them assorted in boxes and another made the backgrounds, passing them to yet another worker who gave the card further embellishment. By the end of 1849 Esther Howland had fully launched her valentine business and perfected her "assembly line" technique. At least during the early years of her business, Ms. Howland reportedly inspected every valentine produced by the women in her family workroom.

Which choice best introduces the information presented in the paragraph?

A) It is estimated that annual US retail sales of greeting cards are more than $7.5 billion, with Valentine's Day the second-most-popular occasion.

B) A room was set aside on the third floor of the Howlands' Summer Street residence, Esther gathered a group of friends to assist in filling her orders, and a valentine business was born.

C) Perhaps we should credit Esther Howland rather than Henry Ford with the development of mass production.

D) Esther Howland was born in 1828 in Worcester, Massachusetts, and her father was a successful stationer and bookseller of the firm S.A. Howland & Sons.

18

Showing Earth from space has long been a way to show how something that might seem very significant up close is at a distance not a particularly big deal. A 1906 cartoon from the humor magazine *Puck* shows two Martians yawning and expressing relief that Charles Evans Hughes has been elected governor of New York. We can see fireworks marking the celebration back in New York from our point of observation on Mars. The caption reads in part, "We can get a little sleep now that we know how the New York election came out." State politics are viewed by many as dull and meaningless in comparison to national politics, but this idea can be tempered by questioning whether they are really being watched with considerable anticipation from 300 million miles away.

Which choice most effectively supports the main idea of the paragraph?

A) NO CHANGE

B) Hughes's governorship introduced policies focused addressing political corruption,

C) It can be easy to get caught up in the feeling that your state's politics are the center of the universe,

D) While events on Earth may not matter to inhabitants of other planets, they do affect us,

19

The One Health concept is a worldwide strategy for expanding interdisciplinary collaborations and communications in all aspects of health care for humans, animals, and the environment. It recognizes the interconnections of human and animal health with environmental health and that no single discipline or sector of society has enough knowledge and resources to prevent the emergence or resurgence of diseases in today's globalized world.

Disease has been with us since the beginning of human society, considering the fact that 2,500 years ago it was Hippocrates who urged physicians to consider where their patients lived, the foods they ate and waters they drank, their lifestyles, and the seasons of the year. In the 19th century, pioneering pathologist Rudolf Virchow stated that "between animal and human medicine there are no dividing lines—nor should there be."

Which choice provides the most logical introduction to the paragraph?

A) NO CHANGE

B) Experts are just beginning to see how interdependent some systems are,

C) Network theory and artificial intelligence are leading the way in One Health initiatives,

D) The concept of One Health is not really new,

20

Food can be wrapped in meaning or symbolism, with state dinners often setting the scene for diplomacy. In a drawing of George Washington's farewell dinner, the outgoing president is seen surrounded by weeping guests who are loath to let him go, while he stands to propose a toast to the incoming president, John Adams. Lyndon Johnson's first state dinner, in December of 1963, was held, not at the White House, but at the LBJ Ranch in Texas. West German Chancellor Ludwig Erhard journeyed to the ranch, sometimes referred to as the Texas White House, where guests ate barbecue and beans prepared by pit master Walter Jetton.

In another example of culinary diplomacy, Richard Nixon, as part of the preparation for his historic trip to China in 1972, spent months mastering the art of eating with chopsticks. He displayed his expertise at a banquet for 600 in the Great Hall of the People, hosted by China's Premier Zhou Enlai and televised live at home…

Which choice establishes the best transition from the previous paragraph to this paragraph?

A) NO CHANGE

B) Richard Nixon was known to favor unusual food combinations, such as cottage cheese with ketchup and baked grapefruit, and he knew just how he liked such concoctions.

C) Likewise, when an American politician travels abroad, as Richard Nixon did to China in 1972, it is important that he or she be familiar with the customs of the host country.

D) Not every state visit is accompanied by a meal, however, as evinced by Richard Nixon's historic trip to China in 1972, which was conceived of primarily as a way to improve diplomatic relations between the countries.

21

Despite the ubiquity of the genre, sales of self-help books are on the rise. According to publishing statistics, 80% of self-help book customers are repeat buyers, which could indicate that the books are not effective. A recent study found that most purchasers read no more than the first twenty pages, if they even open the book. Anecdotal evidence suggests that for some people, simply buying a self-help book makes them feel better.

Which choice most effectively sets up the paragraph?

A) NO CHANGE

B) it's hard to say whether self-help books help anyone.

C) people rarely admit to buying self-help books.

D) it seems that everyone is a self-help expert.

22

22 In the northern hemisphere, the beginning of spring is marked by the passage of the vernal equinox, which is when the sun's path is directly over the earth's equator. It is one of two times during the year when day and night are more or less equal, and it is a significant date on calendars around the world, falling between March 19 and 22 every year. The increasing daylight means the return of life, and those signs of life are how we know that spring has really arrived. There will be buds, flowers, bees, and of course, eggs.

Which choice most effectively establishes the main topic of the paragraph?

A) The earth's orientation to the sun changes throughout the year.

B) How do we know when spring is here?

C) The northern and southern hemispheres experience opposite seasons.

D) With spring comes a controversial practice—the start of daylight saving time.

23

Employment growth for artists <u>is erratic and unpredictable</u>: during good economic times, people and businesses are interested in acquiring more artwork because buyers usually make art purchases when they can afford to invest in nonessential goods. During economic downturns, they generally buy less. However, there is always some demand for art by private collectors and museums.

Which choice most effectively sets up the information that follows?

A) NO CHANGE

B) is threatened by the advent of digital tools that make it possible for anyone to create professional-quality art:

C) is driven by trends among high-end private art investors and museum curators:

D) depends in large part on the overall state of the economy:

24

Costas Karageorghis studies the science behind the systematic use of music to improve sports performance and enhance the exercise experience. He has been a consultant for sports federations, sports and music equipment companies, and Olympic athletes. "Music lowers your perception of effort," he says. "It can trick your mind into feeling less tired during a workout, encourage positive thoughts, and reduce your perception of effort by as much as 10%." Listening to music distracts us from discomfort, interfering with the brain's signals of pain, strain, or fatigue. Our favorite tunes can increase endurance and stamina, especially in the context of low-to-moderate-intensity exercise. 24

Which choice serves as the most effective conclusion to the paragraph?

A) Caffeine is also known to improve performance in exercise, though it is not as widely studied as music.

B) In addition to publishing these findings, Karageorghis was head coach of the Great Britain student athletics team from 2007-2011.

C) It seems that you don't have to be an Olympian to reap the benefit of listening to music during your workout.

D) Furthermore, music has been shown to significantly reduce pain and anxiety in medical patients who listen to it after surgery.

25

The red barn is certainly an iconic image, but <u>why are so many barns this particular color?</u> The practice started in the late 18th century with New England farmers applying a protective varnish to barn surfaces. The varnish usually contained some mixture of linseed oil, lime, or iron oxide, which, under the sun, would then turn to the red ochre hue that we have become so familiar with. Eventually, as red paint became available, many people stuck to the color tradition. It helps that red paint is one of the cheapest colors available for purchase due to the plentiful nature of the iron and oxygen compounds that give the paint its hue.

Which choice most effectively sets up the discussion that follows?

A) NO CHANGE

B) is red really the best choice in an agricultural setting?

C) can the first instance of a barn being painted red be pinpointed?

D) what is the underlying chemistry that makes objects appear red?

26

From the latter half of the 19th century until nearly the middle of the 20th, one of the easiest ways for the average American to obtain a portrait photograph was by approaching a booth at a fair or commissioning an itinerant or street photographer. The process, from posing for the camera to a finished portrait in hand, required only a matter of minutes. And it was inexpensive, costing only a few cents for a likeness of oneself, or perhaps of a child or sweetheart.

<u>It's easy to understand why someone would be interested in such a portrait</u>, as it could be created with minimal equipment on any busy street corner. The metal base (iron, not tin, despite the name) for the photo was far more durable than paper, and so it offered a lasting photographic record...

Which choice provides the most logical transition into the next paragraph?

A) NO CHANGE

B) Despite the low cost, such a photograph often became a treasured possession,

C) Indeed, taking a picture of one's child was the most popular application of the technology,

D) For decades, the tintype was the most likely result of such a transaction,

27

The album *Songs of the Humpback Whale* was produced in 1970 by bio-acoustician Roger Payne, based on recordings of the elaborate vocalizations of several humpbacks. The use of underwater microphones, called hydrophones, showed that not only can whales communicate, but they do so with beauty and complexity. The haunting sounds on *Songs of the Humpback Whale*, along with Payne's liner notes for CRM Records, helped turn the tide of US public opinion against whaling.

In addition to having aesthetic and political significance, the album can also be considered historically valuable. Whales change their songs over time, so these recordings document a cetacean performance practice of a time gone by. . . .

The writer wants a transition that makes a connection to the main topic of the previous paragraph. Which choice best accomplishes this goal?

A) NO CHANGE

B) Because it was eventually chosen to be carried on the *Voyager* spaceship,

C) In addition to selling several million copies,

D) Despite the fact that it contains no music or human dialogue whatsoever,

28

The film *Being There* is ostensibly about a simpleton, a man seemingly born without the capacity for cynicism, but sometimes the best films are the ones that strive to be more than just one thing: the audience sees the story that is presented to them but then, at the best of times, the hidden truth begins to reveal itself.

Which choice most effectively sets up the information provided in the rest of the sentence?

A) NO CHANGE

B) many of Ashby's films explore this same theme:

C) such a character is still deserving of respect:

D) it is still worth watching even after all these years:

Questions 29 and 30 refer to the following passage.

Electrons Get Around

Whether the emptiness between stars or the emptiness between molecules, experiments have shown that upon close examination, any vacuum is not truly empty. All manner of subatomic particles—and their antimatter counterparts—constantly pop in and out of existence and annihilate each other on contact. That environment influences the electron; its round, negative charge is defined by the constant interaction.

The Standard Model of particle physics, a longstanding theory describing most of the fundamental forces and particles in the universe, predicts that an electron's charge should have a perfectly spherical shape. Many other theories—involving such concepts as "supersymmetry" and "grand unification"—posit that some undiscovered subatomic particles would be revealed if researchers were able to look closely at an electron and find that its spherical charge was slightly squashed. That would require an extreme observation, akin to measuring an Earth-sized sphere to a precision of a few atoms' thickness. As part of the Advanced Cold Molecule Electron Electric Dipole Moment Search (ACME), researchers did look that closely at the electron's charge— and found that the sphere appeared to be perfectly round.

29 The study was funded in part by the National Science Foundation, which subsidizes approximately 24 percent of all federally supported basic research. The entire ACME team consisted of only about a dozen researchers, using an apparatus that fits in a basement room at Harvard. Within that relatively small chamber, lasers orient the molecules—and their electrons—as they soar between two charged glass plates inside a carefully controlled magnetic field. ACME researchers then watch for light the molecules emit when targeted by an additional, carefully tuned, set of readout lasers. That light reveals whether the electron's orientation twists during flight, as would occur if it were squashed.

"The Standard Model makes predictions that differ radically from its alternatives, and ACME can distinguish those," noted David DeMille, who leads the ACME group at Yale. **30**

29

Which choice provides the most effective transition into the next point?

A) NO CHANGE

B) Probing the shape of the electron's charge has far-reaching implications for fundamental physics but can be done with an experiment of modest size.

C) The Standard Model is believed by many to be incomplete because it doesn't explain some newly discovered phenomena such as dark matter.

D) Hypothetical subatomic particles outside the electron could create a slight separation between the positive and negative charges, called an electric dipole moment.

30

The writer wants an effective conclusion that reflects on a key implication of the study. Which choice best accomplishes this goal?

A) "Larger apparatuses could probe the same phenomena at higher energies, but it's not clear whether they will ever be built."

B) "Now that this hypothesis has been confirmed, it's time to explore what other questions can be answered by this innovative technology."

C) "Our result tells the scientific community that we need to seriously rethink some of those alternative theories."

D) "However, this calculation assumed a certain explanation for the difference between matter and antimatter in the universe, and that assumption may not hold up in future studies."

☙ Specific Tasks ❧

You Have One Job

Some SAT questions give you a weirdly specific task to accomplish.

It's true that the questions in the last chapter also gave you a task to accomplish, but those were much more generic tasks, such as "provide the best transition from the previous paragraph" or "establish the main idea of the passage."

Specific task questions are much more, well, *specific*. For example:

- ⊙ The writer wants to begin this paragraph with a sentence that emphasizes the amount of time it takes for a bristlecone pine to reach maturity. Which choice most effectively accomplishes this goal?

- ⊙ Which choice best maintains the sentence pattern already established in the paragraph?

- ⊙ Which choice gives a supporting example that emphasizes the range of different spices used in Nashville hot chicken?

- ⊙ Which choice gives a second example that supports the idea that Hewitt tried to reach consumers who were unfamiliar with fabric quality grades?

Very particular, right? It's actually nice to be given such a well-defined job. It takes most of the thinking out of it. Instead of trying to decide whether a sentence really does provide a good transition between paragraphs (which requires some deeper analytical skills), all you have to do is find the one sentence that accomplishes the specific task.

As long as you **stay focused on that specific task**, the job usually isn't too hard. For example, if you get down into the choices with the proper mindset of "must... find... something about the amount of time it takes for a bristlecone pine to reach maturity...," there will typically be only one answer choice that's even close to being in the right ballpark. Find it, and you're done.

There are some things you should **not** do on specific task questions:

- ⊙ **Don't forget about the task.** The task is the one and only reason the question exists, but amazingly, people sometimes forget to read or pay attention to the task. Instead, they assume their job is just to find a nice-sounding sentence, so they jump into the choices without a goal in mind.

> **You have one job:** stay focused on the task.

- ⊙ **Don't worry about grammar.** Like the other Expression of Ideas questions we've looked at, these don't test grammar, and you shouldn't worry about whether you think the sentence "sounds good."
- ⊙ **Don't question the author's intention.** If you saw a question that said, "The author wants a sentence that contains six different synonyms for *moustache*, in reverse alphabetical order" your first thought would probably be, "Well, *that's* a stupid thing to want." But your second thought should be, "Sure, boss! Coming right up. A sentence that does... that."

The following drill has a few examples for you to try. To demonstrate how straightforward they should be as long as you focus on the task, we'll show them here without even giving you the full sentence from the passage! Even with just the question and the choices, you should still be able to get them right.

Drill: Specific Tasks

1. Which choice most clearly communicates the location of Dry Tortugas to those readers unfamiliar with it?
   - (A) which is now a national park.
   - (B) where a massive but unfinished coastal fortress sits.
   - (C) 68 miles west of the Florida Keys.

2. The writer wants to complete the sentence with examples of the types of materials Isaiah Zagar uses in his building-scale mosaics. Which choice best accomplishes this goal?
   - (A) with meticulous attention to detail in the midst of sweeping forms.
   - (B) including bottles, bike wheels, and folk art.
   - (C) winning a grant of $50,000 for work in the interdisciplinary arts in 1995.

3. Which choice is most consistent with the idea that the scientist was "expressing reservations" about the proposed policy?
   - (A) balked at
   - (B) embraced
   - (C) despised

4. Which choice most precisely identifies how infrequently it rains in the Atacama Desert?
   - (A) has soil that has been compared to that of Mars.
   - (B) receives less precipitation than even the polar deserts.
   - (C) may go 400 years between precipitation events.

Of course, not every specific task question on the SAT can be answered without looking at the passage. For example:

> **42**
>
> Archaeologists who study Denisovans still have a lot of unanswered questions about these mysterious ancient hominids. Why is there no trace of them in most modern genomes? What did they really look like? <u>There are questions about why they left no mark of distinctive tools in the archaeological record.</u> Even the experts aren't completely sure.
>
> Which choice most closely maintains the sentence pattern established in the paragraph?
>
> A) NO CHANGE
>
> B) Why did they leave no mark of distinctive tools in the archaeological record?
>
> C) Scientists wonder why they left no mark of distinctive tools in the archaeological record, or have we just not found it yet?
>
> D) Scientists are wondering, "Why did they leave no mark of distinctive tools in the archaeological record?"

Because this question asks you to maintain the pattern from the paragraph, you need to figure out the pattern from the paragraph first! (The answer is B because it, like the previous two sentences, asks a direct question.)

And some specific tasks are more specific than others. For example, if a question like one of the following appeared on your test, it would require a little more work on your part:

⊙ Which choice adds the most relevant supporting detail to the sentence?
⊙ Which choice best supports the statement made in the previous sentence?
⊙ Which choice most effectively sets up the examples that follow?

If your task is to provide a relevant supporting detail, you first need to figure out what claim you're supposed to be supporting, and what would count as "relevant." If you can get a prediction in mind before you dive into the choices, that's always helpful.

It's also worth pointing out a detail about how these questions are structured. In some cases, the question is indicated **solely** by the numbered box (28) embedded within the text. For such questions, you are **adding something new** to the existing passage text at that point.

But in other cases, the numbered box is also accompanied by some <u>underlined text</u>. When that happens, you'll have to decide whether to **remove** the underlined text and **replace** it with something different or leave the existing text **unchanged**.

As we discussed in the last chapter, if the underlined text is a full sentence, you may want to ignore it at first as you read the surrounding content, so you aren't unduly influenced by option A.

StudyLark

Practice Question Set

*The questions in the following practice set all ask you to accomplish a **specific task**. Stay focused on the task.*

1

Despite being the very first exoplanet candidate discovered by NASA's Kepler space telescope, Kepler-1658b had a rocky road to confirmation. The initial estimate of the planet's host star was off, so the sizes of both the star and Kepler-1658b were vastly underestimated. It was later marked as a false positive—that is, scientists thought the data did not really point to a planet—when the numbers didn't quite add up for the effects seen on its star for a body of that size. **1**

At this point, the writer wants to add a sentence that emphasizes the amount of time Kepler-1658b was believed not to be a planet. Which choice most effectively accomplishes this goal?

A) It was quite a while before new software was used to refine the data and reclassify it, changing it from a data anomaly to possible planet.

B) Indeed, Ashley Chontos with the University of Hawaii's Institute for Astronomy was just a middle-schooler when Kepler-1658b was first written off.

C) It was not until ten years later that Ashley Chontos was able to reanalyze the data with new tools and help confirm that Kepler-1658b is in fact a "hot Jupiter."

D) Some time passed, and astronomers moved on to study the thousands of other planets and potential planets identified by the Kepler space telescope.

2

Some of the tools commonly used by glassblowers include a marver (which is often a polished steel, brass, or graphite surface) and a punty (which holds the bottom of the vessel while the top is finalized).

Which choice provides an example that is most similar to the other example in the sentence?

A) NO CHANGE

B) (which forms a cool skin on the exterior of the molten glass blob)

C) (which must be kept clean to prevent the transfer of debris to the molten glass)

D) (which can be hand-held or mounted on a wooden table)

3

Berliner's gramophone, initially powered by a manual crank, was the direct predecessor of the modern record player. Since its inception, improvements in music recording have been substantial. Rudimentary mechanical recording via acoustic horn microphone has been replaced by other things, including electrical microphones and amplifiers.

Which choice most effectively sets up the examples that follow in the sentence and completes the contrast introduced earlier in the sentence?

A) NO CHANGE

B) devices Berliner would not have been familiar with:

C) more sophisticated techniques using

D) more expensive equipment such as

4

The mtDNA and microsatellite data provide strong evidence that the Puerto Rican breeding group of snowy plovers is genetically divergent from that in the continental US.

The writer wants to be consistent throughout the passage in presenting the hypothesis as a possibility rather than as an accepted fact. Which choice best maintains that consistency?

A) NO CHANGE

B) conclusively show

C) have clearly confirmed

D) give proof

5

The 30-year-old Federal Communications Commission sports blackout rule stated that if a team had not sold all tickets for an event 72 hours prior to game time, the game could not be aired on local broadcast television stations. By 2012, fans had had enough. A petition was filed with the Media Bureau of the FCC to lift local blackout rules and allow fans everywhere to watch their hometown teams on TV, regardless of ticket sales; the FCC is an independent agency of the United States government created to regulate interstate communications. In a statement, the FCC welcomed the petition "in light of marketplace changes."

Which choice best maintains the paragraph's focus?

A) NO CHANGE

B) sales, though it is not clear whether those who signed the petition knew the origin of rule.

C) sales, and the number of petitions submitted to other government agencies has increased as well.

D) sales.

6

The Space Experiment Module introduces students to the concept of performing space-based research on the International Space Station. This investigation lets high school students determine objectives and conduct research on the effects of microgravity, radiation, and space flight on various materials. The students are given 20 vials and allowed to select items to go into them. They choose everything from seeds to chicken bones, copper, plastic, human hair, and brine shrimp eggs, using the items to test hypotheses on seed growth after microgravity exposure, how materials protect against radiation exposure, and survival rates of microscopic life forms.

Which choice provides an additional example that demonstrates that some students' hypotheses relate to biological questions?

A) NO CHANGE

B) how structures are affected by the forces of launch and re-entry.

C) the performance of electronics under extremes of temperature and pressure.

D) novel research techniques that can be performed in microgravity.

7

Renowned cellist Katinka Kleijn of the Chicago Symphony Orchestra is joined by composer Daniel R. Dehaan and engineer Levy Lorenzo to transform the traditional concert hall into an experimental theater. To perform *Intelligence in the Human-Machine*, Kleijn wears an EEG headset that monitors brain signals. Dehaan and Lorenzo in turn mix these brain waves with electronic <u>sounds that are dispatched individually to eight different speakers around the space.</u> *Time* magazine describes Kleijn's performance as "a balancing act for her whole body," as she utilizes her physicality and cello to interact with the electronic sounds.

Which choice adds the most relevant supporting detail to the sentence?

A) NO CHANGE

B) sounds that are created by audio production software on a computer.

C) sounds, which will come as a surprise to attendees who have not read the program.

D) sounds, a technique that would not have been possible before the advent of EEG technology.

8

Dr. Janelle Goetcheus <u>hints</u> that much work remains to be done in caring for the homeless. "This country still needs to make a much more fundamental commitment to care for all its people," she insists.

Which choice best shows that Goetcheus is emphatic about expressing the belief stated in this sentence?

A) NO CHANGE

B) says

C) supposes

D) asserts

9

Unlike a traditional glass mirror, a mirror made of polished, reflective metal does not distort the reflected image. When light travels across the interface between air and glass, its rays are refracted, or bent, before they reach the reflective surface behind the glass. They're refracted again on the way out, which can lead to changes in the image, especially when viewed from an angle. A polished metal mirror reflects directly from its front surface, so there is no interface for the light to cross, <u>and metallic mirrors can be more durable, depending on the alloy used.</u>

Which choice most effectively concludes the contrast set up in the paragraph?

A) NO CHANGE

B) and a pleasing metallic tint may be imparted as well.

C) and thus no distortion of the image.

D) but the image may be warped if the metal is not completely flat.

10

Ground water is one of Hawaii's most important natural resources. It is used for drinking water, irrigation, and domestic, commercial, and industrial needs. Total ground water pumped in Hawaii was about 500 million gallons per day during 2015, which is less than 3 percent of the average total rainfall in the state. From this perspective, the ground-water resource appears ample; indeed, ground water provides about 99 percent of Hawaii's domestic water and about 50 percent of all freshwater used in the state.

The writer wants to include a statement that refutes the idea that groundwater supplies in Hawaii are plentiful. Which choice most effectively accomplishes this goal?

A) NO CHANGE

B) however, much of the rainfall runs off to the ocean in streams or returns to the atmosphere by evapotranspiration.

C) nevertheless, ground-water salinity can range from freshwater to that of seawater, which has a chloride concentration of 19,500 mg/L.

D) still, conservation and modernized agricultural practices in recent years have steadily decreased per capital water consumption.

11

A crosswalk is redesigned to incorporate colorful street art. A stormwater garden is installed to add a sliver of urban greenspace. A sidewalk bench is added to create an opportunity for people to linger and socialize.

Which choice best maintains the sentence pattern already established in the paragraph?

A) NO CHANGE

B) To create an opportunity for people to linger and socialize, a sidewalk bench is added.

C) Adding a sidewalk bench can help create an opportunity for people to linger and socialize.

D) On a sidewalk, a bench is added to create an opportunity for people to linger and socialize.

12

While some mathematicians conduct research into mathematical theory, others apply mathematical techniques to solve problems in science, management, and other fields. Big Data will contribute to the expected continued increase in demand for mathematicians. As more sales and business transactions are completed online and as social media and smartphone usage grows, the amount of digitally stored data will also increase. With the vast amounts of new data, new facilities must be constructed to house the needed computer equipment.

The writer wants to further reinforce the paragraph's claim about employment opportunities in the field of mathematics. Which choice best accomplishes this goal?

A) NO CHANGE

B) people with backgrounds in mathematics will probably need to look for new career paths.

C) roles in mathematical modeling and analysis will become more viable and lucrative.

D) the risk of data breaches and malicious activities by hackers will grow as well.

13

Yet for all his many talents, Berle is best known for jokes, gags, and routines. From the vaudeville era to the computer age, Berle always wanted to share the gag—regardless of its creator. He collected jokes from all kinds of sources: radio shows of his peers (including Fred Allen and Bob Hope), subscription joke collections, and topics at which he wanted to poke fun.

Which choice gives a further supporting example that is most similar to the examples already in the sentence?

A) NO CHANGE

B) material prepared by his writers.

C) lyrics to more than 400 songs.

D) a floppy disk containing the searchable text of his entire Private Joke File.

14

One of the first acts of the Office's Music Committee was to recommend Aaron Copland for a nine-country Latin American tour, during which he would promote works by US composers and select Latin American musicians for visits to the United States. Copland was an ideal choice for this government assignment. Not only did he speak Spanish reasonably well, <u>but he was used to traveling, having already visited over twenty different countries at that point in his life.</u> As such, he embraced a fundamental tenet of the Good Neighbor policy, namely, the notion that the Americas are linked by shared historical and cultural experiences.

Which choice best reinforces the main point of the paragraph?

A) NO CHANGE

B) but he more than once enthused over "a new world with its own new music," one that could challenge the European tradition.

C) but he never enrolled as a member of any political party, despite his interest in civic events.

D) but he had perhaps the most distinctive and identifiable musical voice produced by the United States.

15

As a child, Gretchen Shaw had no desire to be stuck in a darkroom, mixing chemicals and developing negatives. <u>Having tried and failed,</u> Shaw's father was unable to interest her in photography.

Which choice best emphasizes how much Shaw's father wanted his daughter to share his fascination with photographic art?

A) NO CHANGE

B) Because of her indifference,

C) Contrary to expectations,

D) Despite his repeated attempts,

16

One factor driving employment growth in veterinary occupations is that pets are increasingly treated as companions or even as members of the family. The Centers for Disease Control and Prevention explains that "studies have shown that the bond between people and their pets can increase fitness, lower stress, and bring happiness to their owners." 16

At this point, the writer wants to include an additional example of a benefit that pets may provide to their owners. Which choice best accomplishes this goal?

A) One survey by the American Pet Products Association estimates the number of dogs kept as pets in the United States increased 50 percent from 1988 to 2017.

B) The average life expectancy for both cats and dogs has increased over time, due to a variety of factors.

C) Demand for veterinary medicine stems, in part, from advances in human healthcare and technology.

D) Some researchers suggest that having dogs and cats can protect against developing allergies and asthma in childhood.

17

Anangula Village was buried beneath deep layers of volcanic ash that have grown over with ryegrass and monkshood. <u>On a slope at the edge of the village are a handful of additional archaeological ruins.</u> Archaeologists found hammerstones, anvil blades, scrapers, retouched blades, and even tools made for right-handed or left-handed use. Seemingly, these artifacts were preserved in their original positions at the time of the ash fall. Outside the houses are several intact stone tool workshops where thousands of stone flakes had been left behind by these ancient craftspeople.

Which choice provides a detail suggesting how the ash may have aided archaeological studies at the site?

A) NO CHANGE

B) The ash was the result of the Okmok eruption about 8,300 years ago.

C) The ash layers protected the site from wind erosion.

D) Volcanic ash is composed of tiny fragments of jagged rock, minerals, and glass.

18

In February 1923, Coleman suffered her first major accident while preparing for an exhibition in Los Angeles; <u>the plane experienced a significant malfunction, and</u> she crashed. Knocked unconscious by the accident, Coleman received a broken leg, some cracked ribs, and multiple cuts on her face. Shaken badly by the incident, it took her over a year to recover fully. Coleman started performing again full time in 1925.

Which choice gives the most specific description of how the crash occurred?

A) NO CHANGE

B) just five months after her first airshow,

C) her Jenny airplane's engine unexpectedly stalled, and

D) despite her excellent training from Caudron Brothers' School of Aviation in Le Crotoy, France,

19

As with other aspects of natural-resource management, the approach to managing wildland fires has evolved over time as scientific understanding has advanced and the broader context surrounding management decisions has changed. Prior to 2000, the primary focus of most fire research was on the physical and ecological aspects of fire; social science research was limited to a small number of studies. However, as more people moved into fire-prone areas, interest <u>waned</u> in understanding relevant social dynamics.

Which choice most accurately portrays the change in fire-related research, as suggested by the paragraph?

A) NO CHANGE

B) was renewed

C) disappeared

D) grew

20

Musical instruments are traditional craft objects that seem to deny the quest for originality. McNally's backpacker's guitar, which he patented in 1980, both contradicts and conforms to this model. Here, necessity was the mother of invention, as the instrument was created to make it easier for hikers and campers to carry their music with them. Since 1980, however, each of McNally's guitars has— <u>surprisingly enough</u>—followed exactly the specifications of its predecessors.

Which choice most clearly establishes that McNally wanted all his instruments to conform to the same design?

A) NO CHANGE

B) as it turned out—

C) not unintentionally—

D) ironically—

☙ Organization ❧

Look for the Hooks

Organization questions ask you to rearrange parts of the passage to create the most logical order. This almost always means moving a sentence to the proper spot within a paragraph. In a few cases, the test has asked people to rearrange the paragraphs within a passage. That's just rude, but it happens.

Because correct answers on the SAT aren't supposed to be a matter of opinion, a sentence's "proper spot" within a paragraph has to be dictated by some kind of **concrete evidence**. The test writers have to provide you with contextual clues that indicate the best order, and there can really be only one spot in the paragraph that is even remotely defensible. So you shouldn't answer based on gut feeling, or guessing, or even what "sounds like a natural flow." Keep working on the question until you've found the concrete evidence that locks the sentence into place.

In other words, look for those contextual clues. A great way to think about these questions is to understand that each sentence must "**hook in**" to the sentence before and the sentence after it. There's got to be some way for adjacent sentences to link up, and to do so in that order. For example, check out these three sentences, which are arranged in the proper order:

Sentence 1	Sentence 2	Sentence 3
DeCampli's lyrics are filled with insight, poignancy, and humor.	A technically skilled instrumentalist as well, he laces his songs with challenging and unusual scales and chord progressions.	It is this unusual blend of heartfelt poetry and sophisticated arrangement that makes his music seem likely to stand the test of time.

You'd probably agree that this seems like a pretty logical order for the sentences, but how would you prove it? What guarantees that the sentences have to hook together in this way?

The **hook** in sentence 2 that links it up to sentence 1 is the phrase *as well*. Sentence 1 introduces the lyrics, and sentence 2 brings up an additional aspect of his songwriting. Those two are logically related, so it makes sense to have them next to each other. And they must be in that order because you couldn't put *as well* first, before you have two aspects.

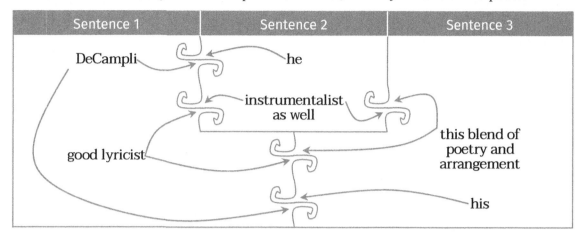

(Those curly things are supposed to be hooks, in case you couldn't tell.)

The **hook** in sentence 3 that links it up to sentence 2 is the phrase *this blend of poetry and arrangement*. Sentence 1 introduces the poetry; sentence 2 introduces the arrangement; you can't talk about blending the two until you've first mentioned them. So sentence 3 must follow sentence 2.

> **Demonstrative pronouns** such as *this*, *that*, *these*, and *those* can be useful indicator words that help point to the proper organization.

Another **hook** to notice is that sentence 1 gives us the musician's name, DeCampli, and sentences 2 and 3 go on to use the pronouns *he* and *his*. That's another common type of ordering clue to look for. A pronoun in an earlier sentence than its antecedent is typically wrong.

You can easily tell when an organization question is coming up. Each sentence in the paragraph will be preceded by a number in brackets, like this: [2]. As soon as you see those numbers, you can tell that one of the sentences may be out of place. In fact, a good habit is to immediately glance ahead at the question, see which sentence it's going to ask you to move, and **mark that sentence within the paragraph ahead of time**.

Then, as you read, be on the lookout for ideas that seem out of order, too far apart from each other, or illogically close. Think about how you would move the sentence to fix the order. You should have a prediction in mind before you read the choices.

> Decide where you want the sentence before you read the choices.

Remember, when the question refers to sentence 5, it's talking about the sentence that comes immediately **after** the bracketed number [5] and not the sentence before [5]. In other words, the *beginning* of each sentence is where its number appears. People sometimes get this backwards, and it messes everything up.

The other careless mistake to avoid is thinking that, since the box indicating the question number (39) shows up at the end of the paragraph, the question must be asking you to move the *last sentence* in the paragraph, the one adjacent to the question number. That's often not the case. You have to check which sentence they actually want you to move.

Drill: Hooking up Sentences

Each exercise below consists of four numbered sentences, which form a complete paragraph. However, the sentences are arranged out of order. Your first job is to figure out the proper order of the sentences. For example, you might decide that the sentences should be rearranged as [2], [1], [4], [3]. Your second task is to explain your reasoning. What are the "hooks," or links between each pair of sentences?

Exercise 1

[1] But soon they were working on the "firing lines" that connected the fighting units in the field with their commanders.

[2] Initially, the female telephone switchboard operators known as Hello Girls handled routine duties, such as calls for supply orders and transportation information.

[3] Hello Girls relayed messages about troop movements and supplies—frequently in military code— and acted as interpreters between American and French units.

[4] At the time of World War I, the telephone was cutting-edge technology, and no one knew for sure the part it would play in battlefield strategy.

1. What do you think is the correct order of the sentences? _____, _____, _____, _____

2. Why do your first pair of sentences belong next to each other, in that order?

   _____

   _____

   _____

3. Why do your middle pair of sentences belong next to each other, in that order?

   _____

   _____

   _____

4. Why do your last pair of sentences belong next to each other, in that order?

   _____

   _____

   _____

Exercise 2

[1] Early cinema brought the character vividly to life, solidifying "Frankenstein" as the monster in the minds of people, taking the character from the context of the novel and putting him into new situations of horror.

[2] Published in 1818, *Frankenstein* was a success and became so popular that the character of Dr. Frankenstein's monster became a well-known image even in the 1800s.

[3] When Mary W. Shelley finished her novel *Frankenstein* over 200 years ago, she could not have imagined the liberties that would be taken with her characters in the future.

[4] But by 1899, the line between Dr. Frankenstein and his monster had blurred: the monster himself was becoming known as Frankenstein.

5. What do you think is the correct order of the sentences? _____, _____, _____, _____

6. Why do your first pair of sentences belong next to each other, in that order?

    _____

    _____

    _____

7. Why do your middle pair of sentences belong next to each other, in that order?

    _____

    _____

    _____

8. Why do your last pair of sentences belong next to each other, in that order?

    _____

    _____

    _____

Exercise 3

[1] When architect John A. Roebling first proposed building a bridge to span the East River between Manhattan and Brooklyn, N.Y., engineers denounced his plan as visionary and impractical.

[2] Fortunately, he'd mentored his son, Washington Roebling, who was appointed chief engineer of the project and wove the great wire cables according to the plans made by his father.

[3] Then tragedy struck: Roebling's foot was crushed while he was surveying the new bridge and he died three weeks later of tetanus.

[4] But Roebling had already created several significant suspension bridges, and with undaunted courage moved forward with the project.

9. What do you think is the correct order of the sentences? _____, _____, _____, _____

10. Why do your first pair of sentences belong next to each other, in that order?

_____

_____

_____

11. Why do your middle pair of sentences belong next to each other, in that order?

_____

_____

_____

12. Why do your last pair of sentences belong next to each other, in that order?

_____

_____

_____

Exercise 4

[1] Discussions of mosquito-borne diseases started in the spring, much earlier than usual, because of the increasing concern about the link between the virus and microcephaly in newborn babies in Brazil.

[2] Not only do mosquitos cause itching and discomfort with their bites, but they can also transmit serious diseases.

[3] In 2016, there was heightened concern due to one such pathogen, the Zika virus.

[4] Since that country was the host country of the Olympics that year, expecting visitors from all over the world, there were serious concerns about travelers facilitating the spread of Zika.

13. What do you think is the correct order of the sentences? _____, _____, _____, _____

14. Why do your first pair of sentences belong next to each other, in that order?

_____

_____

_____

15. Why do your middle pair of sentences belong next to each other, in that order?

_____

_____

_____

16. Why do your last pair of sentences belong next to each other, in that order?

_____

_____

_____

Practice Question Set

The questions in the following practice set test ***organization***.

1

[1] Precious metals have been used in coins throughout history. [2] Cryptocurrencies typically rely on a distributed computing system known as blockchain. [3] Blockchain has several advantages that appeal to cryptocurrency users and designers, but because it relies on computers, it also relies on the minerals that are used to produce computers. [4] So it's somewhat ironic that they have a new, vital role to play in the rise of cryptocurrencies, which are billed as a radical departure from traditional money. [5] One of the unanticipated side effects of the cryptocurrency's growing utilization is a shortage of high-end graphics cards. [6] The blockchain equations that enable cryptocurrencies to function require massive computing power, which relies on the best graphics cards. [7] These cards are made with pricey materials, such as the platinum group metals, and increased demand is leading to rising prices.

To make this paragraph most logical, sentence 4 should be placed

A) where it is now.

B) after sentence 1.

C) after sentence 5.

D) after sentence 7.

2

[1] Nearly four out of five employers, in establishments of all sizes and in all industries, use some form of nontraditional staffing. [2] Among the most common reasons they cite are to accommodate workload fluctuations and to fill positions that are temporarily open due to permanent employees' short-term absences. [3] Some people view this large and growing workforce as one employers relegate to second-class employment—with no worker benefits, little or no mutual loyalty, and all risk borne by the employee—while employers benefit from lower costs. [4] Others see the nontraditional workforce as an opportunity for workers to achieve a flexible work schedule, reach a better balance between work and other interests, gain new experiences, or bridge periods of traditional employment. [5] The increase in nontraditional staffing arrangements may require reexamining definitions of employer, worker, and workplace.

To improve the cohesion and flow of this paragraph, the writer wants to add the following sentence.

The perception of nontraditional work arrangements is mixed.

The sentence would most logically be placed after

A) sentence 2.

B) sentence 3.

C) sentence 4.

D) sentence 5.

3

[1] Maps for navigation can be matters of life and death, and the inability of early navigators to locate themselves accurately on the surface of the Earth has often spelled disaster, as described vividly in Dava Sobel's book *Longitude*. [2] However, mapping crime is a scientific activity—an application of the broader scientific field of cartography, which has undergone a transformation with the advent of geographic information systems (GIS). [3] Many mapmakers now see cartography as a branch of information technology. [4] A decade or so ago, cartography was much broader in scope than GIS with applications in fields as diverse as surveying, navigation of all kinds (including orienteering and highway mapping), geology, space exploration, environmental management, tourism, and urban planning. [5] Today, however, the convergence of cartography and GIS is nearly complete. [6] Both are tools in a broad range of applications, reflecting the most important use of maps—to communicate information. [7] Fortunately, crime mappers do not have to be concerned about such epic matters.

To make this paragraph most logical, sentence 7 should be placed

A) where it is now.

B) before sentence 1.

C) after sentence 1.

D) after sentence 2.

4

[1] In addition to the baseline record, Turner also photographed the panels of prehistoric rock art in infrared wavelengths, yielding some surprising results. [2] Rock art pigments react differently in infrared wavelengths, which are invisible to the human eye, than they do in visible light. [3] The initial expectation was that lighter pigments, such as white, would become transparent, while darker colors, such as red, would become even darker, allowing the observer to see beneath a white outer layer of pigment to the darker image beneath. [4] This would help reveal vandalized or eroded red pigments that could no longer be seen with the naked eye. [5] What was discovered, however, is that rock art pigments don't always follow expectations.

To make this paragraph most logical, sentence 5 should be placed

A) where it is now.

B) after sentence 1.

C) after sentence 2.

D) after sentence 3.

5

[1] Poetry in Motion began when Elise Paschen, the then-executive director of the Poetry Society of America (PSA), visited London on a reading tour and spotted a poem by English poet Michael Drayton displayed publicly on the Tube, London's subway system. [2] Simultaneously, the then-president of New York City Transit, Alan F. Kiepper, was also visiting London and was likewise impressed with the display of word-based art. [3] "It was a case of synchronicity and serendipity," said Alice Quinn, who currently leads the PSA. [4] "When Alan returned to the US, he poked around and landed on our organization as a place to phone. [5] He and Elise put their heads together and launched this program. [6] Immediately, it became immensely popular." [7] Inspired, she began to wonder if publicly placed poetry could elicit a similarly striking effect in the US.

To make this paragraph most logical, sentence 7 should be placed

A) where it is now.

B) after sentence 1.

C) after sentence 2.

D) after sentence 3.

6

[1] Cyanobacteria inhabit water in every corner of the world. [2] These microorganisms possess the qualities of algae and bacteria, and under certain environmental conditions, cyanobacteria multiply rapidly, creating harmful algal blooms. [3] During blooms, cyanobacteria produce toxins, such as microcystins, in amounts that can harm wildlife, pets, and humans. [4] To combat such threats, a fleet of satellites orbiting 700 kilometers above the Earth scans lakes in the continental United States, searching for the characteristic blue-green swirls of cyanobacteria. [5] At the national level, these officials look for ways to protect drinking and recreational waterbodies. [6] At the local level, bloom prevention can include diverting runoff or planting rows of vegetation in areas of high runoff to slow and absorb nutrients. [7] The information they provide can make decisions easier for water managers by prioritizing at-risk bodies of water.

To make the paragraph most logical, sentence 7 should be placed

A) where it is now.

B) after sentence 3.

C) after sentence 4.

D) after sentence 5.

Find a problem?

Report any issues to curriculum@studylark.com

7

[1] While offering workplace accommodations to qualified employees is often a matter of complying with the law, it is certainly not the only reason to implement them. [2] Furthermore, the employers in the study reported that the majority of accommodations cost absolutely nothing, while the remainder typically cost no more than $500. [3] In a recent study conducted by the Job Accommodation Network, employers reported benefits such as retaining valuable employees, improving productivity and morale, reducing workers' compensation and training costs, and improving company diversity. [4] For example, in one case, a valued manager with attention deficit/hyperactivity disorder often missed common errors as he rushed to submit his reports on time. [5] The accommodation provided was a whiteboard with a checklist of important elements to review prior to submitting his reports. [6] According to the employer, the whiteboard was an effective solution, and it cost just $20.

To make this paragraph most logical, sentence 2 should be placed

A) where it is now.

B) after sentence 3.

C) after sentence 4.

D) after sentence 6.

8

[1] Scientists sought ways to increase the number of eggs laid and chicks hatched. [2] In the wild, whooping cranes typically lay two eggs at a time and only one clutch (group) per year. [3] In captivity at Patuxent, scientists removed eggs from the parents' nests for incubation in the lab, which encouraged re-nesting and increased the total number of eggs and chicks produced. [4] If those eggs don't survive or are lost to predators, a whooping crane may lay a second or even a third clutch that year. [5] Sandhill cranes were often used to incubate the extra eggs.

To make the paragraph most logical, sentence 4 should be placed

A) where it is now.

B) after sentence 1.

C) after sentence 2.

D) after sentence 5.

9

[1] She developed several platforms for spreading that message. [2] One of the first ideas was to develop a mobile app, the Domestic Worker App, that could connect users to a call-in radio show that broadcast humorous, educational vignettes about the types of situations domestic workers regularly run into. [3] It was also critical that the radio broadcast feature actual workers' stories using actual workers' voices. [4] Jahn described the programming as "Click and Clack for nannies," referring to the former hosts of NPR's popular *Car Talk* radio program. [5] It was important to Jahn that the program be accessible by any basic cell phone—not just smartphones—so that the workers—many of whom work 60-hour weeks in addition to caring for their own households—could access the show whenever they had free time.

To make the paragraph most logical, sentence 3 should be placed

A) where it is now.

B) after sentence 1.

C) after sentence 4.

D) after sentence 5.

10

[1] In late 2017, the NEA published results from an analysis of business establishments in rural areas hosting performing arts centers. [2] The report concluded that rural businesses clustering near performing arts centers were more likely than businesses in other rural areas to be innovative in their practices and to use fully integrated design processes. [3] This dynamic is not lost on corporate recruiters, who are always seeking ways to attract new skilled workers. [4] These findings stood out even when the researchers controlled for numerous other factors. [5] The report stopped short of identifying a definite reason for this affinity, but one popular hypothesis is that creative talent often migrates to places with arts "hot spots." [6] Economist Tim Wojan notes that we don't know whether the arts are the secret sauce or the cherry on top, but they are certainly worth paying attention to.

To make the paragraph most logical, sentence 3 should be placed

A) where it is now.

B) after sentence 4.

C) after sentence 5.

D) after sentence 6.

11

[1] Waterway barriers come in all shapes and sizes, and there are dozens of different species of fish affected by them, so a single fish passage solution will not work for all fish in all locations. [2] "Scientists have learned a great deal over the past several decades when it comes to fish nature and fish passage design," O'Connell said. [3] "Most species need passages that are designed for their unique physical traits." [4] For instance, most migratory fish face problems with barriers when they are heading downstream out to sea, such as getting caught in power generating turbines, which results in many fish kills each year. [5] Thus, protecting this species could require solutions that might not work for other fish species. [6] "Because of the complexity and needs of so many different migratory fish, there is a tremendous amount of work left to be done to improve passage for the whole range of species," Castro-Santos said.

The author wants to add the following sentence to the paragraph.

> This is especially true for American eels because they spend most of their adult lives in fresh water and travel out to sea for spawning, which is the opposite of most migratory fishes' movement pattern.

To make the paragraph most logical, the sentence should be placed

A) after sentence 1.

B) after sentence 3.

C) after sentence 4.

D) after sentence 5.

12

[1] A nationally significant photographer, Austen resided there from about 1867, when she was an infant, until 1945, near the end of her life. [2] The house is primarily significant as the most important resource associated with the life and work of Alice Austen. [3] Austen is considered one of the first women photographers in America to work outside of the confines of a studio. [4] Her early body of work, which chronicles Staten Island, New York City, and other places and particularly focuses on the lives of her family, friends, and social circle, is considered among the finest produced in America in the late nineteenth and early twentieth centuries. [5] In the 1890s, Austen's work became increasingly public. [6] She ventured into the streets of Manhattan to photograph immigrants at work and also traveled to local Quarantine stations to document their operations, as well as the lives of immigrants living at these stations.

To make the paragraph most logical, sentence 2 should be

A) placed where it is now.

B) placed before sentence 1.

C) placed after sentence 3.

D) DELETED from the paragraph.

13

{Up to this point, the passage has been discussing the Kohler ceramics company and its Arts/Industry residency program, in which artists can use the factory's materials and equipment to create original work}

[1] With the increased presence of onsite creativity, Kohler has the opportunity to learn new techniques, processes, and possibilities for their products. [2] In 1976, artist Karen Thuesen Massaro was watching Kohler glazers and the way they were able to gauge the movement of glazes during firing. [3] This led her to develop a method of layering glazes to look like marbleized paper. [4] Kohler was thrilled with Massaro's technique and introduced a limited edition of marbleized plumbing ware in 1984 as part of Kohler's Artist Editions. [5] The Artist Editions line continues and is a direct result of having artists-in-residence in the factory.

Where is the most logical place in this paragraph to add the following sentence?

> But the artists are not the only ones who benefit from the Arts/Industry program.

A) Before sentence 1

B) After sentence 1

C) After sentence 4

D) After sentence 5

14

[1] Butterflies, for example, find nectar-filled flowers by smell, while mosquitoes are pros at sniffing out people or other potential sources of the blood meals they require. [2] The success of insects—the most diverse group of multicellular organisms on Earth—is linked to their ability to detect and distinguish an enormous variety of volatile chemicals in the environment, allowing them to thrive in a wide range of ecological niches. [3] While humans rely strongly on sight and hearing to navigate their environment, for insects it's all about odor. [4] Butterwick's research reveals how the shape of a key insect "sniffer" molecule makes this olfactory virtuosity possible. [5] To cope with an almost unlimited range of chemical odorants in the environment, insects have evolved a similarly enormous variety of odor receptors. [6] Researchers estimate there are tens of millions of distinct receptors, each capable of detecting a different chemical.

To make the paragraph most logical, sentence 3 should be placed

A) where it is now.

B) before sentence 1.

C) after sentence 1.

D) after sentence 5.

15

[1] Automakers use data to design and then assemble a vehicle, analyzing how small changes affect performance, durability, and safety. [2] Yet despite the best duplication efforts on the factory line, no two vehicles are exactly alike. [3] Like the automaker who uses data and machine learning to find trends, aberrations, and ways to make improvements, the scientists used their data to find and predict genetic variations at each step of the bacterial replication cycle. [4] That information can help them determine whether a given change is likely to result in no disease, mild disease, or severe disease in humans.

The writer plans to add the following sentence to this paragraph.

The same is true for the progeny of bacteria.

To make this paragraph most logical, the sentence should be placed

A) after sentence 1.

B) after sentence 2.

C) after sentence 3.

D) after sentence 4.

16

[1] Controversy still surrounds the origin, abundance, and history of water on Mars. [2] Recently, NASA and an international team of planetary scientists have found evidence in meteorites on Earth that indicates Mars has a distinct and global reservoir of water or ice near its surface. [3] They reached this conclusion by ascertaining that water in the meteorites contained hydrogen atoms with a ratio of isotopes distinct from that found in water in the Red Planet's mantle and current atmosphere. [4] This discovery helps resolve the question of where the "missing Martian water" may have gone. [5] Scientists continue to study the planet's historical record, trying to understand the apparent shift from an early wet and warm climate to today's dry and cool surface conditions.

The writer wants to add the following sentence.

The reservoir's existence may also be a key to understanding the climate history on Mars.

To make the paragraph most logical, the sentence should be placed

A) after sentence 2.

B) after sentence 3.

C) after sentence 4.

D) after sentence 5.

17

[1] The results of genetic tests are not always "yes or no" for the presence or the risk for developing disease, which make interpretations and explanations difficult. [2] In most cases, diseases occur as a result of interaction among multiple genes and the environment—for example, a person's lifestyle, the foods they eat, and the substances to which they're exposed, like sunlight, chemicals, and tobacco. [3] The interactions of these factors in contributing to health and disease can be very complex. [4] A positive result means that the testing laboratory found unusual characteristics or changes in the genes it tested. [5] Depending on the purpose of the test, that result may confirm a diagnosis, identify an increased risk of developing a disease, or indicate that a person is a carrier for a particular disease. [6] It does not necessarily mean that a disease will develop, or if it does, that the disease will be progressive or severe.

To make this paragraph most logical, sentence 3 should be placed

A) where it is now.

B) after sentence 1.

C) after sentence 4.

D) after sentence 5.

18

{The passage is about M&T Bank Stadium in Baltimore, Maryland}

[1] The stadium, built in 1998, is located at the site previously occupied by the William Knabe piano factory. [2] Today, a stone mosaic of piano keys is displayed at the stadium in its honor. [3] Although the practical aspects of designing a stadium took precedence (moving large groups of people safely), the design firm also wanted to include aesthetic elements that related to the community. [4] The closest similarly sized stadium is less than 40 miles away, in Landover, Maryland. [5] Since the stadium was located right in the city (as opposed to many stadiums that live in the suburbs), Baltimore's architecture served as a basis for some of the design. [6] The team drew inspiration from the city—the character, the history of the old industrial buildings, the brick warehouses, and the nearby masonry details.

To make the paragraph most logical, sentence 4 should be

A) placed where it is now.

B) placed after sentence 2.

C) placed after sentence 6.

D) DELETED from the paragraph.

[1] It's impossible to accurately simulate a hurricane eyewall penetration. [2] The training of a commercial pilot and that of a hurricane hunter diverge sharply. [3] The commercial aviation world trains its pilots to avoid inclement weather, while NOAA hurricane hunter pilots are trained to fly through the worst storms on earth, over and over. [4] Expert flying skills are crucial, but most storm-specific training must be done on the job. [5] Thus, doing it in the aircraft in a storm is the only way to experience the responsiveness of the plane, flight characteristics, crew coordination, and visceral response brought on by plowing through a wall of wind and rain. [6] Yet these pilots get satisfaction knowing that their work collects crucial data that helps protect lives and property.

To make this paragraph most logical, sentence 1 should be placed

A) where it is now.

B) after sentence 2.

C) after sentence 4.

D) after sentence 5.

{The passage is about Attention Restoration Theory, or ART}

[1] ART suggests that exposure to nature improves cognitive functioning and overall wellbeing. [2] The theory is based on research that separates attention into two components: involuntary and voluntary attention. [3] Involuntary attention occurs in natural environments where there are inherently intriguing stimuli, while voluntary or directed attention is typically required in urban environments filled with elements that invoke cognitive-control processes. [4] ART proposes that nature appeals to involuntary attention, thereby allowing depleted levels of directed attention to recover. [5] Directed attention is important in cognitive and emotional functioning, but it can become overtaxed.

To make this paragraph most logical, sentence 5 should be placed:

A) where it is now.

B) after sentence 1.

C) after sentence 2.

D) after sentence 3.

❧ Adding or Removing ❧ Information

Should I Stay or Should I Go?

Every test has some questions that ask you whether a piece information—a phrase, or often a whole sentence—should be **added to** or **removed from** the passage. The distinctive thing about these questions is that they are presented as **yes/no questions**. Two choices will vote for *Yes*, and two will vote for *No* (or *Kept* or *Deleted*), each choice accompanied by its own reasoning or justification. For example:

> At this point, the writer is considering adding the following sentence.
>
> > Not a single child at the event cried when the team introduced Gritty, its new furry, orange mascot.
>
> Should the writer make this addition here?
>
> A) Yes, because it …
>
> B) Yes, because it …
>
> C) No, because it …
>
> D) No, because it …

When you first read the question, you may develop a prediction about whether the information should be kept/deleted, or added/not added, and that's not unreasonable. But don't get too attached to your initial prediction.

In fact, perhaps the best way to approach these questions is to **evaluate the reasoning** in each answer choice **first**. Hold off on deciding whether you prefer *yes* or *no*. That's because, regardless of whether you're keeping or deleting something, the reasoning provided in the correct choice must be **a true and relevant statement**.

Here's a critical fact: the main reason people get these questions wrong is that they don't pay close enough attention to the reasons. They decide whether they personally like the extra information or not, and then they casually pick one of the two choices that confirm their preconceived notion. In other words, if they think the answer should be *yes*, they don't even bother to read the *no* choices. They quickly find a reason to weed out one of the *yes* choices, and they settle for the other.

But the answer may not in fact have been *yes*! If the person had read the *no* choices, one of them may have been accompanied by a better reason, one that actually justified getting rid of the extra information.

Don't be one of those people. Look at the reasoning in all four choices first. Doing so gives you more concrete and specific information to work from. You can make better decisions if you give each reason serious consideration.

> To evaluate the reasoning in each choice, ask yourself whether it's **true** and whether it's **relevant**.

Why is that? It's often easier to decide whether or not a statement is **factually accurate** than to decide whether it makes a worthwhile stylistic contribution to an essay. If the justification given in a choice is **a false statement**, then that alone is enough to make the choice incorrect. In fact, you can often knock out all three wrong answer choices just by eliminating untrue statements, and then you're done. You don't even need to bother deciding whether to add or delete the information.

Other times, a choice is wrong because the reasoning it provides is **true but irrelevant**. For example, imagine a choice that says, "Yes [the proposed sentence should be added], because it precisely specifies how many minutes of exercise are recommended." Assuming that's true, the important thing to ask yourself is whether the passage even *should* specify how many minutes of exercise are recommended. Would that be a logical and useful thing to have in the paragraph at that point? If such information not needed, then the reasoning is true but irrelevant—in other words, wrong.

> Something we pointed out for specific task questions is also relevant here. If the question is indicated solely by the numbered box in the text, then you're considering adding something **new** to the passage at that point. But if there is also underlined text in the passage, then you're considering removing or revising an **existing part** of the passage.

Once you eliminate all the choices containing false statements and irrelevant statements, you'll usually be down to just one choice. Occasionally, you might have two left, and then you'll really have to decide whether something belongs in the passage or not. Be sure to consider the overall context of the paragraph—as always, you need to examine the flow of ideas within the passage.

Let's take a look at a couple of examples.

34

Many electronics continue to use energy even when they're turned off. An average household can save about $20 in electricity costs each year by unplugging such devices or using a power strip with an on/off switch. <u>Twenty dollars may not sound like much, but</u> if everyone in a single large metropolitan area got into this habit, the collective action would save enough energy to eliminate the need for an entire 500-megawatt coal power plant.

The writer is considering deleting the underlined portion and capitalizing the next word. Should the portion be kept or deleted?

A) Kept, because it provides an explanation for the continued energy draw of devices that seem to be off.

B) Kept, because it acknowledges a likely objection to the writer's argument.

C) Deleted, because it undermines the claim made later in the sentence.

D) Deleted, because it fails to identify what a more impressive figure would be.

Look at the reason offered by choice A. Does the underlined portion *really* "provide an explanation for the continued energy draw of devices that seem to be off"? No. Such an explanation might be a nice thing to see, but the underlined bit does not provide it. Thus, the justification in choice A is a **false statement**. Choice A is wrong.

How about choice B? Does the underlined portion really "acknowledge a likely objection to the writer's argument"? In fact, it does. The writer thinks we should unplug our devices, but it's easy to imagine someone objecting by saying, "That sounds like a lot of trouble for just $20 a year." The writer acknowledges this. Second, is that a relevant or worthwhile thing for the writer to do? Again, yes. When you're trying to persuade, showing that you understand and can respond to the opposing point of view is generally an effective rhetorical strategy. This reasoning is **true** and **relevant**—it checks out.

Choice C is another **false statement**. What would it look like to really undermine the claim made later in the sentence? Something would have to show that unplugging devices would *not* save enough energy to eliminate the need for a power plant. The underlined bit doesn't do that.

Choice D, on the other hand, provides a true statement. The underlined bit truly *doesn't* provide a number that sounds bigger. However, is there any reason the author *should* have discussed a more impressive figure at this spot? No. It wouldn't contribute to the point being made. Thus, choice D is **true but irrelevant**.

Choice B is the only one left. Without having to make a decision on the keep/delete issue, we can confidently pick B and know it's correct.

Here's another:

35

{From a passage about costume designer Miles White}

Later that year [1940], designer Norman Bel Geddes hired White to design costumes for an ambitious ice revue. *It Happens on Ice*, with songs by Vernon Duke, opened at the magnificent Center Theatre in Rockefeller Center. The ice show project required construction of an extension of the Center's already sizable stage to accommodate the ice production's large cast. **35** The thrust stage projected well into the auditorium, requiring removal of many rows of orchestra seats, giving White enormous space to display his spectacular costumes with a host of accomplished skaters.

At this point, the writer is considering adding the following sentence.

> Modern ice show costumes include sensors that allow spotlights to track the performers' movements automatically.

Should the writer make this addition here?

A) Yes, because it reinforces the main idea of the paragraph.

B) Yes, because it clarifies the problem that White faced during the project.

C) No, because it diverges from the paragraph's emphasis on Duke's music.

D) No, because it contains an irrelevant detail that blurs the focus of the paragraph.

Choice A looks like a false statement. The main point of the paragraph is to recount the story of Miles White and this particular production. The proposed addition has nothing to do with White or this particular production, so it certainly doesn't reinforce the main idea.

Choice B is false as well. There doesn't seem to be a heavy emphasis on any problem faced by White. If anything, perhaps it was the need to extend the stage, but this sentence doesn't have anything to do with that.

Choice C starts out looking good. The proposed addition really does "diverge from the paragraph's emphasis." However, this choice misrepresents what that emphasis actually was. Duke's music was a minor detail, not the overall emphasis of the paragraph. So this choice ends up being an untrue statement too.

That leaves us with D, which indeed checks out. The proposed addition is in fact irrelevant. It does in fact blur the focus of the paragraph. And that would be a good reason to decide against adding the sentence to the paragraph.

Drill: Evaluating Reasons

In each question, you're given a proposed addition to the passage, along with one of the reasons given to justify whether it should or should not be added. The yes or no part of the choice is missing because your job is to focus on the reason. Decide whether the reason is a true statement or not.

Note: *If the reason refers to a part of the passage you can't see, assume for this drill that what it refers to is actually there. For example, if it refers to "the paragraph's discussion of watermelon genetics," you can assume that's what the paragraph's discussion is really about. However, on the real SAT, you can't assume that—you must check, and if the choice doesn't accurately describe the passage, kill it.*

Proposed addition	Reason given	Is the reason a true statement?
Even a short break to stand up and walk can improve energy, creativity, and concentration.	… because it details the methodology of the studies mentioned earlier in the paragraph.	1. The reason is ☐ True ☐ False
The Japanese card game Weiss Schwarz has become increasingly popular in the United States over the past several years.	… because it suggests that card tournaments are not as popular in Japan as the writer claims they are.	2. The reason is ☐ True ☐ False
With nearly 5,400 hostels across every country in Europe,	… because it supports the sentence's point about the widespread nature of hosteling.	3. The reason is ☐ True ☐ False
Ferdinand de Saussure was the first linguist to distinguish between how languages function today and how they evolved over time.	… because it digresses from the paragraph's discussion about the employability of linguistics majors.	4. The reason is ☐ True ☐ False
However, given that household water often had to be hauled several miles, most people at the time were unfazed by washing clothes only sporadically.	… because it undermines the claim in the next sentence that Tierney was a careful planner.	5. The reason is ☐ True ☐ False
Additionally, opening a new manufacturing facility can cost billions of dollars in labor, logistics, equipment, and more.	… because it provides a further example that supports the claim that reorganizing large supply chains presents difficulties.	6. The reason is ☐ True ☐ False

Success is the sum of
small efforts, repeated
day in and day out

— Robert Collier

Practice Question Set

*The questions in the following practice set test—you guessed it—**adding or removing information.***

1

Corazza has been diligently reconstructing the details of Respighi and Diaghilev's working relationship in an effort to shed light on this period in the history of music. Much of the primary evidence is found in their correspondence, as well as in notes left on their scores. What has made this a challenge, however, is that following his death in Venice in 1929, Diaghilev's library and possessions were split between his two closest collaborators. **1** In the summer of 2012, however, Corazza found a record of auction that pointed to the existence of Respighi's lost manuscript.

The writer is considering adding the following sentence.

> These two estates, in turn, were further scattered due to ad hoc sales and international auctions.

Should the writer make this addition here?

A) Yes, because it elaborates on the information presented in the preceding sentence.

B) Yes, because it introduces an idea that is further developed in the next sentence.

C) No, because it conveys information that is unrelated to the passage.

D) No, because it blurs the focus of the paragraph by introducing irrelevant information.

2

In 1859, the idea that solar flares might have some effect on Earth hadn't occurred to anyone yet. There was no such thing as an electrical grid or a telecommunications network. There were, however, telegraph networks, and the long wires of the network in France became the antennae for solar energy, heating up transmitters, some of which caught on fire. **2** Today, the damage potential is far greater: communications satellites can be knocked out, astronauts have to take shelter in a special module in the space station, pipelines can be damaged, GPS systems harmed, flights re-routed, and potentially most damaging of all, the electrical grid could be knocked out across parts of North America for years.

At this point, the writer is considering adding the following sentence.

> France was one of the earliest adopters of telegraph technology, so the effect was particularly widespread there.

Should the writer make this addition here?

A) Yes, because it provides a supporting detail for a general claim made in the previous sentence.

B) Yes, because it provides relevant context for the examination of how solar flares occur.

C) No, because it distracts from the paragraph's discussion of the types of damage that solar flares can cause.

D) No, because it does not explain what led France to invest in telegraph technology.

3

The history of Green River is one of peaks and valleys as the railroad, uranium mining, and a missile base came and went. In the 1970s, Interstate Highway 70 was built but bypassed downtown. When Moab to the south embraced mountain biking and the town's proximity to the national parks, Green River didn't find something on which it might have capitalized. Businesses closed, buildings fell into disrepair, and people left. Today, one in four people in Green River lives in poverty. Despite these challenges, <u>or in part because of them,</u> Forinash was drawn to the town. Green River's strong interest in affordable housing and its western, rural setting appealed to his desire to make a difference in a community's life.

The writer is considering deleting the underlined portion. Should the portion be kept or deleted?

A) Kept, because it provides relevant insight into Forinash's motivations.

B) Kept, because it helps the reader understand why Green River experienced such hardship.

C) Deleted, because it contradicts the claim made earlier in the sentence.

D) Deleted, because it calls into question the idea that Forinash had clear reasoning behind his actions.

4

The partnership got its start when the managers of a fire-fighting operations center in Redding, California, found that they were sending 13 tons of waste—much of it fire hose—to landfills every year. To reduce their waste, they worked with Hose2Habitat, which transformed the hose into enrichment devices and distributed them to organizations in need. <u>Some of the waste, however, was not able to be reused.</u> For animals housed in zoos, aquariums, and wildlife sanctuaries, enrichment helps stimulate their senses by mimicking what they would experience in the wild. Fire hose is durable and malleable by design and allows for enrichment products like "browsers" to be created on limited budgets. Browsers are braided hoses that are filled with leaves and treats, making interaction with them challenging and rewarding for animals like Flemish giant rabbits, parrots, chinchillas, and prehensile-tailed porcupines.

The writer is considering deleting the underlined sentence. Should the underlined sentence be kept or deleted?

A) Kept, because it completes the discussion of the outcome of the waste reduction initiative.

B) Kept, because it anticipates and addresses a likely objection to the partnership between Hose2Habitat and the fire-fighting operations center.

C) Deleted, because it distracts from the paragraph's focus on animal enrichment devices.

D) Deleted, because it fails to explain the nature of the waste that could not be reused and its ultimate fate.

5

Cooperatives are user-owned and democratically controlled businesses. Given this unique business structure, each cooperative has particular goals and objectives. For example, the objective of a cooperative that sells supplies to its members is to provide merchandise on a "best value" basis. The goal of a cooperative that markets products or services produced by the members is to pay fair-market value or negotiate for the highest price. **5** Some cooperatives provide services to their members that are not available from other sources. In such cases, the objective is to provide a needed service, not necessarily to save money or obtain the highest price.

At this point, the writer is considering adding the following sentence.

> Fair-market value is defined as a selling price for an item to which a buyer and seller can agree.

Should the writer make this addition here?

A) Yes, because it clarifies a term that is important in the discussion that follows.

B) Yes, because it provides an example of a specific goal that a cooperative might have.

C) No, because it interrupts the paragraph's discussion of the unique responsibilities of cooperative employees.

D) No, because it weakens the focus by diverging from the paragraph's main discussion.

6

Characterizing species diversity is important to many aspects of scientific research and resource management today, including agriculture. But the practice is not a new one. In many traditions, knowing or assigning something's "true name" held incredible power (think Rumpelstiltskin). That knowledge remains powerful today. Using taxonomy, Messinger will identify the bee species she is cataloging and preserve it in a biological collection. <u>Insect collections have been popular at least as far back as the seventeenth century.</u> This practice helps us to better comprehend and more responsibly protect the world around us.

The writer is considering deleting the underlined sentence. Should the underlined sentence be kept or deleted?

A) Kept, because it counters the misconception that characterizing species diversity is not a new practice.

B) Kept, because it completes the comparison between modern and historical taxonomic methods.

C) Deleted, because a reference to the past is inappropriate in a paragraph that discusses modern procedures.

D) Deleted, because it interrupts the discussion of Messinger's use of taxonomy.

7

In 1998, the World Wide Web was in its infancy. Most personal computers didn't have the ability to display more than 256 colors, processors were tiny and slow by today's standards, and dial-up modems were the way most people connected to the internet. People who had email addresses generally got them through their employers, mostly government agencies or universities. **7** Now, of course, the internet is ubiquitous, and available to people in all levels of society. Cultural repositories always try to keep up with new technology and make their collections accessible to all, but there isn't always agreement on the best way to do so.

At this point, the writer is considering adding the following sentence.

> Political circumstances in many countries were vastly different than they are today.

Should the writer make this addition here?

A) Yes, because it supports the passage's claim that much has changed since 1998.

B) Yes, because it provides an explanation for why most people no longer get their email addresses through government agencies.

C) No, because it restates information about international relations discussed earlier in the paragraph.

D) No, because it diverges from the paragraph's discussion of technological progress.

8

The *Folk Music of America* radio series premiered in October 1939 and featured a wide array of folk music, including works by women composers and African-American performers such as Huddie "Lead Belly" Ledbetter. The broadcast was primarily intended for the classroom and simulated community through on-air singalongs. The Music Educators' National Conference (MENC) helped develop the *Folk Music of America* educational <u>materials.</u> According to the 1939-1940 instructor manual, students were to learn the chorus to "Samson" prior to its broadcast in February 1940.

The writer is considering revising the underlined portion to the following.

> materials, including a workbook with musical notation and instructions so teachers could prepare their students for the singalongs.

Should the writer make this revision?

A) Yes, because it provides specific examples of the materials that were distributed to schools by the MENC.

B) Yes, because it shows how a community atmosphere was fostered by the radio broadcast.

C) No, because it merely repeats information about *Folk Music of America* stated previously in the passage.

D) No, because it distracts from the passage's focus with irrelevant details about the MENC's involvement.

9

Employees' work and home life can influence the amount and quality of sleep they get. As a result, getting enough sleep can be a problem for anyone, no matter the job. People who work in industries that require shift work or spend long hours on the job are at a higher risk for sleep-related disorders and report getting the least amount of sleep. Their lack of sleep may also put others at risk—especially when their responsibilities involve patient care or transportation. By addressing sleep as part of a workplace health program, companies can increase safety and make employees healthier and safer at home.

The writer is considering deleting the underlined portion (ending the sentence with a period). Should the writer make this deletion?

A) Yes, because the underlined portion blurs the focus of the paragraph by introducing extraneous information.

B) Yes, because the information in the underlined portion is provided in the previous sentence.

C) No, because the underlined portion provides a relevant elaboration on the claim made earlier in the sentence.

D) No, because the underlined portion gives examples of the industries in which workers experience the highest rates of sleep deprivation.

10

While in Huntsville, Falkowski also became active in the civil rights movement, working primarily with the Huntsville Council on Human Relations, the bi-racial group fighting for equal rights in the city. As early as 1958, Falkowski argued that segregation was simply unethical and "unbrotherly"—a moral wrong that ought to be ended immediately. Alabama was in fact the center of many civil rights activities. In her position as chair of that group's employment committee, Falkowski worked with volunteers examining local job conditions and observing what happened to Alabama A&M University graduates. She also explored how Civil Service regulations and local organized labor organizations impacted the employment of minority groups in the aerospace industry and beyond.

The writer is considering deleting the underlined sentence. Should the sentence be kept or deleted?

A) Kept, because it contributes to the passage's description of Falkowski's accomplishments.

B) Kept, because it provides historical context central to understanding why Falkowski chose to live in Huntsville.

C) Deleted, because it introduces information that is only loosely related to Falkowski.

D) Deleted, because it fails to acknowledge that many other locations were also associated with the civil rights movement.

11

The story Sonenberg developed focuses on Josh Gibson, a great athlete who played for Pittsburgh's Homestead Grays in the Negro Leagues and once hit a ball completely out of Yankee Stadium. The story chronicles his early success (some had said he was better than Babe Ruth), the discrimination that kept kept him from playing in the major leagues, the death of his wife in childbirth, a stint playing baseball in Mexico, and his tragic early death at 35 from a brain tumor shortly before Jackie Robinson integrated baseball by joining the Brooklyn Dodgers.

The writer is considering deleting the underlined portion. Should the portion be kept or deleted?

A) Kept, because it shows that Sonenberg used a researched approach to write the story.

B) Kept, because it adds validity to the claim that Gibson was a successful athlete.

C) Deleted, because it does not explain precisely how many people held that view.

D) Deleted, because it undermines the primary assertion of the paragraph.

12

Astronomers have come up with several creative ways to deal with problems of magnification. One technique is to make the telescope larger. A larger telescope collects more light from the object, producing a brighter image. Another solution is to use a recording device, such as a photographic film or an electronic detector. These methods have an advantage over the human eye: observations of faint objects can be made over a very long time. The exposures can be as long as 45 minutes per image. Multiple images can be added together to produce effective exposure times of up to 38 hours for each filter. The longer an exposure is, the more light falls on the film. As long as the image is held very still, an image of even a faint target will eventually appear.

The writer is considering deleting the underlined sentence. Should the sentence be kept or deleted?

A) Kept, because it describes why astronomers no longer make unaided visual observations.

B) Kept, because it effectively sets up the information presented in the following sentences.

C) Deleted, because it weakens the paragraph's main argument by adding irrelevant information about human physiology.

D) Deleted, because it fails to take into account the possible disadvantages of photographic film.

13

Genetic information is encoded in DNA, and all the critical work of the cell is done by proteins, from which enzymes are <u>made.</u> By 1966, several researchers began to think about how such a code could have evolved. It seemed like a chicken-and-egg problem: you can't make enzymes without DNA instructions, and you can't read those instructions without polymerase enzymes. Which came first? Several people, including Francis Crick, suggested that RNA, which, like DNA, can store genetic information, might also be able to act like an enzyme.

The writer is considering revising the underlined portion of the sentence to the following.

> made—including a class of enzymes called polymerases, which read off the DNA.

Should the writer make this revision?

A) Yes, because it articulates the main idea of the passage.

B) Yes, because it introduces a detail that is further developed in the paragraph.

C) No, because it contains an irrelevant technicality that blurs the focus of the paragraph.

D) No, because it diverges from the passage's emphasis on genetic material.

14

Lewis Hine, at a certain point in his career, began to refer to himself as an "interpretive photographer" and not a social photographer as he'd been previously termed. What drew Brubacher to Hine's work was one particular aspect of many of Hine's photographs: the extremely limited depth of field. **14** In photographs with deep depth of field, the entire image appears sharp. With shallow depth of field, as in Hine's pictures, only a narrow plane appears unblurred. And unlike some photographers making use of this technique to blur out the background, Hine repeatedly uses it in a way that also blurs the foreground. Brubacher wanted to explore how much of the shallow focus was prescribed by circumstance and how much was an aesthetic decision on the part of Hine.

At this point, the writer is considering adding the following sentence.

> Depth of field refers to the area of a photograph that remains in focus.

Should the writer make this addition here?

A) Yes, because it effectively introduces the explanation of an important term.

B) Yes, because provides background as to why Hine began to describe his work differently.

C) No, because it interrupts the discussion of Hine's work with unrelated information.

D) No, because it repeats claims made earlier in the paragraph.

15

{SDO refers to the Solar Dynamics Observatory, a satellite that studies the Sun}

In the video, the Moon seems to pause and double back partway through crossing the Sun. No, the Moon didn't suddenly change direction in space—this was an optical illusion, a trick of perspective. Here's how it happened: SDO is in orbit around Earth. When the transit started, the satellite was moving crosswise between the Sun and Earth, nearly perpendicular to the line between them, faster than the Moon. **15** But during the transit, SDO started the dusk phase of its orbit, traveling around toward the night side of Earth, moving almost directly away from the Sun but no longer making any progress horizontally to the Sun. The Moon, however, continued to move perpendicular to the Sun and thus could "overtake" SDO. From SDO's perspective, the Moon appeared to move in the opposite direction.

At this point, the writer is considering adding the following sentence.

> SDO helps scientists understand the influence of the Sun on the Earth by studying the solar atmosphere and magnetic field.

Should the writer make this addition here?

A) Yes, because it provides a description of the difference between SDO and other satellites.

B) Yes, because it helps explain the reason SDO recorded the video.

C) No, because it does not adequately describe how the solar atmosphere can affect the Earth.

D) No, because it interrupts the narrative sequence detailing the optical illusion in the video.

16

To get the new ZIP code system going, large bulk mailers such as magazine distributors and publishers were targeted first. As for individual correspondence, acceptance was a bit slower. **16** As usage rose, mail using the code was given priority, and that mail was delivered much faster. Despite the fact that not everyone was enthusiastic, the Postal Service hoped that by the second anniversary people would be more comfortable with the system. Ultimately, the full benefits of the system wouldn't be realized until everyone was using the number.

At this point, the writer is considering adding the following sentence.

> Initially many people didn't even use the new ZIP code, and most personal letters were still delivered in roughly the same time frame.

Should the writer make this addition here?

A) Yes, because it introduces a contrast that is completed in the following sentence.

B) Yes, because it explains why people were reluctant to use the new system.

C) No, because it adds an idea that is not relevant to the focus of the paragraph.

D) No, because it includes information that contradicts a claim made earlier in the passage.

17

While employers are required to protect workers from hazards and unhealthy exposures at work, the Total Worker Health (TWH) approach encourages organizations to do more. TWH efforts emphasize organization-level interventions over individual ones, concentrating on workplace policies, programs, and practices that address the job design and workplace conditions, such as workload, leadership and management practices, and wages and benefits. These initiatives are in addition to the required protections businesses must provide against workplace hazards and health risks. To optimize the TWH approach, workers at all levels of the organization—frontline employees, midlevel managers, and senior leadership—must be engaged and participate.

The writer is considering deleting the underlined sentence. Should the sentence be kept or deleted?

A) Kept, because it introduces an important additional issue for employers considering the TWH approach.

B) Kept, because it clarifies the paragraph's claim that protecting employees from hazards is an employer's main responsibility.

C) Deleted, because it merely repeats an idea stated earlier in the paragraph.

D) Deleted, because it introduces information that is irrelevant to the paragraph.

18

Every individual is aware of the environment that best supports his or her work. Typical work environments are constantly evolving, transforming from the once-traditional office workplace to an innovative, hybrid workplace embracing flexibility and a changing world. Some individuals find themselves working best in a coffee shop, listening to music. Experts caution, though, that distractions such as music may lower productivity. Others perform best in the company of other people. Different people want different options; there are many different styles of working. In order to accommodate different working styles, encourage collaboration, incorporate new technology, and push the boundaries of science, the modern workplace is being redefined.

The writer is considering deleting the underlined portion. Should the portion be kept or deleted?

A) Kept, because it contributes useful advice for choosing a productive working environment.

B) Kept, because it lends credibility to the discussion by citing knowledgeable experts.

C) Deleted, because it blurs the focus of the paragraph by introducing extraneous information.

D) Deleted, because it undermines the author's claim that some people enjoy listening to music as they work.

19

Thaddeus Lowe was inspired by the ballooning pioneer John Wise and quickly became an expert balloonist himself. Knowing the science behind how balloons worked and moved, he held outdoor shows where he would "predict" the movement of the balloon. He also built, sold, and took passengers on rides in his balloons. Lowe resigned as Chief Aeronaut in 1863, and the Aeronautical Corps was disbanded. But this was not the end of Lowe's scientific curiosities. He opened the Lowe Manufacturing Company in Pennsylvania, where he experimented with ice, having become fascinated with ice crystals during his balloon ascents. Lowe invented an ice machine and created the first-ever refrigerated ship that could transport perishable items, mostly meat. Unfortunately, citizens were not ready, nor did they trust this invention, so it failed.

The writer is considering deleting the underlined sentence. Should the sentence be kept or deleted?

A) Kept, because it counters the common misconception that Lowe was only a balloonist.

B) Kept, because it provides an effective transition to the discussion of Lowe's later pursuits.

C) Deleted, because it blurs the paragraph's focus on ballooning by introducing an unrelated detail about curiosity.

D) Deleted, because it disrupts the logical sequence of events recounted in the passage.

20

Electric vehicles powered by hydrogen fuel cells suffer from a refueling problem. The challenge is to recharge the hydrogen safely, quickly, and affordably. One way to do this is to store the hydrogen in safe materials that release the hydrogen on demand via simple chemical reactions. The next question is how to put the hydrogen back into the "spent fuel." Hydrogen for fuel cells can be generated by the electrolysis of water. Scientists at Pacific Northwest National Laboratory discovered cobalt and nickel complexes that activate hydrogen, enabling the spent fuel to be recycled. An advantage to this method is that these materials are not precious metals, which have availability and cost issues.

The writer is considering deleting the underlined sentence. Should the sentence be kept or deleted?

A) Kept, because it makes an important distinction between the release and the generation of hydrogen.

B) Kept, because it establishes a context for understanding how electric vehicles work.

C) Deleted, because it contains information that interrupts the discussion of recharging fuel cells.

D) Deleted, because it contradicts a statement made earlier in the paragraph about the problematic nature of electric vehicles.

☙ Figures & Tables ☜

How Did These Numbers Get In Here?

You may have found yourself wondering what the heck charts and graphs are doing in the middle of the SAT reading and writing sections. Perhaps you dozed off and someone swapped your SAT for an ACT? Maybe the word nerds writing the passages got captured by a roving band of engineers who forced them at calculatorpoint to stick some bar graphs in there?

These are natural questions, and everyone has them at some point. We'll try to explain.

You see, it all comes down to jealousy. When the SAT underwent a major revision in 2015, the test writers were super envious of the amazing ACT science section and its ability to cause great anguish in test takers. However, since the new SAT was already so similar to the ACT, they figured it would look bad to just directly copy *everything* from the competition. So they decided to sneak some figures and tables into the two verbal sections instead.

This doesn't have to mean trouble for you. We tell ACT students every day that the science section is really just another reading section. The only difference is that you're reading charts about mollusks instead of fictional stories. You can apply the same mindset here. The fact that there are charts lurking in the verbal sections just reinforces the idea that interpreting charts is **simply another reading task**. Just because there are numbers and lines and scientific terms, it doesn't change your overall approach. Getting these questions right is still about reading.

> Data Interpretation questions do not test grammar, nor do they test stylistic issues or effective use of language.
>
> Instead, they are totally and completely about **reading comprehension**.

First, make sure you have the right workflow. Because of the way the SAT questions are written, there's no need to look at a figure until you encounter a question about it. Thus, your process should be:

- ⊙ Wait until you see a question about the supplementary material
- ⊙ Get a good careful reading of the supplementary material
- ⊙ Answer any questions about the supplementary material

OK, so that's not exactly rocket surgery, but the point is that you don't need to worry about a figure until you see a question about it. In the writing section, because you're reading the passage and answering the questions in parallel, this is how you will naturally be doing it anyway.

Actually, the much more important point is that you want to **get a good careful reading of the supplementary material before you start answering questions about it.** This is where people usually go wrong. They don't bother to closely examine the figure or table before diving into the questions about it. This can lead to the mistake of latching on to the first piece of information that *seems* to answer the question, even if it's incomplete or doesn't accomplish the given task.

A good way to think about it is this: you wouldn't try to answer the questions about a reading passage without fully reading the passage; the same should be true for the figures. Indeed, you want to consider charts and tables as **part of the story**. Even though they look a little different from the text, you still want to **understand** and even **visualize** the story they tell. Start by trying to absorb as many details as possible. You should especially take notice of:

- The title of the figure
- The titles of the axes
- The scales of the axes and the units of measure
- The row and column headings
- The key and the location on the graph of the different data sets
- Any citations or special notes provided
- **Trends in the data**

> The passage tells a story, and the figure also tells a story. It's your job to see how those stories relate and support each other.

The last point, **trends in the data**, is the most difficult, and the one people are most likely to cut corners on, but it is definitely the most important. As you're looking at the graphs you should ask yourself not only, "What is being measured?" but also, "What do the measurements **show**?" Imagine you're the scientist who did the experiment or the researcher who gathered the data, and it's your job to explain the outcome to someone else. Think about how you would **tell the story of the data.**

Does the data line increase? Do two lines cross? How do the numbers in the table relate to each other? Is one quantity always more than another? Does some factor seem to have an impact on another? How would you summarize what's happening? Most importantly, *what do those trends reveal?*

The most basic chart questions may simply ask you to locate and retrieve a number from a figure, and it's true that you can often answer such questions without a deep understanding of what is going on. However, more complex questions will ask you to tie together the figure and the information in the paragraph. These questions can get much more challenging.

If your job is to get accurate information from the graph that supports the main point of the paragraph, guess what? You're going to need to understand the story in the text and the story that the figure itself tells. Only then will you be able to find the data that effectively reinforces the author's argument.

In other words, whether it's sentences or trendlines, make sure to **read carefully** and **comprehend**.

Practice Question Set

Each page contains a passage excerpt and a pair of questions related to the figure or table. Passages on different pages are not related to each other.

The customer loyalty program was instituted in 1992 as a way to retain customers and keep them from straying to competitors. Over the subsequent years, however, multiple changes to the policy created complexity, and Gardner was concerned that complicated rules and shrinking benefits were reducing interest in the program or even driving customers away. Looking at enrollment in the program since 2010, she noticed that participation first saw a major decline in **1** 2013, when new restrictions were introduced to the policy. The decrease continued steadily until 2018, when the trend finally bottomed out at just over **2** five thousand active members.

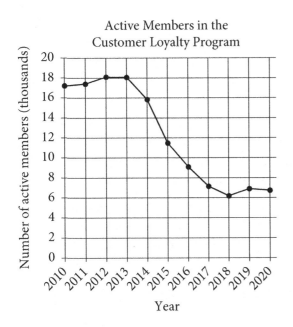

Active Members in the
Customer Loyalty Program

1

Which choice provides accurate information from the graph?

A) NO CHANGE

B) 2014,

C) 2015,

D) 2016,

2

Which choice provides accurate information from the graph?

A) NO CHANGE

B) six thousand

C) seven thousand

D) eight thousand

When Santos and Hart were finally able to arrange an expedition to the hydrothermal vent area in the Pacific, they were surprised by what they found. The team took measurements of dissolved oxygen in the seawater, starting at the surface and continuing to a depth of 1,000 meters (m). They found that, beginning at a depth of 3 100 m, dissolved oxygen content began to drop rapidly. After reaching a minimum of about 50 μmol/kg, oxygen levels 4 quickly returned to normal over the next 500 m of descent toward the ocean floor. Finally, oxygen content began to climb starting at a depth of around 700 m.

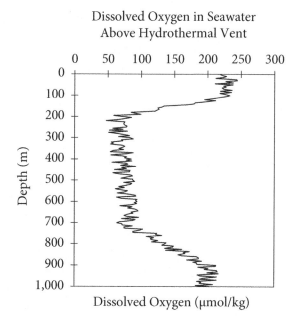

Dissolved Oxygen in Seawater
Above Hydrothermal Vent

3

Which choice provides accurate information from the figure?

A) NO CHANGE

B) 200 m,

C) 250 m,

D) 700 m,

4

Which choice provides an accurate interpretation of the information in the figure?

A) NO CHANGE

B) fluctuated wildly

C) dwindled even further

D) remained relatively low

To investigate whether the beneficial effects of exercise and meditation might be affected by sleep patterns, Hodges repeated the memory experiment but divided the subjects into two groups: those who slept less than 7 hours per night, and those who slept 7 or more hours. Among all subjects, he found performance **5** gains of 12 percent to 46 percent based on their activity before the memory task, but the biggest effect he observed—46 percent better performance on the memory task—appeared when subjects who slept 7 or more hours **6** spent 40 minutes either meditating or exercising moderately, but not both.

Percent Change in Performance on a
Memory Task According to Sleep Patterns
and Activities Prior to the Task

	Subjects who slept less than 7 hours	Subjects who slept 7 or more hours	All subjects
No exercise or meditation (control group)	—	—	—
20 minutes moderate exercise only	–6%	12%	5%
20 minutes meditation only	9%	34%	24%
40 minutes, divided evenly between moderate exercise and meditation	–2%	38%	22%
40 minutes, divided between moderate exercise and meditation according to subject's preference	12%	46%	32%

5

Which choice provides accurate information from the table?

A) NO CHANGE

B) losses and gains of –6 percent to 12

C) losses of –2 percent to –6

D) gains of 5 percent to 32

6

Which choice provides an accurate interpretation of the data in the table?

A) NO CHANGE

B) were allowed to choose how to divide 40 minutes between meditation and moderate exercise.

C) spent 40 minutes meditating and exercising moderately, divided evenly.

D) were instructed to spend 40 minutes exercising moderately and were allowed to meditate according to their own preference.

As the climate in the region shifted in the period from fifteen thousand years ago to five thousand years ago, Park hypothesized, a desert ecosystem would have given way to forest. To test this theory, she examined pollen grains buried in the sedimentary layers. Pollen from one type of tree commonly found in the region today, pine, was relatively rare prior to twelve thousand years ago but has steadily become more prevalent since, suggesting that **7** her hypothesis was mistaken. Indeed, **8** all five samples from less than six thousand years ago showed a pollen count of over 80,000 grains per square centimeter, on par with present-day levels.

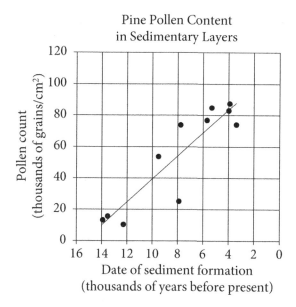

Pine Pollen Content
in Sedimentary Layers

7

Which choice represents the most accurate conclusion that can be drawn from the information in the passage and the data in the graph?

A) NO CHANGE

B) a pine forest did not occupy the region until very recently.

C) the forestation process corresponded to the climate transformation.

D) the pattern of desertification repeats at regular intervals.

8

Which choice provides accurate information from the graph?

A) NO CHANGE

B) three of the ten

C) none of the

D) three of the five

To understand this phenomenon, it is helpful to consider how the number of physicians who specialize in four different areas of medicine [9] has decreased dramatically at the hospital. For example, the number of [10] plastic surgeons dropped below 30 for the first time in 2020 after years of steady increases. By contrast, the hospital has employed a relative stable number of cardiologists, and the number of plastic surgeons has shown a declining trend.

Number of Physicians in Four
Specialty Areas at Westfield Hospital

Year	Medical specialty			
	Oncology	Plastic surgery	Cardiology	Occupational medicine
1960	16	42	63	12
1980	29	31	74	8
2000	52	33	65	13
2020	70	24	68	9

9

Which choice is consistent with the information presented in the table?

A) NO CHANGE

B) has remained remarkably constant

C) varies in lockstep

D) has changed over time

10

Which choice provides accurate data from the table?

A) NO CHANGE

B) cardiologists was higher than any other group

C) oncologists reached a high of 70

D) physicians specializing in occupational medicine was more than 10

Popular subscription services include mobile phone, home internet, video and music streaming, home security systems, wellness apps, newspapers and magazines, meal services, identity protection, cloud storage, and many others. With so many categories to consider, it is difficult for people to accurately estimate how many services they subscribe to, but there is a clear generational divide in the popularity of subscriptions, as demonstrated by a recent survey. Whereas 43 percent of respondents aged 60-75 believed that people their age purchased an average of 5 or fewer subscriptions, **11** 27 percent of respondents in the same group gave the answer of 6-10 services. Indeed, younger people seem eager to welcome subscription services into their lives: **12** 31 percent of respondents in the younger demographic thought that people their age subscribe to an average of 20 or more services.

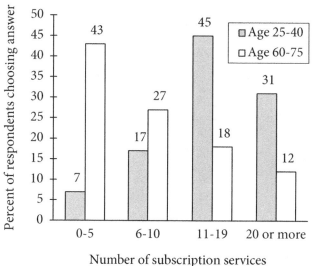

Survey Responses to the Question "What do you think is the average number of subscription services purchased by people your age?"

11

The writer wants to support the claim made in the preceding sentence using accurate, relevant information from the graph. Which choice best accomplishes this goal?

A) NO CHANGE

B) only 7 percent of respondents aged 25-40 said the same about their peers.

C) some respondents aged 25-40 subscribed to as many as 45 different services.

D) more than 20 percent of respondents aged 25-40 believed the average number of subscription purchases per person is 31.

12

Which choice provides an accurate interpretation of data from the graph?

A) NO CHANGE

B) of respondents in the younger demographic, 45 percent

C) 12 percent of younger-demographic respondents

D) 18 percent of respondents in the older demographic

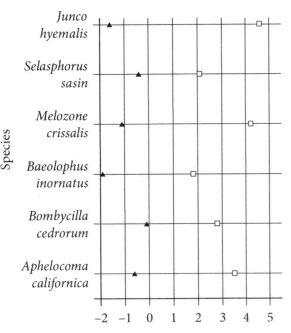

Effect of Dark-Sky Ordinances
on Bird Populations

Percent change in bird population
from previous year

□ location instituting dark-sky ordinances
▲ location without dark-sky ordinances

Proponents believe that dark-sky ordinances—laws aimed at limiting light pollution—have a beneficial effect on insect, amphibian, and bird populations. A 2017 study investigated this claim by comparing two similar locations in California's Central Valley, one of which introduced a package of dark-sky laws. The study found that bird populations increased **13** in the location instituting dark-sky ordinances but not in the location without dark-sky ordinances. Many animals can be harmed by light pollution because they are biologically evolved to be dependent on an environment with a certain number of hours of uninterrupted daytime and

nighttime. Three species in the study, *Junco hyemalis*, *Melozone crissalis*, and *Aphelocoma californica*, all experienced a **14** 1 percent or greater increase in population in the location that introduced the new laws. In contrast, all of the bird populations studied in the location without dark-sky ordinances declined or remained unchanged.

13

Which choice is best supported by the information in the graph?

A) NO CHANGE
B) in both locations but to a different degree depending on the implementation of dark-sky ordinances.
C) in the location instituting dark-sky ordinances for some bird populations but not for others.
D) in the location without dark-sky ordinances but not in the location instituting dark-sky ordinances.

14

The writer wants to use accurate information from the graph to emphasize the beneficial effect of a policy. Which choice best accomplishes this goal?

A) NO CHANGE
B) 2 percent or greater decrease
C) 3 percent or greater increase
D) 4 percent or greater increase

The most popular field of study in postsecondary institutions remains business, but STEM fields have been steadily closing the gap over the last 10 years. According to the National Center for Education Statistics, in the academic year 2017–18, postsecondary institutions awarded 15 18,727 bachelor's degrees for computer and information sciences; they conferred 118,663 degrees for those studying biological and biomedical sciences; and 16 the field of engineering saw 121,956 bachelor's degrees conferred, the most of any STEM field.

Number of bachelor's degrees conferred by postsecondary institutions in STEM fields of study, 2017–18 academic year

Field of study	Number of bachelor's degrees conferred
Engineering	121,956
Biological and biomedical sciences	118,663
Computer and information sciences	79,598
Physical sciences and science technologies	31,542
Mathematics and statistics	25,256
Engineering technologies	18,727

15

Which choice offers accurate information from the table?

A) NO CHANGE

B) 25,256

C) 31,542

D) 79,598

16

Which choice offers an accurate interpretation of the data in the table?

A) NO CHANGE

B) students pursuing degrees in engineering technologies received 25,256 bachelor's degrees, a small increase over the previous year.

C) every STEM field saw at least 20,000 bachelor's degrees conferred.

D) the field of mathematics and statistics appears poised to overtake the field of physical sciences and science technologies in the near future.

Flow rates in rivers vary with the seasons. In temperate climates, a river's discharge—the volume of water flowing past a point each second—is typically high in the early spring, when snow is melting, and low at the end of the dry summer months. Dams affect this range of discharge rates by curbing flooding and regulating flow, but they can also interfere with animal migrations and the transport of nutrients. Hydrologist Carolyn Mathis studied three rivers to determine how the removal of dams may affect the annual variation in discharge rates. In all three rivers she examined, the range of discharge rates after dam removal was **17** roughly double that before dam removal. In the Chemung River, for example, Mathis found an average annual range of discharge rates of **18** 4 m³/s before dam removal; after the dam was removed, however, the range was 78 m³/s.

Average Annual Range of Discharge
Rates for Three Rivers Before and
After Dam Removal

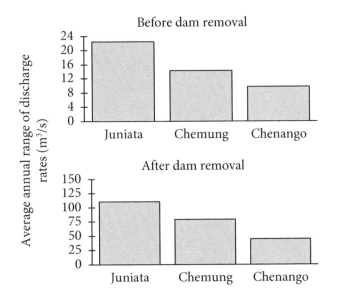

17

Which choice accurate represents the information in the graph?

A) NO CHANGE

B) about the same as

C) much larger than

D) slightly below

18

Which choice offers accurate information from the graph?

A) NO CHANGE

B) 14 m³/s

C) 23 m³/s

D) 70 m³/s

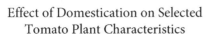

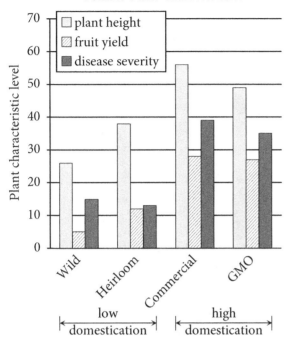

Plant height presented in cm. Fruit yield presented in kg. Disease severity presented in mm^2 (size of *Phytophthora infestans* infection area).

Adapted from Kurt Aguierre, et. al, "Tomato Domestication" ©2018 by Microbiotic Journal.

As agricultural plants become more domesticated, they increasingly differ from their wild relatives. Humans selectively breed plants for certain desirable characteristics, but sometimes these improvements come with tradeoffs. Researchers compared four strains of tomato plants with differing degrees of domestication and found that disease severity **19** in commercial tomatoes is 35 mm^2 according to one method of measurement. By comparison, the levels of **20** fruit yield in commercial and GMO tomatoes are 15 mm^2 and 13 mm^2, respectively. Because the main driver of breeding decisions is fruit yield per plant, these results

suggest that our effort to increase the amount of food produced by tomato plants has the unwelcome side effect of greater susceptibility to disease in highly domesticated strains.

19

Which choice offers an accurate interpretation of the data in the graph?

A) NO CHANGE

B) in commercial tomatoes is 39 mm^2

C) in GMO tomatoes is 27 mm^2

D) in GMO tomatoes is 39 mm^2

20

Which choice uses data from the graph most effectively to set up the information provided in the paragraph's final sentence?

A) NO CHANGE

B) plant height in commercial and GMO tomatoes

C) disease severity in wild and heirloom tomatoes

D) fruit yield in wild and heirloom tomatoes

StudyLark

◑ Putting It All Together ◔

Putting It All together

You've done it!

If you've read this far, done all the drills and practice question sets, and gotten a few real practice tests under your belt (with more to come), then you've seen everything that the SAT writing test has to throw at you. There should be no surprises on test day.

That's not to say there won't be any hard questions. But you'll know exactly what to expect, and you should have the tools to answer just about any question they can create.

If you're not scoring close to perfect yet, that's because the knowledge you need has not yet become reflex or second nature. If you still find yourself thinking, "What were the rules for dashes again?" or "Does *however* work the same as *although*?" then you've still got work ahead of you. You need to do more tests and more review. Those are the kinds of questions you need to be able to answer in your sleep.

Your ultimate goal—and this *is* realistic with enough practice—is to get to the point at which you can look at a question, and within 1 or 2 seconds be able to say,

  ⊙ I know **which** grammar or stylistic issue this question is testing, and
  ⊙ I know **all the rules and techniques** I need to consider to answer it.

The next few pages can help you figure out whether you're there yet. First, let's see whether you can identify what you're looking at.

Drill: Identifying Question Types

This drill contains a series of questions. Your first job is to figure out which grammar or stylistic issue the question is testing. In some cases, the question may be testing multiple issues, so several of the options may be correct—check all that apply. Your second task is to answer the question itself, keeping in mind the rules for the question type you identified.

1

A potential solution to these problems <u>presents</u> itself in March of 2013 when Dr. Mejia reported back to the council with a plan.

A) NO CHANGE
B) presented
C) would have presented
D) will have presented

1. This question is testing
   ☐ Verb agreement
   ☐ Verb tense
   ☐ Word choice
   ☐ Sentence structure

2

In order to illustrate the scientific concepts and specific points in the lectures, Sagan enlisted the help of the legendary technician Bill Coates, <u>who</u> designed and built most of the displays and models used in the lecture series.

A) NO CHANGE
B) he
C) and who
D) being the one who

2. This question is testing
   ☐ Pronouns
   ☐ Redundancy / concision
   ☐ Sentence structure
   ☐ Punctuation

3

If more people ran their daily errands using <u>bicycles, when</u> these accident rates would begin to decrease.

A) NO CHANGE
B) bicycles, afterwards
C) bicycles;
D) bicycles, perhaps

3. This question is testing
   ☐ Punctuation
   ☐ Transition words
   ☐ Sentence structure
   ☐ Logical comparisons

4

The Mütter Museum in Philadelphia, Pennsylvania, is home: to a unique collection of anatomical and pathological specimens, wax models, and antique medical equipment.

A) NO CHANGE

B) is home to

C) is, home to,

D) is home to:

4. This question is testing

☐ Punctuation

☐ Sentence structure

☐ Redundancy / concision

☐ Parallelism

5

Grant Choi, unhappy with the typical tools for creating school posters—crayons made imprecise lines, glued paper letters wrinkled, and what occurred with markers was the problem of bleeding—decided to come up with his own solution.

A) NO CHANGE

B) the problem with markers was that they bled—

C) bleeding was an issue with markers—

D) markers bled—

5. This question is testing

☐ Parallelism

☐ Logical comparisons

☐ Introductory modifiers

☐ Redundancy / concision

6

People who study a foreign language may wonder whether the knowledge he or she acquires in class will ever be put to use in real-world conversations.

A) NO CHANGE

B) they acquire

C) we acquire

D) you acquire

6. This question is testing

☐ Verb agreement

☐ Sentence structure

☐ Logical comparisons

☐ Pronouns

7

Mining companies, which face higher safety and environmental standards in this part of the world, <u>operates</u> in a very different manner.

A) NO CHANGE

B) is operating

C) operate

D) has been operating

7. This question is testing

☐ Verb agreement

☐ Verb tense

☐ Redundancy / concision

☐ Sentence structure

8

Working in an area of journalism that values speed over insightful commentary, <u>article generation software enables financial reporters</u> to quickly publish pieces based on companies' earnings reports.

A) NO CHANGE

B) financial reporters' access to article generation software enables them

C) the use of article generation software enables financial reporters

D) financial reporters use article generation software

8. This question is testing

☐ Punctuation

☐ Sentence structure

☐ Introductory modifiers

☐ Redundancy / concision

9

The idea that there might be habitable planets outside our solar system is no longer restricted to the science fiction genre. It's a research field that has <u>grown dramatically</u> since the first planet orbiting a star like our Sun was discovered by the Kepler space telescope.

A) NO CHANGE

B) grown and expanded dramatically

C) grown dramatically as a field of research

D) grown dramatically and considerably

9. This question is testing

☐ Word choice

☐ Transitions

☐ Logical comparisons

☐ Redundancy / concision

10

What distinguishes chameleons from <u>the camouflage of other reptiles</u> is how they control the color-changing cells within their skin.

A) NO CHANGE

B) that of other reptiles

C) other reptiles' camouflage

D) other reptiles

10. This question is testing

☐ Logical comparisons

☐ Punctuation

☐ Redundancy / concision

☐ Sentence structure

11

Lack of familiarity with the life and writings of Hakim Sanai could have led viewers to gloss over the reference to him. <u>Conversely,</u> had the attribution mentioned a poet more widely recognized by American audiences, such as Rumi, it's much more likely the credit would have attracted attention.

A) NO CHANGE

B) Therefore,

C) Likewise,

D) Surprisingly,

11. This question is testing

☐ Word choice

☐ Transition words

☐ Introductory modifiers

☐ Pronouns

12

The country's independence has led to not only the rebirth of its cinematic tradition <u>as well as</u> the restoration of films from its past.

A) NO CHANGE

B) but also

C) in addition to

D) but also led to

12. This question is testing

☐ Parallelism

☐ Sentence structure

☐ Verb tense

☐ Word choice

You can continue working on this skill every time you take a practice test. You should always be identifying question types as you work, and you can go back later during your test review to check whether you were right. Your tutor, score report, or study partner can help you decide whether you correctly identified the question type.

Final Summary of All the Rules

This is your cheat sheet. It's just a summary, so it leaves out a lot of details. But if you know these rules by heart, then you'll be equipped with the vast majority of what you need for the writing section.

After this summary you'll find a quiz on precisely these rules. Go back and forth—keep studying the summary and keep trying the quiz until you can answer every question from memory. Then revisit it every few days to ensure you haven't forgotten.

Verb Form

⊙ If the choices have two verbs in the same tense, one singular and one plural, then the question is testing subject-verb agreement.

⊙ Nothing inside a prepositional phrase can ever be a subject.

⊙ If a question is testing verb tense, use logic and look at the nearby sentences for context clues.

Pronouns & Nouns

⊙ A pronoun must have the same number (singular or plural) as its antecedent.

⊙ *He or she* and *his or her* are always wrong.

⊙ A pronoun must have a clear antecedent. If you are given the choice between using a pronoun and repeating the noun, you probably want the noun.

⊙ *Its*, *their*, and *whose* are possessive.

⊙ *It's*, *they're*, and *who's* are contractions.

⊙ Sometimes logic dictates that nouns must agree in number.

Parallelism & Comparisons

⊙ Look for parallel structure when you see a list or two things joined by a conjunction.

⊙ Use the second or third item in a list of three to determine the proper format for the other items.

⊙ Any time you compare or contrast two things, they have to be logically parallel.

⊙ Phrases like *that of* and *those of* are frequently used to create logical comparisons.

⊙ A weird-looking *do* or *did* after the word *than* and before a subject is often correct. Find the verb it stands for and put it after the subject to see if the comparison sounds more natural.

Punctuation

⊙ A semicolon is the same as a period.

⊙ A colon needs a full sentence before it. What follows the colon could be a list, a word, or another full sentence.

⊙ Don't ever use a colon after *such as* or *including*.

⊙ A pair of dashes acts like parentheses.

⊙ A single dash acts like a colon.

⊙ Make a singular noun possessive by adding an apostrophe + *s*.

⊙ Make a plural noun possessive by adding an apostrophe after the *s*.

⊙ A possessive is appropriate when it would make sense to say "the second noun **of the** first noun."

⊙ If quotation marks set up as a full, separate sentence of directly quoted speech or writing, use a comma before the quotes.

⊙ If the stuff inside the quotation marks flows as part of the grammar of the sentence, a comma isn't required.

⊙ Parentheses come in pairs, and the sentence should still be properly punctuated if the parenthetical were removed.

⊙ Direct questions need questions marks, but embedded questions don't.

⊙ Coordinate adjectives need commas (if you could put *and* between the adjectives).

⊙ Cumulative adjectives don't need commas (if the adjective closest to the noun creates a single thing that gets further modified).

⊙ If a title or job comes before a name, you don't need commas. If the title comes after the name, use commas.

⊙ You can't use a comma alone to join two clauses. This is the hideous comma splice.

Sentence Structure

- A coordinating (FANBOYS) conjunction can join two clauses. Use a comma before the conjunction.

- A subordinating conjunction can join two clauses. Use a comma when the conjunction precedes the first clause; if it's between them, you don't need a comma.

- A relative pronoun such as *which, that,* or *who* can join two clauses. A relative clause modifies the noun that it refers to.

- A semicolon, colon, or dash can join two clauses.

- A conjunctive adverb such as *however* cannot join two clauses.

- Modifiers should be as close as possible to the thing they modify. Be on the lookout for introductory modifiers and make sure they're next to the right noun.

- Verbals are not verbs. A gerund is a noun. A participle is an adjective. An infinitive is often a noun. Verbals do not have a tense.

- A participial phrase at the end of a sentence can modify the whole situation.

> This is just a summary. Lots of details are left out, and some of the rules are oversimplified here. This list is useful, but it's not a substitute for reading and studying the full chapters.

- *Being* is usually wrong.

- When combining sentences, consider grammar, modifiers, transitions, redundancy, and everything else.

Word Choice

- *Affect* is a verb. *Effect* is a noun.

- *Site* means a location or a website. To *cite* means to refer to something. *Sight* is vision.

Redundancy

- If you see three long choices and a short choice, look for redundancy or wordiness.

- If a question is testing redundancy, the shortest choice is almost always right.

Introductions, Transitions & Conclusions

⊙ Read everything and follow the flow of ideas.

⊙ Examine the ideas before and after a transition and figure out their relationship yourself before you look at the choices.

⊙ If you have the option to delete the transition word, that's probably right.

Specific Tasks

⊙ Stay focused on the task.

Organization

⊙ Each sentence must "hook in" to the sentence before and the sentence after it.

⊙ Don't pick a location for the sentence until you've found concrete reasons for why it must be there and not anywhere else.

Adding & Removing Information

⊙ Evaluate the reasoning in each answer choice before deciding whether you prefer *yes* or *no*.

⊙ The reasoning provided in the correct choice must be both true and relevant.

Figures and Tables

⊙ Ignore the figure until a question asks about it.

⊙ When you see a question about a figure, get a good careful reading of the figure before you worry about what the question is asking.

⊙ Try to absorb all the details of the figure. Look for trends in the data, visualize the situation, and tell the story of what the data reveals.

Drill: Final Summary of All the Rules

Can you remember the rules summary from the last four pages? If you can't, feel free to look back and check. Keep doing this drill until you can recall all the rules automatically.

1. How can you tell if a question is testing subject-verb agreement?
2. What can never be a subject?
3. How can you figure out the right verb tense?
4. What's important about a pronoun's number?
5. Tell me about *he or she*.
6. What's something every pronoun must have? Is it wise to restate a noun when you could use a pronoun?
7. What was that list of possessive pronouns?
8. What was that list of contractions?
9. What is noun number agreement?
10. What occasions call for parallel structure?
11. How can you figure out the right structure for listed items?
12. What's the primary concern when you see a comparison?
13. Which phrases often help to create logical comparisons?
14. What should you do with a strange-looking *do* or *did* after *than*?
15. What's the rule for semicolons?
16. What's the rule for colons?
17. When should you never use a colon?
18. What's the rule for a pair of dashes?
19. What's the rule for a single dash?
20. How do you make a singular noun possessive?
21. How do you make a plural noun possessive?
22. When is a possessive appropriate?
23. When do you need a comma before quotes?
24. When do you not need a comma before quotes?
25. What's the rule for parentheses?
26. Do all questions need question marks?

27. What's the rule for coordinate adjectives?

28. What's the rule for cumulative adjectives?

29. Do you need commas around an appositive that gives someone's job or title?

30. What is the monstrous comma splice, and is it OK?

31. What are the coordinating conjunctions and how are they used?

32. What are some subordinating conjunctions and how are they used?

33. What are relative pronouns, and what do they do?

34. What punctuation is allowed to join clauses?

35. What are conjunctive adverbs not allowed to do? Which one is the primary offender?

36. What should modifiers do? What about introductory modifiers?

37. What are verbals, and what should you not treat them as?

38. What can a participial phrase do at the end of a sentence?

39. Do we like *being*?

40. What topics are fair game when it comes to combining sentences?

41. Explain *affect* vs. *effect*.

42. Explain *site* vs. *cite* vs. *sight*.

43. What's the pattern that should alert you to look for redundancy?

44. What's the rule for redundancy questions?

45. What's the most important thing to do for transition questions?

46. What should you read and do before looking at transition answer choices?

47. Do you always need a transition word?

48. What is your one job when you're given a weirdly specific task to accomplish?

49. What determines the proper order of the sentences?

50. What should you do when determining the organization in a paragraph?

51. What should you do first when deciding whether to add or remove information?

52. What are the two things the correct add/remove justification must do?

53. Should you look at a figure or table right away?

54. When you see a question about a figure, then what?

55. What should you be trying to get out of a figure before attempting the question?

> The answers are on the four pages before the drill.

56.

Failure is the opportunity
to begin again
more intelligently

— Henry Ford

❧ Appendix ☙

Grammar Reference Guide

The SAT will never ask you to name the parts of speech or other grammar terms, but you should know what they are and what they're used for. Here's a quick reminder:

Noun

A **noun** is a person, place, thing, event, substance, quality, or idea.

Examples of nouns: Lisa, doctor, Tokyo, attic, bowl, plaza, pollution, wisdom, water, density, picnic

Verb

A **verb** is an action word.

Examples of verbs: make, know, work, run, meet, study, receive, accept

Adjective

An **adjective** is a word that modifies (describes) a noun.

Examples of adjectives: yellow, useful, independent, complex, fresh, ordinary, soft, scientific

Adverb

An **adverb** modifies a verb, adjective, or other adverb. Adverbs often end in *–ly*, but not always.

Examples of adverbs: quickly, undoubtedly, almost, far, successfully, tomorrow, very, repeatedly

Pronoun

A **pronoun** is a word that substitutes or stands in for a noun (or group of nouns). There are lots of categories of pronouns. We'll list some here, but you can find a more complete list on page 32.

Examples of pronouns: I, you, she, he, it, we, they, me, him, her, us, them

Preposition

Prepositions connect different parts of a sentence and indicate relationships between those parts. They often indicate location, direction, time, possession, or purpose. Explaining prepositions is hard; it's easier to just look at a list and memorize them.

Examples of prepositions: of, in, to, for, with, on, by, at, from, as, into, about

A longer list of prepositions can be found on page 108.

Conjunction

Conjunctions also connect different parts of a sentence. They are often used to make lists or to connect clauses (complete ideas). Again, it's probably best to check out a list of common conjunctions:

Examples of conjunctions: and, but, or, because, unless, if, although

A longer list of conjunctions can be found on pages on page 93-94.

Gerund

A **gerund** is a type of noun. A gerund looks like the base form of a verb followed by –*ing*, but it's not a verb.

Examples of gerunds: <u>Finding</u> a penny is lucky.
She talked about <u>hiking</u> in Maine.

Participle

A **participle** is a type of adjective (or in some cases, adverb). It is a modifier. A present participle looks like the base form of a verb followed by –*ing*. A past participle looks like the base form of a verb followed by –*ed*. Participles are not verbs.

Examples of participles: I finished off the <u>remaining</u> ice cream.
He studies the <u>reflected</u> image.

Infinitive

An **infinitive** looks like the word *to* followed by the base form of a verb. Treat the two words in an infinitive as a single unit. Don't think of the word *to* as a preposition in this case. Infinitives usually act as nouns, but they can do other things too.

Examples of infinitives: to throw, to prepare, to mention, to reveal, to laugh

For much more information about gerunds, participles, and infinitives, see the discussion starting on page 112.

Object

The **direct object of a verb** is the noun that receives the action of that verb.

Direct object of a verb: Jeeves threw <u>the ball</u>.
I visited <u>my sister</u>.
Jen answered <u>the question</u>.

The **object of a preposition** is the noun that comes after a preposition and completes the idea begun by the preposition.

Object of a preposition: There is a book on <u>the table</u>.   (The preposition is *on*)
The chips come with <u>guacamole</u>. (The preposition is *with*)
The piece of <u>paper</u> was crumpled. (The preposition is *of*)

Auxiliary or Helper Verb

An **auxiliary** or **helper verb** precedes the main verb and helps convey the time an event or condition occurred, along with other nuances such as possibility or importance.

Various forms of *be*, such as *am, are, is, was, were*:
She <u>is</u> painting.
He <u>was</u> sleeping.

Various forms of *have*, such as *have, has, had*:
I <u>have</u> finished the novel.
Keith <u>has</u> searched everywhere.

Various forms of *do*, such as *do, does, did*:
I <u>do</u> believe you.
It <u>does</u> smell a bit funny.

One of the modal verbs, such as *will, should, can, might*:
The weather <u>might</u> improve.
I <u>must</u> find that key.

Phrase

A **phrase** is any group of words that work together for a single purpose. Large phrases can be made up of smaller phrases. A **verb phrase** is a main verb plus its auxiliary verbs.

Clause

A **clause** is a type of phrase that conveys a complete idea or full thought. A clause contains both a subject and a verb.

Appositive

An **appositive** is a noun phrase that modifies and gives further information about another noun. It acts to rename or amplify the other noun.

Examples of appositives: Ms. Reese, <u>my former third grade teacher</u>, was at the party.
<u>French philosopher</u> Michel Foucault wrote the book.

A longer discussion of appositives begins on page 110.

It's never right
before it's wrong

— Scott McMicken

❧ Answers ❧

Each prepositional phrase is listed. The first word in each phrase is the preposition. The last word is the object.

1. to graduates
   in all fields
   of engineering

2. for data
   to the request

3. as a goddess
   from the Vedic period
   through the modern era
   of Hindu traditions

4. from his own life
   in his work
   of himself
   throughout the series
   for the most recent exhibition

5. of Basima Castle
   near the cliffs
   above a waterfall
   to a tourist attraction
   in 2002

6. as a writer
   on horticultural and agricultural practices
   to the principal periodicals
   of the day

1. Subject = *challenges*
    (*of raising a child* = prepositional phrase
    without any help = prepositional phrase
    from nearby family = prepositional phrase)

2. Subject = *Margo*
    (*like the managers who held the position before her* = parenthetical element made
    up of prepositional phrases and a relative clause)

3. Subject = *wines*. This sentence has inverted word order.
    (*released* = participle
    earliest = adverb
    in the year = prepositional phrase)

4. Subject = *bass and piano*. This sentence has a compound subject.
    (*on the album's first track* = prepositional phrase)

5. Subject = *move*
    (*in checkers* = prepositional phrase
    in which a … rows = the whole thing is a big relative clause
    Within the relative clause:
    in one = prepositional phrase
    of the back rows = prepositional phrase)

6. Subject = *hexagons, triangles, or squares*. This sentence has a compound subject.
    (*arranged* = participle
    in a repeating pattern = prepositional phrase)

7. Subject = *rain*. This sentence has inverted word order.
    (*into the buckets* = prepositional phrase
    under the eaves = prepositional phrase)

8. Subject = *languages*
    (*spoken* = participle
    in regions = prepositional phrase
    from each other = prepositional phrase
    as southern India and the western part = prepositional phrase
    of Europe = prepositional phrase)

9. Subject = *area*
    (There = adverb)

10. Subject = *Olivia Barber*
    (everything between the commas is a big appositive
    Within the appositive:
    with restaurants = prepositional phrase
    in several cities = prepositional phrase
    across the country = prepositional phrase)

Drill: Using Context to Figure out Verb Tense   page 25

1. began
   We're told that the event was in the past: 2016. The other verbs in the passage (*opened*, *filled*, *seeped*) are all in the simple past tense.

2. had shown
   The past perfect tense is appropriate here because we have one action in the past (the result *came* as a surprise), and one action in the more distant past (the previous studies *had shown* something).

3. release
   The adjacent sentences set up science facts about baking using the present tense. We want the verb *release* to match the present *builds* and *are*.

4. have relied
   The present perfect tense here indicates ongoing action in the past that continues up until the present time.

Drill: Determining the Question Task   page 27

1. Verb agreement. Choice A and C are the same tense but different number

2. Verb tense. All the choices have different tenses

3. Verb agreement. Choice A and D are the same tense but different number

4. Verb tense. All the choices have different tenses

5. Word choice.

Practice Question Set: Verb Form   page 28

1. C) remain
   This is testing subject-verb agreement. When looking for the subject, you can ignore the participial phrase between the commas. You can also ignore the prepositional phrases *of the first acts* and *of Congress*. The subject is *some* (meaning some of the acts), which is plural. Therefore, we need the plural verb *remain*.

2. B) provides
   This is testing subject-verb agreement. To find the subject, ignore the phrase between then commas and the prepositional phrases *by a team* and *of molecular anthropologists*. The subject is the singular noun *analysis*, so we need the singular verb *provides*.

3. A) NO CHANGE
   This is testing verb tense. The story is being told in the past tense. The biggest clue for that is the verb *helped* in the first sentence. Therefore, *implemented*, which is also in the past tense, is appropriate.

4. B) work
   This is testing verb tense. The most appropriate choice is the present tense *work*. The sentence boils down to "most boards no longer function, but others work perfectly well." Because *function* is in the present tense, then choosing *work* creates a logically and grammatically parallel structure.

5. B) there are
    To indicate the existence of something, use *there*, not *their*. In this case, what exists? The plural *benefits* exist, so we need the plural verb *are*.

6. A) NO CHANGE
    This is testing subject-verb agreement. Who's gaining new perspectives? It's the plural *people*, so we want the plural verb *gain*.

7. B) were unique for their
    This is testing subject-verb agreement. To find the subject, ignore the phrases between the commas. The subject is the plural noun *houses*, so we need the plural verb *were*. The question is also testing pronoun agreement. The pronoun also refers to *houses*, so we want *their*, not *its*.

8. C) is
    This is testing subject-verb agreement. The sentence has inverted word order—the subject appears after the verb, not before it. None of the words in front of the underlined verb are nouns, so the subject must be after. You can ignore the prepositional phrases *of quinine* and *from cinchona bark*, so the subject must be *isolation*. That's singular, so you need a singular verb.

9. A) NO CHANGE
    This is testing subject-verb agreement. The subject is technically *which*, but *which* is a pronoun that can refer to either a singular noun or a plural noun. Therefore, to figure out whether you need a singular or plural verb, you need to figure out what *which* is referring to. It should be the noun that it immediately follows—in this case, *engagement*. Since *engagement* is singular, we want the singular verb *is*.

10. A) NO CHANGE
    This is testing verb tense. You can tell the story is being told in the past because of the verbs *released* and *flowed*. So the past tense verb *settled* is an appropriate choice.

11. B) were
    This is testing subject-verb agreement. You can use some logic to figure out the subject: what or who is unprepared for a major shock? Logically, it's the banks. In this case, we have a compound predicate—two verbs working together for the same subject. It boils down to *banks had become ... and were*. Since *banks* is plural, we need a plural verb.

12. D) hypothesize
    This is testing subject-verb agreement. The subject is the plural *geologists*, so we need a plural verb. You can ignore *who have studied the new lunar survey* because it's a separate clause with its own subject and verb.

13. A) NO CHANGE
    This is testing subject-verb agreement. The subject is *technology*, which is singular, so the singular *has* is appropriate. All the stuff between the commas is a bunch of prepositional phrases and other modifiers, so you can ignore it.

14. B) allowed
    This is testing verb tense. The big clue is the past tense *reflected*, which has the same subject as the underlined verb. When you use *allowed*, the sentence becomes *the walls reflected ... and allowed*, which is grammatically parallel and logically appropriate.

15. D) makes
    This is testing subject-verb agreement. The subject is *fact*. The phrase *that chiropractic jobs must be performed in person by practitioners, not computers*, is a separate relative clause with its own subject and verb, so you can ignore it. Since *fact* is singular, we want the singular verb *makes*.

16. C) had supported
    This is testing verb tense. In this story, we have multiple events taking place at different times in the past. First (in the more distant past) came the supporting of the boss. Later (in the more recent past) came the firing by the opponent. Since *were fired* is in the simple past tense, it is appropriate to use the past perfect tense (*had supported*) for the earlier event.

17. B) arises
    This is testing subject-verb agreement. The subject is *ability*, so we want the singular verb *arises*. Between the subject and the verb, you can ignore the infinitive *to process sounds* and the prepositional phrases *at much higher rates* and *than humans*.

18. B) held
    This is testing verb tense. The story is being told in the past tense, as demonstrated by the verb *approved* and the dates in the past. So the past tense *held* is appropriate.

19. B) contributes
    This is testing subject-verb agreement. What exactly is contributing to this phenomenon? It's *the way*, so that's the subject. *In social groups* is a prepositional phrase, and *knitters* has its own verb, *come*. (Everything between *way* and *contributes* is a big relative clause based on the word *which*.) Since *way* is singular, we need as singular verb.

20. A) NO CHANGE
    This is testing verb tense. There are two tenses used in the sentence, so it's a bit tricky, but the underlined verb is for the building, not the photographer. Since the other verb that applies to the building is in the present tense (*the building is normal*), then it makes sense to stick with the present tense for the underlined verb as well.

Drill: Finding Antecedents   page 33

1. attitudes

2. document

3. entrepreneurs

4. government

5. organisms

Drill: Possessive Pronouns and Contractions   page 36

1. it's

2. their

3. its

4. who's

5. they're

6. it's

7. there

8. whose

Practice Question Set: Pronouns & Noun Agreement   page 38

1. B) it also allows
To figure out the antecedent for the underlined pronoun, ask yourself, "*What* is allowing us to create new bonds?" The answer is *world travel*, which is singular. So we need the singular pronoun *it*, as well as the singular verb *allows*.

2. D) their
What has the ability to filter pollutants? The answer is *silt and clay*. Even though each of these nouns is singular, they become a plural antecedent when you join them together with *and*. To make this more obvious, try replacing *silt and clay* with *these two things*. We need a plural, possessive pronoun, so *their* is appropriate.

3. B) a skilled debater and fundraiser.
This is testing noun number agreement. *Anyone* is singular—it refers to any one person. One person can't be *debaters*. One person has to be *a debater*. We need singular nouns, so we're looking at choice B.

4. D) who actually try
To decide between *who* and *whom*, figure out whether the pronoun is acting as a subject or an object. In this case, it's the subject of the verb *try*. *Who* is for subjects; *whom* would be for objects. We also need to figure out whether we need the singular verb *tries* or the plural *try*. The pronoun's antecedent is *people*, which is plural, so *try* is appropriate.

A little trick to help with *who/whom* is to create a mini-sentence based on the first verb after the pronoun, and see whether you would replace the pronoun with *he/they* (subjects) or *him/them* (objects).

For example, "… the person *who* invited me to the party" becomes "…*he* invited me to the party." In contrast, "… the person *whom* I invited to the party" becomes "I invited *him* to the party."

Yet another trick is to use the rule of thumb that says to use *who* immediately in front of a verb, and to use *whom* immediately in front of a noun or after a preposition. This rule is not foolproof, but it works in most situations.

5. A) NO CHANGE
What has a limited ability to expand? The answer is *businesses*. We need a plural, possessive pronoun, which would be *their*.

6. B) their
Who is expected to share insights? The answer is *members of the class*. That's plural, so we need a plural, possessive pronoun. *Their* does the trick.

7. D) you
Be sure to read the whole sentence. Toward the end of the sentence, we see "inventions *you* had never seen," so this sentence is actually written in the second person, using the pronoun *you*. To stay consistent, use *you* in the beginning of the sentence as well.

8. D) Study abroad programs usually grant
Notice the pattern in the answers: Choices A and B use the pronouns *it* and *they*. Choice C uses the noun *things*, which is pretty vague. Choice D uses the noun phrase *study abroad programs*. This is the best choice because it is the most specific and clear. The other choices are too ambiguous. When given the choice between a pronoun and a noun, you probably want the noun.

9. C) they
Who could not be more engaged? The answer is *the fourth-graders*. We want the plural pronoun *they*.

10. C) For help in interpreting the document,
Just as in question 8, you can see the telltale pattern in the answer choices: some choices use ambiguous pronouns, such as *it* or *them*, but choice C makes it specific and clear that we're interpreting *the document*. Choice D uses a different structure, but it still fails to specify what's being interpreted.

11. B) each painting in its
Each painting is singular, so choices A and C are wrong because they use the plural pronoun *their* with a singular antecedent. Choice D is wrong because it uses the plural antecedent *all the paintings* with the singular pronoun *its*. Choice B gets it all right.

12. C) who help
You can use the relative pronouns *that, who* and *whom* to refer to people, but avoid *which*. (It's not nice to call people witches.) To decide between *help* and *helps*, notice that it's the *great thinkers* helping us to frame important questions, so we want the plural verb *help*. And to decide between *who* and *whom*, notice that the pronoun is acting as the subject of the verb *help*, so *who* is appropriate.

If you want to try the mini-sentence trick (see the explanation for question 4), notice that "… *they* help us frame and answer important questions" sounds better than "… *them* help us frame and answer important questions." Thus you want *who*, not *whom*.

13. B) the form of snow crystals.
Three choices use ambiguous pronouns (*their* and *its*). But one choice uses the clear and specific noun *snow crystals* to make it obvious what form we're talking about. That's the choice you want.

14. A) NO CHANGE
What's being followed for another week? The answer is *a different routine*. Singular noun, singular pronoun. Here's an example where you **don't** prefer the noun in choice D over the pronoun. The problem in D is that it has bad noun number agreement. Each participant is following a single routine, so *routines* is inappropriate. The pronoun *it* is acceptable because it has a clear and unambiguous antecedent.

15. C) this question.
Two choices offer ambiguous pronouns (*those* and *them*). The other two choices give us clear and specific nouns, but we have to figure out which one makes sense. The previous sentences don't raise any *objections*, but they do give us a *question*. So choice C is more logical.

16. D) their
Who do the feet belong to? The answer is *geckos*. Since the antecedent is plural, we want the plural pronoun *their*. Be careful with animals: it's also perfectly acceptable to refer to a species in the singular. If the sentence had started out with, "The gecko has millions of tiny hairs…," then the appropriate pronoun would be *its*. So be sure to notice how the sentence is structured. Another reason to be careful with animals: they can bite.

17. D) this movement
Notice the pattern in the answer choices: we have three vague pronouns and one clear, specific noun. The noun is the one you want.

18. C) they have

    What has since become well known? The answer is *David McDermott and Peter McGough*. Even though each person is singular by himself, the antecedent becomes plural when you join the singular nouns with *and*. Think of the antecedent as being *these two people*. Choice D is wrong because the past perfect tense (using the auxiliary verb *had*) is inappropriate when referring to action that started in the past and continues up to the present day.

19. C) as guides

    This is testing noun number agreement. Plural *librarians* can't be a singular *guide*. They have to be plural *guides*. Choice B goes off track because of the word *each*, which is singular and doesn't agree with *guides*.

20. C) its

    Whose ancestors are we talking about? The answer is the singular *bamboo*. We want the singular possessive pronoun *its*.

Drill: Completing a List   page 45

1. (C) books

2. (B) increasing tourism

3. (B) look for people in need of aid

4. (C) dress like druids

5. (C) congested

6. (A) in a member's home

Drill: Demonstrative Pronouns in Comparisons   page 48

1. testimony

2. forts

3. output (the daily output of crude oil)

4. patterns (the acoustic patterns)

5. (A) that for (meaning *the public's support for*)

6. (B) those in (meaning *plot lines in*)

7. (C) Nothing additional is needed. (the comparison is *products* vs. *foods*)

8. (B) those of (meaning *the voices of*)

9. (C) Nothing additional is needed. (the comparison is *cola* vs. *acid rain*)

10. (A) that displayed by (meaning *the outlook on life displayed by*)

Drill: Using Formal Structures in Comparisons page 51

1. France produces more cheese than does Italy.

2. Hybrid vehicles emit less carbon dioxide than do conventional cars.

3. People who speak several languages learn music more easily than do those who speak just one language.

4. The wings of a falcon produce more power per downstroke than do those of a robin.

5. High school student athletes scored 15% higher on a fitness test than did students who exercised on their own.

6. The stomachs of participants in the experimental group contained more diverse bacteria than did those of participants in the control group.

Practice Question Set: Parallelism & Comparisons page 54

1. D) those of conventional vehicles.
   We have a comparison here. Something is *similar to* something else. The first part of the comparison is *prices* (meaning the prices of new electric cars). Therefore, we need the second part of the comparison to be another set of prices. Choice A compares prices to a vehicle. Choice B uses the singular pronoun *that* to refer to plural prices. Choice C contains the singular *vehicle*, but we need plural vehicles and plural prices to make a logical comparison. Choice D gets the job done, using *those* to refer to prices.

2. D) that of a gilled fish.
   There is a comparison here. Something *can resemble* something else. The first part of the comparison is the *respiratory system* of an amphibian. So we need the second part of the comparison the be another respiratory system. Choice A compares a system to an animal. Choice B compares a whole system to just one component of another respiratory system. Choice C, despite all the distraction, is still comparing a respiratory system to gills. Choice D does it right, using *that* to refer to the respiratory system.

3. D) minimizing noise pollution.
   This question tests parallelism in a list. It should be a list of three gerunds: *improving*, *reducing*, and *minimizing*.

4. C) those in similar programs
   This questions is testing logical comparisons. Something was *compared to* something else. The first part of the comparison is *them*, meaning the *graduation rates* in one program. So we need to make sure the second part of the comparison is another set of graduation rates in another program. Choice A compares rates to programs. Choice B could be tricky, since it is possible to use possessives to create logical comparisons, but the first part of the comparison here is the rates *in* one program, not the *program's* rates or the rates *of* one program. Choice C works, using *those* to refer to graduation rates. Choice D goes wrong with the singular *that*.

5. D) those who said they ate no
   We have a comparison here. The right structure should say that *people who said one thing* were less likely to develop heart disease than *people who said another thing*. In other words, both parts of the comparison need a noun (people) and a verb (said). Only choice D puts it all together in the right way, using *those* to refer to people.

6. C) stay

    This question tests parallelism in a list. It's a list of three infinitives, starting with *to work*. You need to figure out whether to repeat the word *to* in each infinitive on the list, or just let the first *to* apply to all of them. The easy way to check is to make sure the second and third items match. Here the third item is *decrease* (without the *to*), so the second item should also skip the *to*. The list is *work, stay*, and *decrease*.

7. C) chemicals

    Here we have a list of three items. The first item is *contamination from gasoline*, and the choices are testing whether we need to repeat the words *contamination* and *from*. Just make sure the second and third list items match. Here, the second item is *road salts*, so for parallelism the third item should just be *chemicals*. The list becomes *gasoline, road salts*, and *chemicals*.

8. A) NO CHANGE

    We need to make a logical comparison here. Something is *more … than* something else. This is a somewhat complicated comparison. The first part of the comparison has a noun (one set of programs) and a predicate (how much self-awareness they lead to). So the second part of the comparison should also have a noun (a different set of programs) and a predicate (a different amount of self-awareness that they lead to). Choice A gets the job done by using both the word *programs* and the word *do*, which refers to the action of *leading to* an amount of self-awareness. Choice B lacks a word to refer to the action of leading to something. The double-dog-hyphenated adjective in C is super awkward, and D uses the pronoun *it*, which lacks a clear antecedent.

9. D) century but also starred

    In this question, we need to create parallelism in a correlative conjunction. When you see *not only*, you need to look for *but also* later in the sentence. Choice D gets the job done by not only completing the structure but also creating parallelism in the two verbs joined by the conjunction. We get *not only illuminated … but also starred*.

10. A) NO CHANGE

    When a comparison starts with *more*, it should finish with *than*, not *then*. Choice B is wrong because there's just no need for that comma.

11. D) that of the Beatles' George Harrison.

    This sentence gives us a little list of things on display. The first thing is a *guitar*, so the second thing should be another instrument or other item that could logically be on display at a museum. Choices A, B, and C all put George Harrison on display, which is a little too macabre for the SAT. Better to put his instrument on display, which choice D accomplishes with the word *that*, referring to his guitar.

12. B) taking time

    This question tests parallelism in a list. We want a list of three gerunds, which choice B accomplishes: *listing, paying*, and *taking*.

13. D) Japan's Mount Fuji.

    We're looking for a logical comparison here. Something is *as tall and symmetrical as* another thing. The first part of the comparison is one mountain; the second part should be another mountain. The extra verbs in A and B are unnecessary, and *those of* in C doesn't have any logical antecedent (we're not talking about the *changes of* Mount Fuji).

14. B) the extraction of DNA from other bones.

    Another opportunity to make a logical comparison. Something *has distinct advantages over* something else. The first something is *extraction*, specifically the extraction of DNA from teeth. So the second part of the comparison should be another kind of extraction or another method. Choices A and D compare extraction to *bones*, which is not logical. Choice C compares extraction to *DNA*, which is likewise absurd. Choice B gets it right.

15. D) propose initiatives

    Looks like we're making a list. At the beginning of the list, we see that *members can meet*. Do we need the *members* in every item on the list? Do we need the word *can*? The second list item provides the answer: it just has the verb *connect*, so the third list item should also be just a verb. The list becomes *meet, connect,* and *propose.*

16. A) NO CHANGE

    When a comparison starts with *more*, it should finish with *than*, not *then*, so choice B is out. In C, you don't need a comma between *more* and *than*. You also don't need a comma after *phrase* because *a phrase or a line* is a list of just two things. In D, you don't need a comma after *than* because it's never appropriate to separate a preposition from its object.

17. D) those of players who did not smile

    Create a logical comparison. The researchers *compared* something *with* something else. The first something is the *lifespans* of group. So the second half of the comparison should be another set of lifespans. Choices A and C compare lifespans with players, which is illogical. Choice B uses the singular *that* to refer to plural lifespans.

18. A) NO CHANGE

    This question is about using a correlative conjunction properly. *Either* must be followed by *or*. Choice A creates the grammatical and parallel structure *either to refund … or to replace.*

19. B) those of

    If you choose A, C, or D, you're comparing *Langston Hughes's works* with other *people*. That's illogical. Choice B creates a logical comparison by contrasting his *works* with the *works of* any other poet or writer.

20. B) their peers who followed

    In this comparison, one group had *higher levels than* another group. The first half of the comparison has both the people (*younger men*) and what they did (*who altered*). So the second half needs both of those components as well. Choice B gets it done with the different group of people (*their peers*) and the different thing they did (*who followed*). Choice A lacks the other group. Choice C seems to refer to the original group using *they*. And choice D compares people to a path.

21. D) reached twelve feet in height.

    In this question we're making a list. The subject is *statue*, and we have three verbs working for that subject. The second item on the list starts with a verb in the past tense, *weighed*. For parallelism, the third item should have the same structure. The list is *had, weighed,* and *reached.*

22. B) that of conversing through

    We need to make a logical comparison. Something is *superior to* something else. The first part of the comparison is one kind of *experience*, specifically the experience of conversing in person. So the second part of the comparison should be another kind of experience. Choices C and D are wrong because they compare an experience to *conversations* or to *conversing*. Choice A is tricky because *that of* does indeed refer to the *experience of* something, which at first looks good. But if you read the whole sentence with A, it becomes *the experience of a screen*, which is illogical. Choice B gets it right. We should be talking about *the experience of conversing through a screen.*

23. D) those published by the traditional method.
    Another opportunity to make a logical comparison. Here, something is *less expensive than*
    something else. The first thing is one set of *titles*. So the second part of the comparison should be a
    different set of titles. Choice A compares *titles* to a *method*. Choices B and C go wrong with the
    ambiguous pronoun *it*. Choice D is right, using *those* to refer to *titles*.

24. D) sports stadiums, and
    This question is about lists. This time, it's not about making sure the list items are parallel. Instead,
    it's about using the proper structure for the list itself. If you have a list of 3 or more items, the right
    structure is *X, Y, and Z*. You need a conjunction such as *and*. Depending on the list, *or* can also
    work (*X, Y, or Z*); so can *but* (*X, Y, but not Z*).

    But you **cannot** say *X, Y, as well as Z*. You also can't say *X, Y, also Z*. That knocks out choices A and
    B. In choice C, *places such as* is unnecessary and redundant because it's already clear that we're
    listing examples of places. Choice D is what you need.

25. D) similar to that of
    We should be comparing two experiences here: the experience of the elephant and the experience
    of the child. Choice A is wrong because *such as* is appropriate for giving an example within a
    category, not for comparing two separate things. Choice B compares the *experience* of the elephant
    to *a child*, which is illogical. Choice C attempts to use the word *as* to make the comparison, but
    that's just not a valid structure. Choice D works, using *similar to* to make the comparison and
    that of to ensure we're comparing one experience to another experience.

26. B) than
    There is a comparison here. Something is *more influential than* something else. The first part of the
    comparison is a set of *forces*, specifically gravitational forces. So for logical parallelism, the second
    part of the comparison should be another set of forces. And we've already got that: *mechanical ones*
    refers to mechanical forces, so the comparison is already in good shape with just the word *than*. In
    choices A and C, what noun do *that of* and *those of* refer to? Forces? If so, then the sentence
    basically says *forces of mechanical forces*, which would be illogical. In choice D, if a comparison
    begins with *more*, then it must finish with *than*, not *compared with*.

27. D) but they were also clapping
    This sentence is testing a more complex version of the correlative conjunction *not only X … but
    also Y*. First, get rid of C because it lacks *but*. Next , notice that the first half of the conjunction has
    both a subject (*these Ghanaian girls*) and a verb (*were engaged*). So to ensure parallelism, you need
    to make sure the second half also has a subject and a verb. Choice D works. It has a subject (*they*)
    and a verb (*were clapping*). In this kind of structure, the word order may seem strange, but you
    should be in good shape if you just look for the necessary pieces and not worry about the order. It's
    likely that only one choice will have all the right parts.

28. B) other methods did.
    We need to make a logical comparison. The first part of the comparison has both a subject
    (*meditation*) and a predicate (*tended to reduce stress*). Choice B creates a logical and parallel
    comparison because it also has a subject (*other methods*) and the predicate *did*, which refers to how
    the other methods *tended to reduce stress*. In choices A and D, *those of* and *the ones* don't have a
    clear and logical noun to refer to. Choice C makes an illogical comparison between two different
    actions (*tended* and *found*).

29. A) NO CHANGE

    In this comparison, something is *easier than* something else. Choice B is wrong because when a comparison starts with *easier*, it should finish with *than*. Choice A is logical and parallel because the first part of the comparison is the infinitive *to reuse*, and the second part of the comparison is another infinitive, *to rework. Them* refers to the familiar ideas. Choices C and D introduce full clauses instead of just sticking with an infinitive.

30. A) NO CHANGE

    This question is testing the correlative conjunction *both X … and Y*. We need to ensure that *X* and *Y* have parallel structure. The first piece is *its technical evolution*, a possessive pronoun and a noun. Choice A has the same structure: *its use* is also a possessive pronoun and a noun. The other choices are simply not parallel.

Drill: Semicolons   page 60

1. Correct

2. Incorrect

3. Incorrect

4. Correct

5. Choices B and D are certainly wrong because they're the same (if you treat a semicolon as identical to a period).

Drill: Colons   page 62

1. Incorrect. Never put a colon after *such as*.

2. Incorrect. The phrase *taking advantage of the opportunity to network* is a participial phrase that modifies the earlier part of the sentence. You shouldn't have a grammatical link like that across a colon. The grammatical structure in front of the colon should be complete by the time the colon arrives.

3. Correct

4. Correct

Drill: Dashes   page 64

1. Use a comma. The comma, along with the one after *Cross*, sets off *which solicited donations in the wake of Hurricane Floyd in 1999* as a nonessential relative clause.

2. Use a dash. The dash, along with the earlier one, sets off *though still unexplained* as a parenthetical.

3. No punctuation needed. The structure before the dash is complete, and everything after the dash is part of its own different structure. The phrase *who are retired or deceased* is a relative clause modifying *figures*.

4. Use a dash. A single dash here acts like a colon. The full sentence before the dash sets up a thought that gets completed by the full sentence after the dash.

5. Use a comma. The comma, along with the one after operator, sets off *in this case a mine operator* as a parenthetical.

6. Use a dash. The dash, along with the later one, sets off *referred to variously as an internet viewer, interface, or browser* as a parenthetical.

Drill: Apostrophes   page 67

1. (C) stomach's ability

2. (C) area's competitive swimmers

3. (B) its own employees

4. (B) region's residents'

5. (B) diet's effects

6. (D) it's clear that crows

7. (A) lengths of the brushstrokes

8. (B) a house's electrical system

Drill: Commas with Quotes   page 69

1. Use a comma. It's a full sentence of quoted speech.

2. Don't use a comma. The term flows as part of the grammar of the sentence.

3. Use a comma. The term flows as part of the grammar of the sentence, but a comma is needed because *when measured using fMRI* is a parenthetical that is set off at the start with a comma. So we need one on the back end too. The comma has nothing to do with the quotation marks.

4. Use a comma. It's a full sentence of quoted speech.

5. Don't use a comma. Even though it looks like a full sentence of quoted speech, it's not quite. The subject *branch* is outside the quote, and the verb phrase *would have to get* is split across the quotation mark. Thus, the quoted speech actually flows as part of the grammar of the sentence.

6. Don't use a comma. This is like the previous one. The quoted material is part of the relative clause set up by the relative pronoun *that*. It flows with the grammar of the sentence.

Drill: Coordinate and Cumulative Adjectives   page 76

1. Incorrect
    The comma between the coordinate adjectives *noisy* and *erratic* is fine.
    But the comma between *erratic* and the noun *lurches* is wrong.

2. Correct

3. Incorrect
    The coordinate adjectives *steep* and *twisty* need a comma between them.

4. Correct
    Underwater is a cumulative adjective that creates the single concept *underwater journey*. *Harrowing* and *dangerous* are coordinate adjectives that separately and independently modify that concept.

5. Incorrect
    The adjectives *personal* and *documentary* are cumulative, so they shouldn't have a comma.

6. Correct

7. Incorrect
    The lack of a comma between the cumulative adjectives *loud* and *buzzing* is fine.
    But the comma between *buzzing* and the noun *noise* is wrong.

1. Correct

   The appositive *Australia native* precedes the noun *Priya Cooper.*

2. Correct

   The appositive *a Native American storyteller* follows the noun *Te Ata*. The comma after *New York* sets off the introductory element; it has nothing to do with the appositive.

3. Incorrect

   The appositive *German mathematician* precedes the noun *Emmy Noether*, so there should not be any comma.

4. Incorrect

   The appositive *A leading expert in the field of occupational health* is an introductory element, so it needs a comma after *health*.

5. Correct

   The appositive *fellow arranger* precedes the noun *Scott Snyder*, so there is no need for any appositive-related comma. The comma after *Snyder* sets off the introductory prepositional phrase.

6. Incorrect

   The appositive *the founder of the Bauhaus Movement* follows the noun *Walter Gropius*, so it should be set off with commas on both ends. We're missing the second comma.

7. Correct

   There's all kinds of fun here. Two appositives, *chemist* and *materials scientist*, precede their nouns (*Anthony Mendoza* and *Pedro Mendoza*, respectively) and thus don't require commas. The entire phrase *materials scientist Pedro Mendoza* is a big appositive (with a little appositive in it) that follows the noun it modifies, *son*, so we need commas around that entire phrase. The comma after *year* sets off the introductory element.

8. Incorrect

   The appositive *professional surfer* precedes the noun *Kelly Slater*, so there should not be any comma there. The comma after *2015* sets off the introductory prepositional phrase.

Drill: Finding Comma Errors   page 82

In the paragraph below, each comma is marked as correct or incorrect, as well as numbered. See the discussion afterward for an explanation of each comma's valid or erroneous usage.

Even from 512 miles above the Earth,[1✓] holiday lights shine bright and,[2✗] now we're able to measure just how much. Miguel Román,[3✓] a research physical scientist and remote sensing specialist at NASA Goddard Space Flight Center,[4✓] has been looking at daily data,[5✗] from the Suomi National Polar-orbiting Partnership (Suomi NPP) satellite and has identified how patterns in nighttime light intensity change during major,[6✗] holiday seasons—Christmas and New Year's in the United States and the holy month of Ramadan in the Middle East. In comparing the six weeks,[7✗] between Thanksgiving and New Year's in the U.S.,[8✓] he and his team,[9✗] noticed large areas where night lights were 20-50% brighter than during the rest of the year.

Suomi NPP,[10✓] which circles the Earth from the North Pole to,[11✗] the South Pole and back about 14 times a day,[12✓] carries an instrument that can observe the dark side of the planet and detect the glow of lights in cities and towns across the globe. The analysis of holiday lights uses an innovative,[13✓] advanced,[14✗] algorithm that filters out moonlight,[15✓] clouds,[16✓] and airborne particles in order to isolate city lights on a daily basis. The data from this algorithm,[17✗] provides high-quality satellite information on light output across the globe,[18✓] allowing scientists to track when—and how brightly—people illuminate the night. Holiday light displays have become more affordable,[19✗] people are pushing them to new limits every year.

Dr. Román believes we need to better understand the driving forces behind energy use,[20✓] including how dominant social,[21✗] phenomena,[22✓] the changing demographics of urban centers,[23✓] and socio-cultural settings affect energy-use decisions. The satellite data can help cities estimate the timing of their peak energy use,[24✗] it can also predict how much electricity they will use in a given time period.

1. Correct. This comma sets off the introductory element.

2. Error. This comma is after the coordinating conjunction *and*. It should be before the conjunction instead.

3. Correct. The phrase *a research physical scientist and remote sensing specialist at NASA Goddard Space Flight Center* is a nonessential appositive that follows the noun it modifies. Thus, it needs commas on both ends. This is the front comma.

4. Correct. This is the back one.

5. Error. The prepositional phrase *from the ... satellite* modifies the noun *data*. This comma comes between a prepositional phrase and the word it modifies.

6. Error. *Major* and *holiday* are cumulative adjectives modifying the noun *seasons*. Thus, they shouldn't be separated by a comma.

7. Error. The prepositional phrase *between Thanksgiving and New Year's* modifies the noun *weeks*. This comma separates the prepositional phrase from the word it modifies.

8. Correct. Everything in front of this comma is a big introductory element. This comma sets it off from the main clause.

9. Error. This comma separates the subject *he and his team* from its verb, *noticed*.

10. Correct. The phrase *which circles the Earth from the North Pole to the South Pole and back about 14 times a day* is a nonessential relative clause. Thus, it needs commas on both ends. This is the front comma.

11. Error. This comma separates the preposition *to* from its object, *the South Pole*.

12. Correct. This is the back comma for the relative clause (paired with comma #10).

13. Correct. *Innovative* and *advanced* are coordinate adjectives working for the noun *algorithm*. A comma belongs between the adjectives.

14. Error. This comma separates the adjective *advanced* from the noun it modifies, *algorithm*. Don't put a comma after the final coordinate adjective.

15. Correct. The phrase *moonlight, clouds, and airborne particles* is a list of three things. So we need this comma after the first list item.

16. Correct. And we need this comma after the second list item.

17. Error. This comma separates the subject *data* from its verb, *provides*. The presence of the prepositional phrase *from this algorithm* doesn't create any need for a comma.

18. Correct. The stuff after the comma, starting with *allowing*, is a big participial phrase that modifies the entire situation that comes before. Thus, it should be set off with a comma.

19. Error. This is a comma splice. The stuff before the comma is a clause with subject *displays* and verb *have become*; the stuff after the comma is a clause with subject *people* and verb *are pushing*. The only thing joining the clauses is a comma, which is the dreaded comma splice. You could fix it by swapping the comma for a semicolon or period.

20. Correct. The word *including* typically kicks off a nonessential phrase that introduces extra information about an already specific noun. Thus, it is typically preceded by a comma. Here, the nonessential phrase modifies the noun phrase *driving forces behind energy use*.

21. Error. This comma separates the adjective *social* from the noun it modifies, *phenomena*. *Dominant* and *social* are cumulative adjectives, but don't put a comma after the final cumulative adjective.

22. Correct. This clause sets up a list of three things, which boils down to *how these 3 things affect decisions*. The 3 things are the nouns *phenomena*, *demographics*, and *settings*, along with the words that modify them. So we need this comma after the first list item.

23. Correct. And we need this comma after the second list item.

24. Error. This is a comma splice. The first subject-verb pair is *data ... can help*. The second is *it ... can predict*.

Practice Question Set: Punctuation   page 84

1. D) States: Uncle
    Kill choices A and B right away. They are identical according to the semicolon = period rule. Choice C is a comma splice. Choice D works because the stuff in front of the colon could stand alone as a complete sentence. Furthermore, it sets up a thought that needs completion, and *Uncle Sam* completes the thought.

2. D) narrative, Messenheimer
    Choices A and B are identical according to the semicolon = period rule. Choice C is wrong because the stuff before the colon is not a complete sentence. Choice D works because the stuff before the comma is a big introductory phrase before the main subject and verb.

3. A) NO CHANGE
    The sentence should say *it is obvious*, so choices C and D are out because they use the possessive *its*, not the contraction *it's*. Choice B is wrong because there is no reason for *attempts* to be a possessive. It's just plural. There is no noun after *attempts*, and you can't say (*something*) *of the attempts*.

4. D) reasons, such as
    You never want any punctuation immediately following *such as*, even if you have a list.

5. C) an unanswered question: Why is the Milky Way warped?
    Direct questions need a question mark, while embedded questions don't. The choices get that punctuation issue right, so it's then a matter of looking for effective sentence structure. Choice A is redundant when it says *the issue … which is a question*. Choice B is awkward when it says *address why*, among other problems. Choice D is awkward and wordy, especially when you compare it with C, which says the same thing more directly and using fewer words.

6. C) warm, fluffy blueberry
    The words *blueberry* and *delights* work together to create a single idea, so you don't want a comma after *blueberry*. Think of *blueberry delights* as a single noun. We have two adjectives (*warm* and *fluffy*) independently modifying that noun. They're coordinate adjectives. So you do want a comma between *warm* and *fluffy*, but you don't want a comma after the second adjective.

7. C) technologies—the microphone, the gramophone player, and the flat recording disc—
    The list of technologies Berliner developed is a parenthetical phrase. It interrupts the flow of the sentence and could be removed without changing the meaning of the sentence. So you want something that can set off a parenthetical phrase. Dashes work. Semicolons don't. You can't use a colon after *technologies*, even though the stuff before could stand alone. That's because there is a grammatical connection between what comes before the colon and what comes after: *Berliner* is the subject for the verb *is responsible*. You can't separate a verb from its subject with a colon.

8. B) zebras, for example:
    The stuff after *for example* could stand alone as a complete sentence, and *consider zebras* is actually a complete sentence too. It's a command, which is why you don't see a subject, but it still counts as a complete sentence. So choices A and C are wrong because they attempt to join two complete sentences with just a comma—it's the unspeakable comma splice. Choice D has acceptable punctuation, but it's wrong because it puts *for example* in an illogical spot in what has become a third sentence. Zebras are an example of what was said in the *first* sentence, so *for example* really belongs in the next sentence after that. Choice B gets it in the right place, attached to *consider zebras*.

9. D) professions; the median annual salary for translators
    Professions should be simply plural, not possessive. There is no noun after *professions* that you can say is *of the professions*. So you don't want an apostrophe on that word. Same thing with *translators*, so you don't want an apostrophe on that word either.

10. B) families:
    Families should be simply plural, not possessive. There is no noun after *families* that you can say is *of the families*. That's why A and C are wrong. Choice D is wrong because it's a run-on sentence. It has clauses joined by nothing at all. The colon in choice B works because the stuff before the colon could stand alone. What comes after is also a full sentence, which is fine.

11. B) words—
    When you see the other dash earlier in the sentence, check whether the sentence is trying to create a parenthetical phrase that could be removed. In this case, the answer is yes. *People who study the origins of words* provides the definition of *etymologists*, but that's nonessential information. Since the parenthetical is set off with a dash at the beginning, you need a second dash to finish it up.

12. D) nicknamed "brickmaking capital of the world"
    Because the stuff inside the quotation marks flows as part of the grammar of the sentence (and it's not a full sentence of directly quoted speech), you don't need a comma after *nicknamed*. You also don't need a comma after *world*, since it would inappropriately separate the prepositional phrase *for supplying* from the preceding phrase it modifies.

13. D) or exposure to the sun's rays, on
    One way to provide a definition or clarification of a term is to use the word *or* and put the definition after the term, surrounded by commas. The *or* goes inside the commas. For example, "Zizania, or wild rice, is a cereal grain." In this sentence, the definition of *insolation* is *exposure to the sun's rays*. So choice D gets the structure right.

14. C) poetry, publishing a collection of poems—titled *A Book of Verses*—in 1898.
    Choice B is wrong because the stuff after the semicolon is not a complete sentence. In choices A and D, if you want to use a single dash, then there can't be any grammatical connection between the stuff before the dash and the stuff after. But *in 1898* modifies the participle *publishing*, so these choices are wrong. Choice C is good because the stuff between the dashes forms a parenthetical phrase that could be removed from the sentence.

15. B) program, the Department of Folklore and Folklife at the University of Pennsylvania,
    The whole long phrase *the Department of Folklore and Folklife at the University of Pennsylvania* is an appositive explaining what her ideal program is. Thus, it should be set off with a pair of commas, dashes, or parentheses at the beginning and end of the appositive. Choice B is the only one with an acceptable pair in the proper positions.

16. C) is Death Valley, California—the
    Choice A is wrong because the stuff after the semicolon is not a complete sentence. Choice B is wrong because the stuff before the colon is not a complete sentence. Choice D is wrong because we have an opening parenthesis without a closing one. Choice C works because the stuff before the dash can stand alone, and the stuff afterward completes the thought that was set up.

17. D) sculptor Constantin Brancusi's
    Sculptor is the appositive, and *Constantin Brancusi* is the noun it modifies. The appositive is before the noun, and that's the situation in which we don't need commas around either the appositive or the noun.

18. A) NO CHANGE
    The phrase *particularly the younger members* is a nonessential or parenthetical phrase that could be removed from the sentence. So it should be set off on both sides with appropriate punctuation, which could be commas, dashes, or parentheses. Choice A is the only one with acceptable punctuation on both sides of the nonessential phrase.

19. A) NO CHANGE
    You never want any punctuation immediately following *such as*, even if you have a list.

20. C) activity: "farming"
    The word *farming* flows as part of the grammar of the sentence, so we should punctuate the rest of the sentence as if there were no quotation marks. Choices B and D are wrong because there is no reason to separate *farming* from *aphids* with a comma. Choice A is wrong because the stuff after the semicolon is not a complete sentence. Choice C works because the stuff before the colon is a full sentence that sets up a thought in need of completion. The stuff after the colon completes the thought.

21. A) NO CHANGE
    According to the sentence, we need a list of three things. The number of commas in choices B and D create lists with too many items. Choice C is illogical because *rice cayenne* is not a thing, but *cayenne pepper* in choice A is a thing.

22. C) Disabled, there
    Choices A and B are identical according to the period = semicolon rule. Choice D is wrong because the stuff before the dash cannot stand alone. Choice C is appropriate because everything before the word *Disabled* is a very long introductory phrase, which should be set off from the main clause using a comma.

23. D) cover in the Stillwater,
    You need a comma separating the city name from the state name, so choices B and C are incorrect. Choice A is wrong because there is no reason to separate the prepositional phrase *in the Stillwater, Oklahoma, area* from the preceding phrase it modifies.

24. C) counterparts; she graduated
    The prepositional phrase *on time* modifies the adjacent verb *graduated* and doesn't create a distinct pause in the sentence, so there is no need to separate them with a comma. Choices B and D are out for that reason. Choice A creates the vile comma splice. *Thorpe … caught up* is a subject-verb pair, and *she graduated* is another, so we can't connect them with just a comma. But a semicolon works.

25. C) single scrap of paper?
    Because it begins with the interrogative word *what*, this is a direct question, not an embedded question, so it must end with a question mark. Choice D is wrong because there is no reason to separate the adjective *single* from the noun it modifies, *scrap*.

26. B) hawk feathers.
    There is no noun after *feathers*, and you can't say *something of the feathers*, so it's inappropriate to use an apostrophe. *Feathers* is simply plural, not possessive. *Hawk* is something called an attributive noun: when you put two nouns in a row, the first one becomes an adjective modifying the second one. The attributive noun should be singular, not plural. For example, we say *coat rack* and *potato peeler*, not *coats rack* or *potatoes peeler*.

27. B) watermelons, however. The
    There are multiple clauses here, and the adverb *however* is not allowed to do the grammatical heavy lifting of connecting them. When it comes to punctuation, clauses can be joined by a semicolon, colon, or dash, or the sentence may be broken into two with a period. One subject-verb pair is *objection … had*, and another is *problem was*. So choices A and D are wrong because they join those clauses with just commas, or worse, nothing at all. Choice C has acceptable punctuation, but it is wrong because it puts *however* in an illogical spot. Logically, the story boils down to this: they scrapped the note, *but* not because of the font. We can use *however* to show this contrast, and we can even shift the *however* to appear after the discussion of the font. But if you put it after the dash, it creates an illogical contrast: the problem was not X—*however* it was Y. Explaining the true problem is not a contrast to pointing out what was not the problem. It's more like further explaining what you meant by the first statement.

28. B) Perenyi's neighbors'
    We want *Perenyi* to have apostrophe + *s* because it's singular and possessive. We can say *the neighbors of Perenyi*. We want *neighbors* to have an apostrophe after the *s* because it's plural and possessive. We can say *the displays of the neighbors*.

29. A) NO CHANGE
    Seventy-one-year-old is the appositive, and *Frank Goss* is the noun it modifies. The appositive is before the noun, and that's the situation in which we don't need commas around either the appositive or the noun.

30. C) Dempsey, vice president for public policy
    James Dempsey is the noun, which is modified by the very long appositive *vice president for public policy at the Center for Democracy and Technology*. Because the appositive follows the noun, it should be set off by commas. We just need one comma in this case because the sentence ends with the appositive.

31. A) NO CHANGE
    A subject-verb pair is *precision … is dependent*. Between that subject and verb is the relative clause *with which measurements can be made*, which modifies the noun *precision*. Some relative clauses are nonessential and should be set off with commas; others aren't and shouldn't. Because there is no comma after *made*, you can tell this is an essential relative clause that doesn't need a comma at the beginning either.

32. C) witty, irreverent poems
    Here we have two adjectives modifying a noun. The adjectives are *witty* and *irreverent*, and the noun is *poems*. You never want a comma between the final adjective and the noun, so choice B is out. Are the adjectives coordinate or cumulative? They each independently tell you something about the poems, so they are coordinate adjectives and need a comma between them. That's why D is wrong. Finally, do you need a comma after *poems*? It depends on whether *similar to limericks* is an essential or a nonessential phrase. If it's nonessential, then it needs to be surrounded with commas. A valid argument could be made either way on that point, but since you don't have an option to put a comma after *limericks*, then you shouldn't put one in front of *similar*.

33. D) is *storge*, for example,
    The entire second sentence provides examples of the topic introduced in the first sentence. Thus it would be natural to put *for example* at the beginning of the second sentence, but it's also acceptable to put it in the middle or even at the end of the second sentence. Wherever it appears, it needs to be surrounded by commas because it's nonessential and interrupts the flow of the sentence.

34. D) eyes' lachrymal glands
    Glands should not be possessive because there is no noun *of the glands*. That kills choices A and C. It could be possible to discuss a biological concept like *the eye* in the singular, but later in this sentence we see the plural pronoun *them*, whose antecedent needs to be the plural noun *glands*, not the singular *gland*. That's why choice B is wrong.

35. C) dinosaurs went extinct.
    This sentence has a question *why*, but it's embedded in the statement that *paleontologists have long wondered…*. Embedded questions don't end in a question mark, so choices A and B are wrong. Choice D is awkward, wordy, and somewhat illogical. It also has a problem with word order. Direct questions put auxiliary verbs in front of the subject (*"Why were dinosaurs caused to … ?"*). But embedded questions should put all verbs after the subject (*"… wondered why dinosaurs were caused to …"*).

36. C) that
    The material between the quotation marks flows with the grammar of the sentence, since *was* is the verb for the subject *that*. Therefore, we must punctuate as if the quotation marks were not there. In this case, there is no need for any punctuation. The second half of the sentence is an essential relative clause modifying the word *something*.

37. B) quality, catfish, bass, perch, and shad inhabit
    Thanks to improved water quality is an introductory phrase, so it should be followed by a comma. In the list of four fish, we need a comma after each of the first three list items. We don't need a comma after *shad* because it would needlessly separate the subject (the four fish) from the verb *inhabit*.

38. B) interview, Russian expressionist painter
In an 1893 interview is an introductory phrase, so it must be followed by a comma. (The comma after *interview* has nothing to do with the appositive that follows.) After that, *Russian expressionist painter* is an appositive modifying the noun *Wassily Kandinsky*. The appositive is before the noun, so we don't need any additional commas around either the appositive or the noun.

39. A) NO CHANGE
The stuff inside the quotation marks is set up as a full, separate sentence of directly quoted speech or writing, so we need a comma after *proclaimed*. Choices B and D are out. However, there is no reason to use a comma to separate the prepositional phrase *in the Chicago Daily Tribune* from the noun it modifies, *headline*. That's why choice C is wrong.

40. C) cheetah's pattern of spots
Cheetah needs an apostrophe + *s* because the cheetah possesses the pattern of spots. However, *spots* does not need an apostrophe. It's true that you could say *the pattern of the spots*, but in fact the sentence already says exactly that. You can show possession **either** by saying *spots' pattern* **or** by saying *pattern of spots*, but combining both structures into *pattern of spots'* is like double overkill.

Drill: Finding Clauses and the Words that Connect Them   page 102

1. Clause: *postseason ... has been*

2. Clause: *cornerstone ... was laid*

3. Clause 1: *jade ... was revered*
Connector: *and*
Clause 2: *variety ... have been found*

4. Clause 1: *games ... are*
Connector: *because*
Clause 2: *they ... have*

5. Clause 1: *everything ... is*
Connector: *but*
Clause 2: *things ... are*

6. Clause 1: *we ... can develop*
Connector: *if*
Clause 2: *programs ... can be improved*

7. Clause 1: *you ... should be*
Connector: *that*
Clause 2: *you ... post*

8. Clause 1: *paper ... is*
Connector: *which*
Clause 2: *which ... was read*

9. Clause 1: *Carl Sagan ... was*
Connector: *although*
Clause 2: *imagery ... verges*

10. Clause 1: *feature ... was*
    Connector: *which*
    Clause 2: *speakers ... understood*

11. Clause 1: *lyrics ... carry*
    Connector: the colon
    Clause 2: *you ... should* (not) *forget*

12. Clause 1: *ejection ... is*
    Connector 1: *but*
    Clause 2: *you ... could see*
    Connector 2: *if*
    Clause 3: *it ... would cause*

13. Clause 1: *sneeze ... is*
    Connector 1: *that*
    Clause 2: *that ... is triggered*
    Connector 2: *when*
    Clause 3: *endings ... are stimulated*

14. Clause 1: *city ... hosts*
    Connector 1: *and*
    Clause 2: *judges ... allow*
    Connector 2: *which*
    Clause 3: *which ... help*

Drill: Connecting Clauses page 106

1. Correct. There are 3 clauses, joined by *and* & *when*.

2. Incorrect. This is a comma splice. The first subject-verb pair is *Moon ... will slip*. The second is *this ... has been happening*.

3. Incorrect. We have the conjunctive adverb *however* posing as a conjunction. It tries to join the clauses *Balch ... served* and *she ... was known*.

4. Correct. There are 3 clauses, joined by *and* & *that*.

5. Correct. There are 3 clauses. *Piece ... becomes* is joined to *it ... can lose* by *if*. The second clause is joined to the third, *that ... made* by the relative pronoun *that*. The word *however* is just hanging out, not attempting to connect clauses, so it's cool.

6. Incorrect. We have the conjunctive adverb *therefore* posing as a conjunction. It tries to join the clauses *milling ... strips* and *choosing ... is*.

7. Incorrect. This sentence has the same problem as the example in the chapter that begins, "Experts advocate plenty of vitamin C..." We have the relative pronoun *which*, but that pronoun is neither the subject of *delivered* (that's *he*) nor the object of *delivered* (that's the *speech*). Thus, it's wrong. A good fix would be to insert the word *in* before *which* to create ... *an address in which he delivered* ... In that case, *which* would be the object of the preposition *in*.

8. Correct. There are a whopping 5 clauses, joined by *and*, *that*, *after* & *that.*

9. Correct. There are 3 clauses. The first two are joined by the semicolon. The third is attached with *while.*

10. Incorrect. There are 2 clauses but 2 conjunctions as well—one too many. You could fix the sentence by removing the *as* at the beginning or the *and* after *cities.*

Drill: Finding Appositive Phrases   page 111

1. author of *The Awakening*

2. a University of Chicago Professor Emeritus

3. a patent medicine heavily advertised in old newspapers

4. the words above the door on a building in the background

5. something we tend to take for granted in the twenty-first century

6. French professor

7. a phrase coined by O. Henry in "The Admiral" from his *Cabbages and Kings*

8. a school that taught skills useful in the business world

Drill: Distinguishing Verbs from Verbals   page 115

1. Participle. It modifies *pumpkin.*

2. Verb. The clause is *everything ... has changed.*

3. Participle. It modifies *industry.*

4. Infinitive. It acts as an adverb modifying *able.*

5. Verb. The clause has a compound predicate (two verbs): *cooks ... were* and *embraced.*

6. Gerund. It's the direct object of the verb *was changing.*

7. Verb. The clause is *options ... were becoming.*

8. Infinitive. The word *be* turns this into what's called a "passive infinitive."

9. Gerund. It's the subject of the verb *featured.*

10. Participle. It modifies *pies.*

11. Infinitive. It acts as an adverb modifying *ready.*

12. Verb. The clause is *pies ... caught.*

13. Infinitive. It's the direct object of the verb *continue.*

14. Gerund. It's the direct object of the verb *mean.*

15. Verb. The clause is *boomers ... grew up.*

16. Verb. The clause is *people ... are putting.*

17. Participle. It modifies *variety*.

18. Participle. It modifies *spices*.

19. Gerund. It's the object of the preposition *in*.

Drill: Introductory Modifiers   page 120

1. (A) the posters celebrated...

2. (C) van Gogh was considered...

3. (B) the komuz is related to...

4. (A) the treaty provided...

5. (A) Luciana pointed out that...

6. (B) Ecuador is the same size as...

7. (B) he continues to collect...

8. (C) the researchers were surprised to find...

Drill: Combining Sentences   page 129

Written responses will of course vary. You should check whether the same major problems were identified, and certainly whether the correct answer was chosen.

4A. Incorrect. This sentence has no main verb. It looks like *nesting sites* is supposed to be the subject, but *built with wooden boxes* is a participial phrase, *forty-five in total* is a parenthetical, and *mounted on posts within the preserve* is another participial phrase. We just have a bunch of modifiers without a main clause.

4B. Incorrect. *After being built with wooden boxes* is the kind of awkward and wordy phrase based on *being* that the SAT generally frowns upon.

4C. Correct. This sentence trims the modifier down to the participial phrase *built with wooden boxes*. We've dropped the awkward and unnecessary *after being*. The modifier is properly next to the noun it modifies. The rest of the sentence is streamlined and efficient.

4D. Incorrect. This is again a wordier and more awkward version of the modifier. Instead of the 4-word participial phrase *built with wooden boxes* (from the correct answer), we have the 7-word clause *and these were built with wooden boxes*. The extra words don't do us any good. Another problem here is that the other part of the sentence uses inverted word order for no good reason. Instead of the more straightforward *45 sites ... were mounted*, we see the more awkward *mounted ... were 45 sites*.

5A. Incorrect. The pronoun *it* is somewhat ambiguous here. What raises questions exactly? The aim? The painting? The overall situation?

5B. Correct. Using the relative pronoun *that* makes it clear that the second clause refers to the painting. We want a painting that has two attributes: 1) it's dramatic, and 2) it raises questions. This sentence is unambiguous, logical, and grammatically efficient.

5C. Incorrect. One problem here is redundancy. The sentence repeats the word *painting*, which is typically enough to make a choice wrong in this type of question. The logic of the sentence is a little funky too. The clause after the semicolon makes it sound as if the painting already exists and is currently raising questions. However, the correct answer makes it clear that such a painting is a goal, not a reality.

5D. Incorrect. Again we have redundancy, as the sentence repeats the phrase *the aim*. Another issue is the badly misplaced modifier *dramatically*. As an adverb, it appears to be linked to the verb *raises*. It is better to put the adverb next to the verb when you can, so *dramatically raises questions* would be a grammatical improvement, though still logically problematic. *Dramatic* should be properly be modifying the painting, not the manner in which we're raising questions. Yet another logical problem is *the painting*, not *the aim*, is what's supposed to be raising questions. This choice is a hot mess.

Practice Question Set: Sentence Structure   page 132

1. B) Board, state
    In a process overseen and guided by the Public Employment Relations Board is a big introductory phrase. *Overseen* and *guided* are participles, not verbs, so it's just a phrase, not a clause. Introductory phrases should be joined to the main clause with a comma.

2. C) a nearby farm that raises zubron, a cross between a cow and a European woods bison.
    This question is testing the proper placement of modifiers. They should be as close as possible to the nouns that they modify. The cane fiber is sent to a farm, so choice B is out because it suggests that the fiber is sent to an animal. Choice A makes it sound like the farm is a cross between two animals. In choice D, the phrase *known as zubron* should be modifying the noun *cross*, but it's much closer to the noun *bison*, which creates an unclear or unintended meaning.

3. D) DELETE the underlined portion.
    The stuff before the comma is a full sentence that can stand alone. The stuff after the comma is an appositive that gives more information about the noun *proprionate*. Choices A and C create comma splices, and *being* in choice B is just, no.

4. C) efficacy: some studies do show
    One subject-verb pair is *question … relates*. In choice A, another subject-verb pair, *studies … show*, is connected with just a comma, forming the vermicious comma splice. Choice C has the same two subject-verb pairs but connects them with a colon, which is acceptable. In choice B, changing *show* to the participle *showing* means the second clause has no verb. Choice D has a similar problem: by putting *show* inside the relative clause beginning with *that*, there is no verb for the subject *studies*.

5. B) which he subsequently donated
Choices A, C, and D all create the fiendish comma splice. *Ashmole ... acquired* is a subject-verb pair, and those choices all have a second subject-verb pair connected by only a comma. Choice B uses the relative pronoun *which* to properly join the two clauses.

6. B) who gained national recognition
If you look outside the commas, you'll see a subject and a verb: *Michael Larson ... had figured out.* Therefore, the stuff inside the commas must be either a phrase or a properly joined clause. Choices A and C are wrong because they are full clauses with subjects and verbs, but they're joined to the main clause with nothing but commas—the filthy comma splice. Choice B is correct because the relative pronoun *who* creates a proper relative clause. Choice D might seem acceptable at first because it could create a participial phrase based on the participle *recognized.* However, it uses an unidiomatic construction. It's OK to use the prepositional phrase *by winning* to modify the verb *gained,* as choice B does, but it's wrong to use *by winning* to modify *recognized.* The correct idiom would be to say *recognized for winning.*

7. D) DELETE the underlined portion.
Where is the main clause of the sentence? *Rather than being part of a complete mold* is just an introductory phrase, since *being* is a gerund. Between the commas, *which would ... patterns* is a clause, but it's a relative clause that modifies the word *mold,* and it's properly joined to the rest of the sentence with the relative pronoun *which.* So the main clause must come after the second comma. The subject-verb pair is *designs ... were stamped.* Since there is no other independent clause, we don't need any of the coordinating conjunctions offered by choices A, B, and C.

8. A) NO CHANGE
Choices C and D are identical according to the period = semicolon rule. (The stuff after the period is not a full sentence because *happening* alone is not a verb.) In choice B, we have the clauses *students ... don't come* and *part ... happens* joined by just a comma. Choice A fixes the wicked comma splice by properly joining the two clauses with a colon.

9. B) typically extending
Choice A has a comma splice. The clauses *headache ... is* and *it ... extends* are joined by nothing but a comma. The consecutive pronouns *which it* in choice C create an illogical meaning. They seem to suggest that the headache extends the headache. Choice D is also illogical because it suggests that the headache is triggered from the forehead. Choice B works by turning the last part of the sentence into a participial phrase based on the participle *extending.* The phrase modifies the entire preceding idea of the headache.

10. B) bonds, most
It's a long sentence, but there are only two clauses. The subject-verb pairs are *side chains ... associate* and *polypeptide chains ... fold.* The clauses are already properly joined by the subordinating conjunction *because* at the beginning of the sentence. The comma indicates the end of the first clause and the beginning of the second. So you don't need the coordinating conjunction *so* in choice C or the colon in choice D because they would introduce too many connectors. The word *therefore* in choice A is awkward and unnecessary, since the idea of causality is already provided by *because.*

11. C) government creates a stable economic structure
What is *providing services and protection?* The answer is *government,* so that's the word that should immediately follow the introductory modifier.

12. B) Pearl Lang clearly identified with
Who is *feeling the tension?* Why, it's *Pearl Lang,* of course, so she should immediately follow the introductory modifier.

13. C) engineers created a new prototype that
Who is *identifying the source*? It must be *engineers*, so they should immediately follow the introductory modifier.

14. A) NO CHANGE
What could be *challenging and stressful*? The answer is *social work*, so that's the noun we want immediately after the introductory modifier.

15. D) Emma Dusenbury's version has stayed closest to the song's roots in the theater.
What is *suggesting* something? It's the song. This one is tricky, but by beginning with *Emma Dusenbury's version* (of the song), choice D is correctly putting a song next to the introductory modifier.

16. C) knocking
Choices A, B, and D all create the horrible comma splice. They all contain a verb for the subject *each one*, and there is nothing but a comma to join the clause to the rest of the sentence. Choice C works because *knocking* is not a verb—it's a participle. You can tell because an *-ing* word without some form of *be* as an auxiliary verb cannot be a verb. Therefore, choice C creates an absolute phrase. The sentence before the comma is complete. Then we have a comma. Then a noun (*each one*). Then a modifier (the participle *knocking*) that modifies that noun. It's the perfect recipe for an absolute phrase, and it's correct.

17. D) process, supplying
Choice A is the terrible comma splice because *they ... supplied* is a full clause connected with just a comma. Choice B is wrong because *whereby* (a word you surely use on a daily basis) is a relative adverb—in other words, it should create a relative clause and modify a noun that it follows. But that doesn't happen. In choice C, the stuff after the semicolon could not stand alone. Choice D is good because *supplying* kicks off a participial phrase that modifies the entire situation that comes before the comma.

18. C) they hope
This is a tricky one, but it becomes easier to see why C is right if you realize it's an elliptical construction (page 97). The word that has been left out is the relative pronoun *that*. When you put the missing word back in, the sentence becomes ... *a special hydrogel that they hope can one day act as ...* In other words, the researchers hope the special hydrogel can one day act as a power source. We're allowed to use an elliptical construction (i.e., drop the word *that* from the sentence) because we have an essential relative clause in which the relative pronoun *that* is not the subject.

19. C) of which
With choices A, B, and D, we have a full clause with a subject (*half*) and a verb (*had to be*) between the commas. That's a nasty comma splice. Choice C fixes the issue by introducing the relative pronoun *which*, which can do the grammatical work of connecting the little clause between the commas to the rest of the sentence.

20. A) NO CHANGE
All the choices properly use a conjunction or punctuation to join up the clauses. This question wants you to choose the most logical conjunction or transition word. In this case, there is a contrast. On the one hand, we have new innovative companies with advanced technology. But on the other hand, drug discovery is difficult and time-consuming. Because of that conflict, the conjunction *but* is the most logical choice.

21. D) who
    Choice B connects the clauses *cases ... will increase* and *they ... may lose* with just a comma. You know what that is. The other choices all use relative pronouns to try to properly connect the final clause, which is a step in the right direction. But *that* in choice A is used for essential relative clauses, which should not be preceded by a comma. Choice C is wrong because we should use *who* to refer to people, not *which*. It's not nice to call people witches, even if they are fugu consumers.

22. A) NO CHANGE
    The word *being* in choices C and D should make you very nervous. Because *being* is not used as a helper verb, a gerund, or to refer to a living creature, it's likely to be awkward and unnecessary, and indeed there is no reason to use it here. Choice B is wrong because the stuff after the semicolon cannot stand alone. Choice A is good because the stuff before the colon can stand alone, and it sets up a thought that is completed by the nice parallel contrast after the colon.

23. C) be one of the most beneficial ways to practice
    This question asks you to find a clear and concise sentence structure. One problem that all the wrong choices share is the use of the word *technique*. Since we already have the words *method* and *ways* in the sentence, *technique* is wordy and redundant.

24. B) puppets," which
    Choice A connects the clauses *there ... are* and *these ... are* with nothing but a comma. It's the evil comma splice. Choice B correctly joins the clauses with the relative pronoun *which*. Choice C has too many connectors, with both the conjunction *and* and the relative pronoun *which*. Choice D uses the dreaded *being*, which don't even.

25. B) researchers identified a previously unrecognized current that provides a rare ...
    Did you notice that this sentence begins with a big introductory modifier? Make sure whatever follows the comma is the appropriate noun. Check out the beginning of the sentence—who was *investigating*? It was the *researchers*, so we need them to be the first noun after the comma.

26. C) eye, and
    We have two clauses here that need to be properly joined. The plain comma in choice A ain't gonna do the trick. In choice B, *thus* is a conjunctive adverb (like *however* or *therefore*), not a conjunction, so it's not allowed to connect clauses either. In choice D, *and so* would be acceptable if there were a comma before the conjunction *and*. But there isn't, so it's not. Choice C uses "comma-FANBOYS," so it works.

27. B) developed
    First, make your life simpler by ignoring the parenthetical phrase between the dashes. Choices A and C have subjects and verbs—they create full clauses, which have nothing to properly connect them to the first clause. Choice B works because *developed* is a participle (an adjective) that modifies the noun *process*. Now the stuff after the dash is just a participial phrase, so we don't have to worry about properly joining clauses.

28. B) which says
    Choice B uses the relative pronoun *which* to create a big relative clause between the commas, which tells us exactly what *this story* is. That's valid. Choice A is the nefarious comma splice.

29. D) Graham explained the meaning behind the choices of colors …
This question wants you to ensure that modifiers are clearly positioned next to the nouns they modify. Choices A and C are wrong because they suggest that the person *Graham* is decorated with hundreds of sequins. Choice B is wrong because it suggests that *the meaning* is decorated with hundreds of sequins. Choice D is correct because it makes it clear that *the mask* is the thing with all those glorious sequins.

30. B) damage;
We have two clauses here, *actuaries … have spent* and *they … recommend*, so we need to make sure they're properly joined. Choice A is the despicable comma splice. Choice D is no better because it tries to use the conjunctive adverb *therefore* to connect clauses. *Therefore* (like *however*) is just not strong enough for the task. The relative pronoun *which* in choice C seems like an improvement, but because the noun it modifies, *damage*, is neither the subject nor the object in the relative clause that follows, this is an invalid sentence structure. Choice B works; it appropriately joins the clauses with a semicolon.

31. B) Because
There are two clauses here. Before the comma, we have the subject *sheets* and the two verbs that work for it, *were printed* and *had to be*. After the comma, we have *symbols … were included*. The first task is to get the clauses joined up properly. Choice D is no good because it would create a commas splice. Choice C has a coordinating conjunction, which should appear between the clauses it connects, not before the first clause. Choices A and B work because they give us a subordinating conjunction in front of the first clause, and a comma to separate the first from the second. Next, figure out which conjunction is logically appropriate. The first clause explains the *reason* the symbols were included, so *because* is logically appropriate.

32. D) published,
Before the first comma, there are two clauses, and they're already properly joined with the subordinating conjunction *as*. The clauses are *organization … pioneered* and *it … conducted*. After the comma, we can't have another full clause because this sentence provides no valid way to connect another clause to the first part of the sentence. Choices A and B are out for that reason. Choice C provides just the noun *publication* after the comma, which isn't a valid option either. Choice D works because *published* is a participle. It turns the second half of the sentence into a big participial phrase that modifies the noun *assessment*.

33. B) molecules, a
Choices A and C can be eliminated right away because of the semicolon = period rule. Choice D doesn't work because the stuff after the semicolon cannot stand alone as a complete sentence. Choice B is good because it turns everything after the comma into a big absolute phrase.

34. D) tuberculosis,
Choices A and B don't work because the stuff in front of the semicolon/colon cannot stand alone as a complete sentence. Choice C gives us a comma and a coordinating conjunction, which would be appropriate for connecting two full clauses. But again, the stuff before the comma is not a full clause. Instead, it is a participial phrase—an introductory modifier built on the participle *working*. So choice D works because it joins the phrase to the rest of the sentence with a comma and also puts it next to the noun it properly modifies (the doctor).

35. C) Armstrong takes over manual control and steers the craft to a smoother spot.
Everything in front of the first comma is a big introductory modifier. It's a participial phrase built on the word *seeing*. Who is *seeing* something? It must be *Armstrong*, so he should be the first noun after the comma. Choice B tries to trick you into thinking *Armstrong* is first, but the first noun there is really his *takeover*, which is not what we want.

36. A) NO CHANGE
The sentence is correct as written because the subordinating conjunction *when* at the beginning of the sentence properly joins the stuff before the comma to the clause that follows. Choice D is wrong because the stuff before the semicolon could not stand alone as a complete sentence. Choices B and C introduce illogical and unnecessary conjunctive adverbs.

37. D) issues,
This sentence uses a somewhat unusual structure. There are two things going on here. First, we have a full clause (*women … document*) followed by a comma and an absolute phrase. In the absolute phrase, the noun is *some* and the adjective that modifies it is the participle *gravitating*. That's all correct. Next we have the structure in which you can use a comma to indicate a contrast, a shift, or a distinct pause (see page 78). It's a bit like saying, "She has 25 cats, some large, others small." In this case, the sentence boils down to a contrast between two absolute phrases: "…, some gravitating to …, others focusing on …" That's what choice D gives us. Choices B and C are wrong because we don't have a full sentence after the semicolon. Choice A uses the subordinating conjunction *while*, but the stuff after the conjunction is not a full clause, so that's inappropriate.

38. D) as demonstrated
The word *being* in choice A is just yuck. It appears to be trying to form a participial phrase, which is a violation of the laws of nature. Choice C is the contemptible comma splice. The pronoun *this* in choice B does not have a logical noun to refer to. In choice D, the back half of the sentence becomes a big modifier giving us further information about the situation described in the first half.

39. B) Now referred to as Hubble's
After the comma we have the clause *relationship … allowed*. So we'd better not put another full clause before the comma; otherwise we'll have the villainous comma splice. But that's just what choices A and C do. Choice B works because without a subject, *referred to* becomes a participle , and the first part of the sentence becomes a participial phrase that properly modifies the following noun, *relationship*. Choice D just provides a weird, disconnected noun before the main clause, which is not a valid structure.

40. C) parts,
Choices B and D are no good because the stuff in front of the semicolon cannot stand alone. Choice A gives us a comma and coordinating conjunction, but that's likewise no good because we don't have a full clause before the conjunction. Choice C works because the beginning part of the sentence is an introductory phrase that acts as a big adjective. It is joined to the main clause with a comma, and it is next to the noun it properly modifies, *ceramic components*.

41. C) and
    Before the comma we have the clause *there … are*. After the comma, we have another clause, *experts … predict*. So we need a proper way to join them. Choice D creates the foul comma splice, and choice B is no better because *indeed* is just a conjunctive adverb—useless when it comes to connecting clauses. Choice A is no good because *with* is a preposition, and prepositional phrases can't have subjects and verbs. Choice C gives us a comma and a coordinating conjunction which is a perfect solution.

42. B) Bendire, who
    Choice D is no good because the stuff after the semicolon cannot stand alone. Choice A creates a comma splice, and, well, you know we feel about *them*. Choices B and C both use relative pronouns to join up the clauses. That's a good choice, but since we're talking about a person, we should use *who*, not *which*. Despite his pointy hat, it's not nice to call Mr. Bendire a witch.

43. B) storm, so it wasn't until later that year that the team was
    In the correct version of the sentence, there are three clauses, so of course they have to be appropriately joined. The clauses are *they … were deterred*, *it … wasn't*, and *team … was*. The second and third clauses are properly joined by the relative pronoun *that* in every choice, so we're good there. In choice A, nothing joins the first two clauses but a comma, so we've got the dreadful comma splice. Choice B gives us the coordinating conjunction *so* to go along with the comma, so that fixes the problem. Breaking the sentence into two, as choices C and D do, would also be a fine solution, but both choices create a new problem by dropping the verb *was* from the third clause.

44. B) of which
    We've got two clauses here, so we need to make sure they're correctly joined. The first clause is *Cassini … made*, and the second is *closest pass … was*. Choice A gives us the loathsome comma splice, and choices C and D don't fix the issue. Just dropping the word *pass* or changing it to a pronoun doesn't change the fact that we still have a clause after the comma. Choice B works because now we have the relative pronoun *which* properly connecting the clauses. This is an example of the structure discussed on page 100.

45. D) DELETE the underlined portion.
    There are two clauses here. The first is *programs … may provide*, and the second is *they … do not focus*. Of course they need to be properly joined, and the subordinating conjunction *while* before the first clause has already got it covered. The comma indicates the end of the first clause and the beginning of the second. The coordinating conjunctions in choices A, B, and C give us too many connectors.

46. C) Treaty, which was
    Choice A has problems. If *that* is a noun and the subject of the verb *was based*, then we've got the repulsive comma splice; if it's a relative pronoun, then it shouldn't be preceded by a comma. Choice C gives us the relative pronoun that *should* be preceded by a comma, *which*, so the clauses are properly joined. In choice B, the sentence after the period is a fragment. In choice D, the auxiliary verb *was* has mysteriously disappeared.

47. D) debate, the abundance
    Choices A and C can be axed right away using the semicolon = period rule. In the proper version of the sentence, the phrase *whose potential listing as a federally threatened species has been the subject of legal debate*, is a big relative clause that modifies *bear*. It is properly joined to the rest of the sentence with the relative pronoun *whose*. It is nonessential, so it's surrounded by commas and could be removed from the sentence without affecting the meaning or the grammar. If you do in fact remove it from the sentence, then there is only one clause left (*abundance ... is*), so the coordinating conjunction *and* in choice B is hanging around with nothing to connect.

48. D) skills,
    In choice D, we have one clause (*Judge Beezer ... helped*). It's followed by a comma and then a big participial phrase, which is based on the participle *advising* and modifies the whole situation that comes before. That's a good structure. Choice A introduces the subject *he* and changes the participle into the verb *was advising*, so we've got the odious comma splice. Choice C needs a comma at the very least. And choice B is wrong because it tries to create a relative clause, but the noun it modifies, *skills*, is neither the subject nor the object of the relative clause. That's an invalid structure.

49. A) NO CHANGE
    In the correct version of the sentence, *dunes* and *help prevent* are a subject-verb pair. Between those words, we have the participial phrase *lining the sugar-white sand beaches of the Gulf of Mexico*, which modifies *dunes*. That all works, so there's no reason to mess with it. In choice B, the comma and pronoun *they* take away the verb for the noun *dunes*. In choice C, the relative pronoun *that* hides the verb *help* inside a relative clause. Choice D creates a similar error by hiding the word *help* inside the relative clause kicked off by relative adverb *where*.

50. C) that,
    This sentence becomes easier to understand when you realize that you can remove the entire nonessential phrase *unlike creamware, which was almost exclusively undecorated*. Now we have the simplified structure *one of the reasons ... was X*. We just need a valid structure for *X*. The right answer provides us with this reason: *that pearlware employed ...* It looks like a relative clause because it starts with *that* and contains the subject *pearlware* and the verb *employed*. But instead of modifying a noun, it's acting as a noun itself—it *is* the reason for the popularity. This is something called a **complement clause** because it completes the meaning of the verb *was*. Choice C properly creates the complement clause, and the other choices... don't.

51. C) award-winning Afrobeat musicians begin to enjoy commercial success as well.
    Choices B and D use the highly suspicious word *being* in unjustifiable ways. Choice A is illogical because *bestow* means to present an honor or award. That's not how commercial success works. Choice C contains all the necessary meaning in a concise and grammatical package.

52. B) Although tardigrades are active only when surrounded by a film of water, they ...
    The phrase *tardigrades do their activities* in choice A is more awkward and less concise than *tardigrades are active* in choice B. Choice C uses the conjunction *and*, but it would be better to use a conjunction that indicates a contrast, as *although* does in choice B. In choice D, *which would be in response to* is more awkward and wordy than choice B's *in response to*.

53. C) task:
In choice C, the colon accomplishes everything we need. It tells us that the sentence has set up a thought that needs completion—what exactly *is* the essential task? It provides the completion of the thought—*mapping the seafloor* is the essential task. It links everything together with proper grammar and punctuation. And it gets bonus points for being the shortest choice. The other choices are all some combination of more wordy, less logical, and less grammatical.

54. A) Although there were once gold and iron mining operations in some …
Choice B is redundant; there's no reason to say both *gold and iron mining operations* and *mining operations for gold and iron*. Among other problems, choice C uses the conjunction *and* when it would be better to use a conjunction that indicates a contrast. Choice D puts the modifier *in some Virginia Piedmont parks* too far from the noun it modifies. It should be next to the noun *operations*, but instead it's next to the verb *closed down*, which obscures the intended meaning of the sentence.

55. A) painting, providing
Choice A provides everything we need in the most concise package. The stuff before the comma is a complete sentence, and the stuff after is a participial phrase built on the participle *providing*. The phrase modifies the entire situation that comes before. Choices B and C needlessly repeat the word *versions*, and choice D commits the grammar crime of using *being* as a participle.

56. D) speak, to work for change, and to inspire others
Choice D is the most concise. It creates the parallel list *to speak, to work*, and *to inspire*, and it avoids the grammar mistakes in some of the other choices. In choice A, the stuff after the semicolon cannot stand as a complete sentence. Choice C creates redundancy by repeating the word *compelled*. The word *besides* in choice B is unnecessary, and the comma after *others* has no reason to be there.

57. A) measuring, over the course of several days, operating speed, the speed …
Choice B is redundant; it says *measuring operating speed, … which they measure*. Choice C has some similar redundancy, and the pronoun *it* doesn't have a clear noun to refer to. Choice A might sound a little odd, but it's the best of the bunch, and you can see why by comparing it to choice D. In D, the modifier *known as operating speed* is very far away from the noun it modifies (*speed*). And the modifier *over the course of several days* is also far away from the word it modifies (*measuring*). These problems create an awkward structure and some potentially unclear meanings. In choice A, all the modifiers are next to the words they should properly modify. The prepositional phrase *over the course of several days* is next to *measuring*, and the appositive *the speed that 85 percent of drivers are traveling at or below* is next to the term *operating speed*.

58. C) Unable to read the text of the poem he'd written for the inauguration because …
Choice A seems to suggest that Frost was unable to read one poem while he was in the middle of reciting a different poem, which is illogical. Choice B similarly presents the events in backward chronological order for no good reason. It also switches to a different verb tense: *would recite* instead of *recited*. In choice D, *reading was something he was unable to do* is much wordier than choice C's *unable to read*.

59. D) Studies show that children who learn to play chess have better …
In choice A, *and also with* is awkward and ungrammatical. In choice B, the sentence begins with a long introductory prepositional phrase, but the noun after the comma, *studies*, is not the noun that the phrase logically modifies. Choice C needlessly separates the three benefits of chess into distant parts of the sentence, but choice D puts them in a nice logical and grammatically parallel list.

60. D) chicken, and people use a shocking amount of hot sauce, but
    In choice A, *in light of this* is an illogical fit given the intended meaning of the story. The best way to understand the story is to realize that the author is taken aback by two things that are, if not exactly negative, at least surprising: the weird biscuit size and the hot sauce. But then the author creates a contrast by mentioning two positive things that make it clear why this is the friend's favorite spot: the welcoming atmosphere and the good food. Choice D is the best because it uses *and* to join the first pair of similar things, *and* again to join the second pair of similar things, and *but* between the pairs to show their contrasting nature. Choice D has the added benefit of using all coordinating conjunctions to clearly and properly join up all the clauses.

Practice Question Set: Word Choice   page 152

1. C) into
    This is testing Required Words. The right preposition to go with *convert* is *into*. We say *convert* (something) *into* (something else).

2. B) affected
    This is testing Commonly Confused Words. We want the verb *affect*, not the noun *effect*. And since this sentence uses the passive voice, we need the participle form of the verb: *grassland … can be affected by…*

3. D) When growth is excessive,
    This is testing Style and Tone. *Gets out of hand* and *goes haywire* are too informal. *Occasions of disproportionate multiplication* is too formal. Choice D is just right.

4. D) allowed
    This is testing Vocabulary. When used in this sense, *allowed* means the shape made it possible for the thing to be mounted. The other choices just aren't used in this way.

5. A) NO CHANGE
    This is testing Vocabulary. To *engage in* an activity means to participate or become involved in the activity. The other choices don't have the right definitions or aren't used in a way that fits this situation.

6. B) create
    This is testing Style and Tone. *Bring into being* is too stuffy. *Churn out* is too informal. *Forge* has a weird medieval feel that isn't appropriate for graphic design. *Create* has the right tone.

7. B) upon
    This is testing Required Words. When *confer* is used to mean grant or bestow, the right preposition to go with it is *on* or *upon*. We say *confer* (something) *upon* (someone).

8. D) sites
    This is testing Commonly Confused Words. An internet page is a *website*, or simply a *site*.

9. A) NO CHANGE
    This is testing Commonly Confused Words. His friends told him something positively or confidently to dispel any doubts he might have had. That's the definition of *assure*.

10. B) way to

This is testing Required Words. *To give way to* (something) is a figure of speech that means to be replaced or superseded by that thing. The other choices mess up that figure of speech or propose things we just don't say.

11. B) complications

This is testing Vocabulary. A *complication* is a difficulty or a circumstance that complicates something. The other choices don't have the right definitions or aren't typically used in a way that fits this situation.

12. A) NO CHANGE

This is testing Style and Tone. Choices B and C are too informal, as well as poor logical fits for the situation. The pronoun *it* in choice D is ambiguous and lacks a clear antecedent.

13. B) discount

This is testing Style and Tone as well as Vocabulary. To *discount* a possibility means to regard it as being unworthy of consideration. That's a perfect fit for this situation. *Diminish* doesn't have the right definition, and choices C and D are too informal.

14. C) disclosed

This is testing Vocabulary. To *disclose* means to reveal, or to make secret or new information known. The other choices don't have the right definitions or aren't used in a way that fits this situation.

15. C) respectfully

This is testing Vocabulary. If something is *respectfully received*, it is treated with politeness and civility. In other words, the critics may not have raved about the novel, but they didn't trash it either. The adjective *respectable* means having some merit or importance, but the phrase "respectably received" is almost nonexistent in natural English, probably in part because using the adverb *respectably* to modify the verb *received* seems to suggest that the way the critics received it had some merit, not that the novel had some merit. According to the Oxford dictionary, *respectively* means "separately or individually and in the order already mentioned (used when enumerating two or more items or facts that refer back to a previous statement)." Whether or not you can understand that definition, it's just not the right word here. *Responsibly* is also just the wrong word.

16. C) pales in

This is testing Required Words. *To pale in comparison to* (something) is a figure of speech that means to seem less impressive or important than that thing. The other choices mess up that figure of speech by using the wrong prepositions.

Practice Question Set: Redundancy   page 158

1. D) schools
    The sentence already says *few*, so *a small number*, *not that many*, and *just a handful* are all redundant.

2. D) initial appeal
    First and *initial* are redundant in choice A. Choice B uses an awkward four-word phrase, *in the beginning times*, instead of the concise single word *initial*. In choice C, *usefulness* and *appeal* are redundant.

3. A) NO CHANGE
    By definition, a vaccine provides immunity against disease, so choice B provides no new information. *Protective container* is redundant in C when the sentence already says *safely storing*. And we already know we're talking about a refrigerator, so there's no need for D to tell us it will keep things cold.

4. A) NO CHANGE
    In choice B, *appreciate* and *value* mean the same thing. In choice C, *appreciative* and *grateful* mean the same thing. And choice D uses seven words to do the job of one.

5. C) vehicle lanes
    Here's a case in which the shortest answer is **too short**. It leaves out some necessary information. In the passage, the main idea is that one type of lane has been converted to a different type of lane. It's important to be specific about the contrasting types. In choice D, it's not clear what *kind* of lane is being removed, so we end up with a confusing sentence that says they're removing lanes and replacing them with lanes. Choices A and B say the same thing as C but in much wordier ways.

6. D) DELETE the underlined portion and end the sentence with a period.
    The sentence already says artists have higher levels of education, so A is redundant. The sentence already says that artists are entrepreneurial, so B is redundant. And the sentence already says this information is coming from the report, so C is redundant.

7. B) needs,
    The sentence already tells us about the sensors, about the fact that they move across the field, and about the water needs. So choices A, C, and D are repetitive.

8. B) uncommon,
    Uncommon, *unusual*, and *rare* all mean the same thing. Just one is enough.

9. C) test masses separated by a distance
    Here's another case in which the shortest answer is **too short**. After the underlined portion, the sentence refers to *that distance*. If you pick choice D, it becomes unclear what distance we're talking about. Choice C explains it. In choice A, *separation* and *gap* are repetitive, and *on either side of* is a longer way of saying *separated by*. Choice B is redundant because it's already clear that we're discussing how the measurement is done.

10. C) destinations.
    Choice A is redundant because the sentence already says the counties are *attracting retirees*. The sentence already says *rural*, so B is repetitive. And the sentence already says *scenic*, so D is redundant.

11. A) NO CHANGE
    Miniature, minute and *small-scale* all mean the same thing, so you only need one of those. And *frozen-over* is unnecessary when the sentence already says *icy*.

12. C) spreading
    Spreading, expanding, enlarging, and *increasing* all get at the same idea. One is all you need.

Practice Question Set: Intros, Transitions & Conclusions   page 170

1. C) For example,
   Before the transition word, we get a general statement: "some occupations have higher employment levels in smaller areas." After the transition word, we learn about a couple of specific instances of the same idea. In other words, we're getting some examples, so *for example* is appropriate.

2. B) In fact,
   Before the transition word, we learn that "not all bacteria present in food products are harmful." The stuff after the transition word amplifies that idea—not only are the bacteria not harmful, they actually are essential for making some foods delicious and safe. To amplify or reinforce an idea, *in fact* is a good choice.

3. D) In addition,
   Before the transition word, we learn about some of the growing risks from forest fires. After the transition word, we learn about even more growing risks. The author is adding to the list of dangers, so *in addition* is a good choice.

4. C) though,
   This one is a little tricky because the transition word is buried in the middle of the second sentence. But you actually want a word that helps clarify the relationship between the first sentence and the second sentence. You can imagine moving the transition word to the spot at the beginning of the second sentence. In the first sentence we learn that it's easy for people to name classical musicians from the past. In the second sentence we learn that it's hard for them to name classical musicians from modern times. That's a contrast, so a contrast word like *though* is a good fit.

5. D) DELETE the underlined portion.
   All the choices are true transitions words (not conjunctions or other things related to sentence structure), so before you even read the sentence, you should be strongly considering the option to go naked. It's likely you don't need a transition word at all. And that is in fact the case here. The passage already has a good phrase in this spot that explains the relationship between the first sentence and the second: *with this problem in mind*. Choices A, B, and C are unnecessary or illogical.

6. B) For these reasons,
   The sentences before the transition spot give a list of ways the atmosphere can negatively affect images. After the transition spot, we learn about the astronomers' response to those problems: put a telescope above the atmosphere. Because the list of problems helps us understand why they want a telescope up there, *for these reasons* is a good logical fit.

7. C) Instead,
    Before the transition, we learn what Lansing did not do. After the transition we learn what she did do. That's a contrast, so *instead* is a good choice. You might have been tempted by choice D, which also has a flavor of contrast, but *in spite of* is more appropriate in a situation where you want to say "in contrast to what you might have guessed" or "without being affected by the particular factor just mentioned." That's not exactly the right fit here.

8. A) NO CHANGE
    The first sentence tells us about a phenomenon: housing prices doubled. The second sentence gives us one reason for why that happened: gains in employment and income. After the transition, the third sentence gives us an additional reason why housing prices rose: low interest rates and wider availability of loans. Because we're adding another reason to the list, *furthermore* is appropriate.

9. A) NO CHANGE
    Johannes Gutenberg is the best known of the early printers. Why? The reason for his fame is his innovative moveable type. We're learning the cause of something, so *because of* makes sense.

10. D) DELETE the underlined portion.
    Just like in #5, all the choices are true transitions words and phrases, so before you even read the sentence, you should be thinking the right answer is likely to be DELETE. In this case, the second sentence is neither providing an example of an idea from the first sentence nor setting up a contrast, so choices A, B, and C are all illogical.

11. D) however,
    In the first sentence, we learn that she continued her life as a philanthropist and a society woman. In the second sentence, we find out that she started to build a second life—one that sounds very different from the first! That's a contrast, so *however* is a good choice.

12. B) Indeed,
    Before the transition, we get a general fact: this practice has found its way onto some golf courses. After the transition, the passage gets more specific and amplifies that same idea: not just some golf courses, but a full 42 percent of them. To reinforce or amplify an idea, *in fact* is makes the most sense.

13. C) on the other hand,
    Before the transition, we learn that April Fools' Day pranks are quick and funny. After the transition, we see that hoaxes are long-term and intended to deceive. That's pretty different! A contrast phrase such as *on the other hand* makes the most sense.

14. A) NO CHANGE
    Even though the transition word is in the middle of the second sentence, it should be clarifying the relationship between the first sentence and the second. So what's the relationship? The *reason* she decided to build a career in Europe is that she was unable to have an active career in the US at that time. Because we're learning the cause of something, *therefore* is the most logical fit.

15. A) NO CHANGE
    There's a bunch of junk in space. One place you can find it is in the outer atmosphere (2nd sentence). That's a problem for satellites (3rd sentence). In the 4th sentence we learn about *another* place you can find space junk: the moon and other planets. That's not a contrast or an example. Instead, it's an addition to the list of spots you can find this pollution. So *moreover* is appropriate.

16. C)   Everything changed dramatically when Fitzgerald entered the …
We need the best transition from the previous paragraph, so the right answer should have some connection to both the previous paragraph and the information that follows. When choice C says "everything changed dramatically," it provides a good contrast between her career as a dancer in the first paragraph, and her transition to a singer in the second paragraph. Choice C also has the added bonus of explaining the Amateur Night competition at the Apollo Theater, which is helpful in understanding the following sentence. The biggest problem with choices A, B, and D is that they don't even mention Fitzgerald, so they don't have a strong connection to the previous paragraph.

17. B)   A room was set aside on the third floor of the Howlands' Summer Street residence …
How would you summarize the information in the passage? We learn all about how Esther Howland and her associates created the cards "during the early years of her business." Choice B does a good job a touching on all these points. Choice A is about the modern greeting card industry; it has nothing to do with Howland. Choice C is wrong because Howland didn't "develop mass production." She just had some friends help her make the cards. Furthermore, choice C makes it seem like the paragraph is going to be about mass production instead of Esther's card business. In choice D, her birthplace and her father's job have nothing to do with the story.

18. C)   It can be easy to get caught up in the feeling that your state's politics are …
The main idea of the paragraph is captured by the first sentence: we can reinforce the idea that some things may not be quite so important after all by imagining them from far away. The structure of the final sentence is also important. We need an *idea* that *can be tempered by* adopting a broader perspective (*tempered* in this sense means moderated or reduced). A good choice would be the idea that something up close is very significant. That's exactly what choice C gives us.

19. D)   The concept of One Health is not really new,
Choice A isn't a good fit because the paragraph never mentions disease. Choice B is the exact opposite of what we want, because the idea of interdependence is not something that we're "just beginning to see." Choice C doesn't work because the paragraph has nothing to do with network theory and artificial intelligence. Choice D works: One Health is all about the interconnections of human and animal health with environmental health, and people were already talking about those ideas back in the 19th century and 2,500 years ago. The idea is not new.

20. A)   NO CHANGE
We're looking for the best transition from the previous paragraph, so the right answer should link to both the preceding information and the stuff that follows. Choice A does both. It begins by saying, "In another example of culinary diplomacy." Did the previous paragraph really provide examples of culinary diplomacy? Sure did. Does this paragraph really give another one? Sure does. Another important factor is that the next sentence says he "he displayed his expertise." What expertise are we talking about, exactly? Only choice A provides a good answer—it's his expertise at using chopsticks.

21. B)   it's hard to say whether self-help books help anyone.
We need to know the contents of the paragraph so we can set it up. What's in there? First, self-help books may not be effective. Second, most people don't read them. Finally, any benefit might come just from the act of buying the book, not from the book itself. Sounds like the books are not really helping anyone.

22. B)   How do we know when spring is here?
The main topic of the paragraph is all about the arrival of spring. The topic in choice A is only mentioned in one sentence. The southern hemisphere is never mentioned, and the northern hemisphere only once, so choice C is too narrow. And daylight saving time is never mentioned, so choice D is out of scope.

23. D)   depends in large part on the overall state of the economy:
What do we learn from the paragraph? When the economy is good, people buy more art; when it is bad, they buy less. That sounds like a predictable and well-understood relationship, so choice A is the opposite of what we want. Digital tools are never mentioned, so B is out. In C, the curators and investors are mentioned, but the paragraph never says that trends drive demand—in fact, it never mentions trends at all. Choice D works: the economy makes a big difference.

24. C)   It seems that you don't have to be an Olympian to reap the benefit of listening …
You don't want to introduce a completely new topic in a conclusion. Caffeine was never mentioned, so choice A is out. Surgery was never mentioned, so choice D is out. Choice B introduces a random detail—the paragraph's main focus is music, not Karageorghis, and certainly not some random job he had many years ago. Choice C is perfect. It sticks to the main topic of the benefits of music, and the idea that "you don't have to be an Olympian" ties back both to the fact that Olympic athletes were mentioned and to the idea that it helps with low-to-moderate-intensity exercise.

25. A)   NO CHANGE
The paragraph does a good job of explaining why so many barns are red—we learn where the red color came from in the first place, and we learn why people stuck with it (tradition and cost). There is no discussion of whether it's the best choice, and there's no pinpointing of the first red barn. It's true that there is some discussion of chemical compounds, but there is no deep explanation of underlying chemistry, and the passage is not about red objects in general, so choice D is not a good fit.

26. D)   For decades, the tintype was the most likely result of such a transaction,
The most important reason why D is right comes between the parentheses in the next sentence. Without explaining that we're talking about the *tintype* in particular, that parenthetical does not make much sense. D also makes sense with the second half of the sentence: the fact that the tintype could be created easily explains why it was the most widespread type of portrait. In choice A, just because something is easy to make does not explain why someone would want it. The second paragraph doesn't discuss treasured possessions or pictures of kids, so choices B and C don't connect to the information in the paragraph.

27. A)   NO CHANGE
Choice A is a good transition because it both connects to the previous paragraph and leads into the information that follows. The album has aesthetic significance because the vocalizations have beauty and complexity. It has political significance because it helped turn the tide of US public opinion against whaling. And choice A creates a logical sentence structure: *in addition* to this kind of value, it *also* has another kind of value. Choices B and C introduce topics that have no connection to the previous paragraph. Choice D is somewhat related, but it creates an awkward sentence structure. Pairing *despite* with *also* is weird.

28. A) NO CHANGE
Be sure to notice what the question stem asks for. You have to set up the information provided in the rest of the sentence. What's in the rest of the sentence? We have two competing phenomena: the story as it is presented and the hidden truth. Choice A sets that up perfectly by saying the film is more than just one thing. Choices B, C, and D don't really connect to the information that follows.

29. B) Probing the shape of the electron's charge has far-reaching implications …
Make sure you're paying attention to "the next point," as the question stem asks you to do. What is that point exactly? The next sentence says the experiment was done with a *small team* ("only" a dozen researchers) with a *small apparatus* (it fits in a room, unlike particle accelerators, which can stretch for miles). Choice B is a perfect fit because it introduces the idea of *an experiment of modest size*.

30. C) "Our result tells the scientific community that we need to seriously rethink …
This question takes some work because you have to figure out the "key implication of the study." For big-picture questions, you can often get some help from the title of the passage. Here, it's "Electrons Get Around." What's that supposed to mean? The whole experiment is aimed at figuring out whether the electron is round or squashed. A round shape would be consistent with the Standard Model theory. A squashed shape is predicted by the alternative theories. So what was the ultimate finding of the experiment, and what does it mean? The result is stated at the end of the second paragraph: the researchers "found that the sphere appeared to be perfectly round." That's a win for the Standard Model and a problem for the alternative theories. Choice C perfectly addresses this implication.

Drill: Specific Tasks   page 181

1. (C) 68 miles west of the Florida Keys.

2. (B) including bottles, bike wheels and folk art.

3. (A) balked at

4. (C) may go 400 years between precipitation events.

Practice Question Set: Specific Tasks   page 184

1. C) It was not until ten years later that Ashley Chontos was able to reanalyze …
The specific task here is to emphasize the amount of time Kepler-1658b was believed not to be a planet. Choice C gets the job done. That period of time was ten years. In choices A and D, we get vague and nonspecific phrases like *quite a while* and *some time passed*. Choice B might seem tempting, but it never tells us when astronomers realized Kepler-1658b is actually a planet, so we don't know how long it was thought not to be one.

2. B) (which forms a cool skin on the exterior of the molten glass blob)
Your job is to provide an example that is most similar to the other example. So what does the other example do? It tells us what the punty tool *accomplishes* within the context of glassblowing. That's what choice B does too. Choice A tells us what the marver is made of, choice C explains how it must be maintained, and choice D tells us where it can be put. Not the same.

3. C) more sophisticated techniques using
    Focus on completing the contrast with the earlier part of the sentence. We first hear about *rudimentary mechanical* techniques. What could be a better contrast than *sophisticated electrical* techniques?

4. A) NO CHANGE
    Your task is to show possibility, not fact. *Conclusive, confirm,* and *proof* are all very absolute words that leave no room for doubt. But *provide evidence* in choice A allows for some uncertainty, so that's what you want.

5. D) sales.
    The best way to maintain a paragraph's focus is to not go off on random tangents. You don't want to introduce unrelated information that "blurs the focus," as the SAT likes to say. But choices A, B, and C do exactly that. It's best to skip all that junk and just go with choice D.

6. A) NO CHANGE
    There are lots of things that the students could possibly study, but the question here wants you to pick a choice that relates to *biological questions*. In choice A, *microscopic life forms* fits the bill. The other choices mention structures, electronics, or novel research techniques, but those don't address biological questions.

7. A) NO CHANGE
    This specific task is a little less specific than others, because it's up to you to figure out what makes a supporting detail "relevant." So what is this sentence all about? It explains what the performance consists of and the details of how the team creates it. Choice A is definitely relevant because it gives us a detail about the logistics of the performance. Crucially, it also adds new information—notice that the question stem asks you to *add* a detail. Choice B fails in this regard because it just says the sounds were created by a computer. That's not really new information because the sentence already says the sounds are electronic. Choice D is similar because you already know that the EEG headset monitors her brain signals. Obviously you can't use an EEG headset before EEG technology is invented. Choice C doesn't add any new information either. It just says uninformed people won't know what's going on—that's pretty much the definition of uninformed, so yeah.

8. D) asserts
    Which choice is the most emphatic? Not *hints* or *supposes*. They're too indirect or uncertain. *Says* is neutral. To *assert* is to state a belief confidently and forcefully. That's our winner.

9. C) and thus no distortion of the image.
    You have to do some detective work to find the "contrast set up in the paragraph." In this case, it's all about comparing traditional glass mirrors with polished metal mirrors. One thing we learn about glass mirrors is that they "can lead to changes in the image." So a great way to complete the contrast is to say that polished metal mirrors don't lead to changes in the image. That's what choice C gives us, and you can feel confident about it because the rest of the sentence helps explain why there is no distortion.

10. B) however, much of the rainfall runs off to the ocean in streams or returns to …
    At first, it sounds like ground water is ample, since we learn that the amount pumped is just
    3 percent of annual rainfall. Plenty of rain, so plenty of ground water. But your task is to refute the
    idea that it's plentiful. Choice A makes groundwater sound plentiful because it can provide almost
    all the drinking water needed. Choice C is irrelevant because salinity doesn't tell you anything
    about quantity. In choice D, if people have figured out ways to use less water, then perhaps there is
    even more extra ground water to go around. But choice B works because it tells us there is not so
    much extra rain water after all. If much of the rainfall escapes, then perhaps there is not as much
    ground water as you might think.

11. A) NO CHANGE
    Your first job is to figure out the sentence pattern already established. In the first two sentences, we
    start with a noun (*a crosswalk, a garden*). Next comes a verb in the passive voice (*is redesigned, is
    installed*). After that comes an infinitive (*to incorporate, to add*). Now it's your job to maintain that
    pattern in the third sentence. Choice A is a perfect match.

12. C) roles in mathematical modeling and analysis will become more viable and lucrative.
    Stay focused on your task. You have address employment opportunities for mathematicians, so
    choice A is out because it only talks about facility construction. Same with choice D. Security risks
    don't have any direct connection to employment opportunities. Choice B could be tempting, but
    it's wrong because you also need to "reinforce the paragraph's claim." What's the claim exactly? The
    paragraph says we should expect a "continued increase in demand for mathematicians." But choice
    B makes it sound as if there will be *less* demand for mathematicians, so that's not what you want.
    Choice C gets it right. Jobs in math will be more viable and lucrative.

13. B) material prepared by his writers.
    The two examples already in the sentence tell us some of the sources from which Berle collected
    jokes. So we need to add a third source of jokes for his collection. Choice A tells us what the jokes
    are about but not where they're from. Choice C is about songs, not jokes. Choice D is about the
    collection itself, not a source of material for the collection. Choice B is what we want. Another
    place the jokes came from was Berle's writers.

14. B) but he more than once enthused over "a new world with its own new music," …
    The paragraph is about cultural diplomacy and creating musical ties between the US and Latin
    American countries. Choice B is the most directly related to this topic. If Copland believed that the
    new world had its own new music, then his vision perfectly aligned with the idea that the
    Americas are linked by shared historical and cultural experiences. Choices B and D are more about
    Copland and not so much about the ties between Latin America and the US. In choice C, political
    parties are off topic.

15. D) Despite his repeated attempts,
    Your job is to best emphasize the father's desire to get her interested. Choices B and C have nothing
    to do with her father's efforts. Choice A is not terrible because we learn that he *tried*, but choice D
    is better because *repeated attempts* gives us more emphasis.

16. D) Some researchers suggest that having dogs and cats can protect against …
    Your task: provide an additional example of a benefit that pets may provide. Choice A gives us
    more dogs but no benefit. Choice B gives us longer pet lives but no benefit. Choice C is about
    veterinary medicine, not pets or their benefits. Choice D is the best because protection against
    allergies is a benefit for pet owners.

17. C) The ash layers protected the site from wind erosion.
All the choices provide interesting and relevant details, but only one accomplishes the task you've been given. You need to show that the ash may have aided archaeological studies. Choice C gets it done. If the ash protected the site from wind erosion, then the tools and artifacts would have been better preserved for the archaeologists to find.

18. C) her Jenny airplane's engine unexpectedly stalled, and
Your job is to get specific about how the crash occurred. Choice C works because it tells us the airplane's engine unexpectedly stalled, which is more specific that choice A. Choice B tells us when it happened but not how, and choice D has nothing to do with the crash.

19. D) grew
What does the paragraph tell us about fire-related research has changed? In the past, there was little interest in social science research. There were just a few studies on it, while the primary focus was elsewhere (the physical and ecological aspects). However, that has changed. So we should expect that there is now *more* interest in understanding relevant social dynamics. *Grew* is a good fit. Choices A and C go in the wrong direction. Choice B doesn't quite fit because for interest to be *renewed*, we would need it to be high, then low, and then high again. That doesn't match what the paragraph says.

20. C) not unintentionally—
You have to establish that he *wanted* them all to be the same. So it should not be a surprise or ironic that they followed the same specifications. Choice B makes it sounds like it was an unplanned situation. But choice C gets the job done because *not unintentionally* is just a fancier way of saying *intentionally*. He did it on purpose.

Drill: Hooking up Sentences   page 192

Written responses will vary.

1. [4], [2], [1], [3]

2. Sentence 4 introduces the topic, so it belongs first. And it introduces the uncertainty as to what role the telephone would play. Sentence 2 talks about the first role the telephone played (using *initially*), so it hooks up well to sentence 4.

3. Sentence 2 introduces the Hello Girls, who then appear in the next two sentences. That's one hook that puts sentence 2 before sentence 1. Another hook is that sentence 1 begins with *but soon*, which is a nice transition to follow the *initially* at the beginning of sentence 2. It shows that we're moving to a new role for the technology and the Hello Girls.

4. Once sentence 1 introduces the idea that Hello Girls are now on the firing lines, taking a more active role in the fighting, we get sentence 3, which hooks in by elaborating on the details of that role.

5. [3], [2], [4], [1]

6. Sentences 2 and 3 both talk about the earliest part of the chronology, but sentence 3 should be first. It introduces *Frankenstein* by telling us the author and

telling us that it's a novel. Sentence 2 just refers to it by name. Furthermore, sentence 2 tells us what happened *after* publication—the monster became a well-known figure. Sentence 3 seems to be just a snapshot of the moment of publication itself.

7. First, the dates match up. Sentence 2 refers to the 1800s, while sentence 4 refers to 1899. Another hook is the word *but*, indicating a contrast, and indeed there is a contrast between these two sentences. In sentence 2, the monster is known as Dr. Frankenstein's monster, but in sentence 4, the monster himself was becoming known as Frankenstein.

8. Again, the chronology works. Now in sentence 1 we're talking about early cinema, which would have been around the beginning of the twentieth century. So it belongs after sentence 4. We're also taking the idea from sentence 4 (that the monster is Frankenstein) and "solidifying" it.

9. [1], [4], [3], [2]

10. A big part of this exercise is chronological order. This event comes first: John Roebling proposed the bridge. We also get a nice introduction of the man: we get his full name along with his title in sentence 1. In sentence 4, he's just called *Roebling*. The word *but* also creates a logical transition between the contrasting sentences. First he was denounced. But he proceeded anyway.

11. Sentence 3 moves on to the next chronological step, so the word *then* is an appropriate hook. It also makes sense in the sequence of events. After he decides to move forward with the project (sentence 4), he next surveys the new bridge (sentence 3).

12. Sentence 2 makes sense chronologically after sentence 3. After the father's death, the son is appointed chief engineer. Also, after the surveying step, we now have the builders weaving the great wire cables.

13. [2], [3], [1], [4]

14. The phrase *one such pathogen* in sentence 3 is the main hook. Sentence 2 introduces the idea of serious diseases that can be transmitted by mosquitos. The phrase one such pathogen makes reference to that idea, so sentence 3 must follow sentence 2. Sentence 3 also introduces the idea of the Zika virus, so it must come before the remaining sentences, which refer to the virus.

15. There are two main reasons sentence 1 must follow sentence 3. First, sentence 3 introduces the year 2016, and sentence 1 continues the discussion of that year by talking about the spring. Second, sentence 1 says "the virus," so we need to have introduced it first, which sentence 3 does.

16. Sentence 4 must follow sentence 1 because sentence 1 introduces Brazil, and sentence 4 makes reference to "that country."

Practice Question Set: Organization   page 196

1. B)   after sentence 1.
   The word *they* in sentence 4 refers to precious metals, which are mentioned in sentence 1. That's one hook. Another hook is the *irony* mentioned in sentence 4. In sentence 1, we see that precious metals are used in traditional money (coins). So the fact that precious metals are also important for something that's supposed to be a departure from traditional money is indeed ironic. It's most logical to put sentence 4 here so that we can understand the irony.

2. A)   sentence 2.
   The added sentence introduces the idea of a mixed reaction. It makes sense to first bring up the idea of a mixed reaction and to then to explain the various opinions. So where do we find the ambivalence? Sentences 3 and 4 give us the mixed reaction. Sentence 3 tells us a negative view, and sentence 4 discusses some positives. So the new sentence should go before sentence 3 (after sentence 2).

3. C)   after sentence 1.
   The hook here is the phrase in sentence 7 *such epic matters*. What are the epic matters exactly? The answer is in sentence 1: maps can be a matter of life and death, and bad maps can spell disaster. The hook in sentence 7 makes the most sense if you place it after sentence 1. In that position, it also hooks in well to the word *however* in sentence 2. Crime mapping is not about life and death; *however*, it is still an important scientific activity.

4. A)   where it is now.
   The hooks here are the *initial expectation* set up in sentence 3, and the contrast in sentence 5 that says the actual discovery didn't follow expectations. So logically, sentence 5 definitely belongs after sentence 3. We shouldn't separate sentence 3 and 4 (not that you have the option) because sentence 4 continues the discussion of what the initial expectation introduced in sentence 3.

5. B)   after sentence 1.
   One hook is the word *inspired* in sentence 7. What was she inspired by? It was the publicly displayed poem in the subway, mentioned in sentence 1. Another hook is that sentence 1 talks about poetry in London, and sentence 7 wonders whether it could be similar in the US. The contrast makes sense there. Yet another hook comes in sentence 2: Kiepper was simultaneously "likewise impressed." It doesn't make sense to use the word *likewise* unless you have already given an example of someone being impressed. That's what the word *inspired* does in sentence 7, so we want sentence 7 before sentence 2.

6. C)   after sentence 4.
   The biggest hook is that sentence 5 mentions *these officials*. This phrase doesn't make sense until we introduce the officials. The officials show up in sentence 7: they are the water managers. So sentence 7 certainly must be placed before sentence 5. Choices B and C are possibilities there. However, choice B is wrong because it would split up sentences 3 and 4. Those two sentences should be hooked together because sentence 3 mentions some threats to wildlife, pets, and humans. Then sentence 4 mentions *such threats*. Putting sentence 7 after sentence 4 also puts *water managers* and *these officials* as close as possible, so that's the best choice.

7. B) after sentence 3.

One hook is that sentence 2 mentions *the study* before any study has been mentioned. Sentence 3 introduces us to the study, so sentence 2 certainly belongs somewhere after sentence 3. Choice A is out. You should also notice that sentence 4–6 belong together because they tell the little story of the manager and the whiteboard. There is no reason to break up the story, so choice C is out. Finally, does sentence 2 belong before or after the story? There are two hooks that show it belongs after sentence 3. The first is the word *furthermore* in sentence 2. Sentence 3 gives a list of positives found by the study (improved morale, etc.), and sentence 2 gives some more (low cost). So *furthermore* makes sense there. The other hook is the phrase *for example* in sentence 4. Sentence 2 tells us that many accommodations are cheap, and sentences 4–6 give us an example of a cheap accommodation. The example belongs after the general statement.

8. C) after sentence 2.

Choice B is no good because it would mean we're talking about clutches before sentence 2 has a chance to explain what a clutch is. One important hook to notice is the phrase *those eggs* in sentence 4—which eggs are those? It must be the typical two eggs in the first clutch laid. Since the first clutch is discussed in sentence 2, it makes the most sense to put sentence 4 after sentence 2. Putting sentence 4 in that place also helps sentence 3 make more sense because now we can understand why the scientists removed eggs from the nests and how that would have led to an increase in the total number of eggs.

9. D) after sentence 5.

The biggest hook is a pair of phrases: sentence 5 says *it was important*, and sentence 3 says *it was also critical*. They're both talking about significant features of the radio program, so it only makes sense to put sentence 3 after sentence 5 so it can continue the list of important things.

10. C) after sentence 5.

Sentence 3 mentions *this dynamic*, so we need to make sure that phrase refers to something logical. The best thing to hook it up to is the idea in sentence 5 that creative talent often migrates to places with arts "hot spots." This is right on target for recruiters who are seeking ways to attract new skilled workers. Set up an arts hot spot, and just watch the creative talent roll into town!

11. C) after sentence 4.

There are two major hooks to notice. The first is where the new sentence says *this is especially true*. *What* is especially true? The most logical answer is the issue discussed in sentence 4: problems with barriers when heading downstream. It's especially relevant for eels because eels head out to sea for spawning. So we need to place the new sentence after sentence 4. The other big hook is where sentence 5 says *this species*. The only species mentioned by name is the eel, which appears in the new sentence, so we need the new sentence to come before sentence 5.

12. B) placed before sentence 1.

Two hooks in sentence 1 help make it clear that sentence 2 belongs before sentence 1. The first is that sentence 1 refers to the photographer as just *Austen*. It makes more sense to give us her full name (*Alice Austen* in sentence 2) before we start referring to her by just her last name. Second, it makes sense to explain what place we're talking about (*the house* in sentence 2) before we refer to it as *there* in sentence 1.

13. A) Before sentence 1

The new sentence raises a question: if the artists are not the only ones who benefit from the program, *who else* benefits? The answer comes in the first sentence of this paragraph: the company also benefits because it gets the opportunity to learn new techniques, processes, and possibilities. So the most logical place for the new sentence in before sentence 1. The new sentence functions as a transition from the previous paragraph (which presumably discusses benefits to the artists) to this one.

14. B) before sentence 1.

The phrase *for example* in sentence 1 should stick out. What are these examples of exactly? The paragraph is most logical if you put sentence 3 before sentence 1. Sentence 3 tells us that for insects, navigating the environment is all about odor. Sentence 1 gives us some particular examples of this general phenomenon: butterflies and mosquitoes use smell in specific important ways.

15. B) after sentence 2.

The paragraph starts off talking about automakers but ends up talking about genetic variations in bacteria. Clearly, some kind of transition is necessary to help relate the two topics. The transition is provided by the new sentence when it says *the same is true*. Something about car manufacturing also happens with bacteria, and the most logical reference is to the idea that no two are exactly alike, despite the effort to make perfect duplicates. Thus the new sentence makes the most sense after sentence 2.

16. C) after sentence 4.

Between sentences 4 and 5 is a great place for the new sentence. In sentence 4, we learn about one question the discovery can help answer. In the new sentence, we learn that the discovery can *also* answer another question about Mars's climate history. The word also is a good hook. Another hook is that the new sentence introduces the idea of climate history, and then sentence 5 gets more specific about exactly that same topic.

17. A) where it is now.

Sentence 3 refers to *these factors*, and the best place to say *these factors* is right after a long list of interacting factors. That's what sentence 2 gives us, so just leave sentence 3 where it is.

18. D) DELETED from the paragraph.

This paragraph is all about M&T Bank Stadium and its aesthetic design elements. So the distance between this stadium and some other unrelated stadium is pretty irrelevant. The sentence doesn't hook in to any other sentence in the paragraph, so it's best to get rid of it.

19. C) after sentence 4.

Notice how sentences 1 and 5 will hook together perfectly if you put them next to each other. Sentence 1 tells us that it's impossible to accurately simulate a hurricane eyewall penetration. It makes sense to follow up that idea by saying that *doing it* (penetrating the hurricane eyewall) in the aircraft in a storm is the *only way* (because it cannot be simulated) to experience … all those things brought on by plowing through a wall of wind and rain.

20. D) after sentence 3.

Sentence 3 is the place where the idea of *directed attention* is introduced and defined. Sentence 3 tells us it that directed attention is another name for voluntary attention. Since sentence 5 also uses the term *directed attention*, it should appear after sentence 3. Sentence 5 also makes sense just before sentence 4 because in sentence 5 directed attention becomes *overtaxed*, and then in sentence 4 it is allowed to *recover*.

Drill: Evaluating Reasons   page 210

1. False
    This sentence doesn't give any details about a study or a methodology.

2. False
    Just because something is becoming more popular in the US, that doesn't give us any information about how popular it is or isn't in Japan. So this sentence can't undermine any claim about popularity in Japan.

3. True
    If there are lots of hostels in lots of locations, that supports the idea that they're widespread.

4. True
    If the paragraph really is a discussion about the employability of linguistics majors, then this sentence certainly represents a digression. It has nothing to do with job prospects or people who are currently graduating. It instead talks about something from a long time ago.

5. False
    This sentence just tells us about people in general at the time and how they felt about laundry. It has nothing to do with the specific person of Tierney, nor her planning abilities. Thus it can't undermine any argument on that topic.

6. True
    The word *additionally* makes this look like a "further example." It certainly has to do with "supply chains," because it's talking about manufacturing facilities. And it shows that "reorganizing" them (by, for example, opening a new facility) "presents difficulties," because of the billions of dollars in costs.

Practice Question Set: Adding or Removing Information   page 212

1. A) Yes, because it elaborates on the information presented in the preceding sentence.
    The reason given in choice B is false because the following sentence does not elaborate on the idea that their possessions were scattered by sales and auctions. The reasons given in choices C and D are also false because the information in the new sentence is related to the passage and relevant to the discussion at this point. Choice A is right because in the previous sentence we learn about one factor that made it challenging to understand the working relationship between Respighi and Diaghilev, and the new sentence gives us additional information on the same topic.

2. C) No, because it distracts from the paragraph's discussion of the types of damage that ...
    The reason given in choice A is false because the previous sentence does not make a general claim; it's already pretty specific itself, and the proposed new sentence doesn't provide a supporting detail for the claim that the transmitters caught on fire. The reason given in choice B is also false because the idea that France was an early adopter of the telegraph tells us nothing about how solar flares occur. Choice C works because the discussion in the paragraph really is about the types of damage that solar flares can cause, and the proposed sentence really does distract from that discussion. Choice D gives us a reason that is true but irrelevant. There is no reason the paragraph *should* explain what led France to invest in telegraph technology because that's way off topic.

3. A) Kept, because it provides relevant insight into Forinash's motivations.
    The reason given in choice A is definitely true because it shows that Forinash was motivated by the challenges facing the community, and that's a reasonable thing for the paragraph to do at this point. The reason given in B is false because the underlined portion refers to Forinash's motivations, not to the factors that led to Green River's problems. The reasons given in choices C and D are false because the whole *despite / because of* dynamic is not a contradiction or a sign of unclear reasoning. It just means that Forinash saw the problems as a reason to go to Green River, not a reason to avoid it.

4. C) Deleted, because it distracts from the paragraph's focus on animal enrichment devices.
    Choice A doesn't give us a good reason because the paragraph's main discussion is not about the waste reduction initiative. Instead, the focus is on how the partnership between firefighters and Hose2Habitat led to the creation of animal enrichment devices. Choice B gives a false reason because it's unlikely that anyone would object to the partnership by saying it didn't completely eliminate the fire station's waste. No one would expect it to do that. The reason given by choice D is true but irrelevant. There's no reason the paragraph should be explaining the unused waste because that's way off topic. Choice C is true and relevant. The underlined sentence truly does distract from the main discussion.

5. D) No, because it weakens the focus by diverging from the paragraph's main discussion.
    Choice A gives a false reason because the discussion that follows never even mentions fair-market value. The reason in choice B is also false because the proposed addition doesn't mention cooperatives and their goals; it only defines a term. Choice C's reason is also false because the paragraph never mentions cooperative employees, so they're certainly not the focus of the discussion. Choice D is accurate and gives a good reason not to make the addition.

6. D) Deleted, because it interrupts the discussion of Messinger's use of taxonomy.
    Choice A gives a false reason. If the practice has been going on for hundreds of years, that would *reinforce* the idea that it's not new, not *counter* it. Choice B's reason is false because the paragraph doesn't contain a comparison between modern and historical taxonomic methods. The reason in Choice C is false because there is no rule that says we're not allowed to reference the past in a paragraph about modern procedures. In fact, this paragraph already mentioned the idea that the practice is not new, and discussed "traditions" and old stories. Choice D is true because both the sentence before and the sentence after the underlined sentence are about Messinger's use of taxonomy. So the underlined sentence really does create an interruption, and that's a good reason to delete it.

7. D) No, because it diverges from the paragraph's discussion of technological progress.
The reason in choice B is false—even if political circumstances are different, that doesn't tell us anything about where people are getting the email addresses. The reason in choice C is way off base because there is no information about international relations in the passage. Choices A and D are the ones that deserve a closer look. To decide between them, you have to figure out what the main focus of the discussion is. Is it that much has changed since 1998? Or is it technological progress? Every change mentioned is within the realm of technological progress, and the last sentence isn't really about making a comparison to 1998, so it's more accurate to say that the discussion is about technological progress. That makes D a better answer.

8. A) Yes, because it provides specific examples of the materials that were distributed …
The reason given by choice A is true, because we really do get specific examples of the materials. And that's reasonable information to include at this point in the paragraph, so it's a logical revision to make. The reason given in choice B is false because a workbook and teacher instructions don't have anything to do with a community atmosphere, which comes instead from the on-air singalongs. Choice C's reason is false because there is no repeated information. Choice D is also false because MENC is not irrelevant. It was specifically mentioned earlier in the paragraph, and it's central to the discussion.

9. C) No, because the underlined portion provides a relevant elaboration …
In choice A, it's not extraneous information because it directly relates to the point about sleep deprivation and safety. Choice B is false because it's not repeating information that was already provided. Choice D gives a false reason because those are industries in which sleep deprivation could present a risk to others, not industries with the most sleep-deprived workers. Choice C gives us a true and relevant reason, and a good basis for keeping the underlined bit.

10. C) Deleted, because it introduces information that is only loosely related to Falkowski.
The reason given by choice A is false because the underlined sentence has nothing to do with Falkowski's accomplishments. The reason given in choice B is slightly trickier but also false because it's not clear that Falkowski chose to live in Huntsville specifically *because* Alabama was the center of many civil rights activities. Perhaps she ended up there for other reasons. Choice C gives us an accurate statement—the underlined sentence doesn't relate to Falkowski directly. And since the main focus of the paragraph is on her accomplishments, choice C gives us a good reason to get rid of the sentence. Choice D is true but irrelevant. There's no reason this paragraph should be making a list of all the locations that were associated with the civil rights movement.

11. B) Kept, because it adds validity to the claim that Gibson was a successful athlete.
We definitely do have a claim that Gibson was a successful athlete. The passages calls him *great* and mentions his *early success*. And if people thought he was better than the great Babe Ruth, then there is some validity to that claim. So choice B is both true and relevant, and it gives us a good reason to keep the underlined bit. Choice A is false because *some said* sounds more like an anecdote or hearsay, not hardcore research. And this sentence is more focused on Gibson's life story, not on Sonenberg's authorship. Choice C is true but irrelevant. Who cares about the exact number of people who thought he was great? Choice D is definitely false because the underlined portion reinforces, not weakens, the main idea of the paragraph.

12. B) Kept, because it effectively sets up the information presented in the following sentences.
Do astronomers *really* no longer make unaided visual observations? That seems unlikely, and anyway the paragraph never said that, so choice A is false. In choice C, the reason is false because the underlined sentence reinforces, not weakens, the paragraph's main argument. Choice D is true but irrelevant. Perhaps photographic film does have some disadvantages, but the focus here is explaining one of the creative solutions to the problem of magnification and how exactly it works. If the author wants to discuss downsides, that can be done elsewhere. Choice B is true and relevant. The underlined portion introduces the idea that observations of faint objects can be made over a very long time, and the following sentences explain the details of how that process works.

13. B) Yes, because it introduces a detail that is further developed in the paragraph.
Choices C and D give us false reasons. Polymerase is not irrelevant, and it's definitely related to genetic material. Choices A and B give reasons that are more worth considering, so let's compare them. Is does the revision give a *detail* or a *main idea*? The main focus here is the quest by scientists to figure out the chicken-and-egg problem of DNA and enzymes. The fact that polymerase is an enzyme that reads off DNA is important, but it's not the main idea, so the reason in choice B is the winner.

14. A) Yes, because it effectively introduces the explanation of an important term.
Choice B gives a false reason because the proposed sentence simply defines "depth of field." It doesn't say anything about Hine. Choice C's reason is false because the entire following discussion is about depth of field, so the idea is certainly not unrelated. The new sentence does not repeat anything that was already stated, so choice D is false. Choice A works. The following sentences definitely explain depth of field and why it was an important aspect of Hine's work. The new sentence provides an effective introduction, so it makes sense to add it.

15. D) No, because it interrupts the narrative sequence detailing the optical illusion in the video.
The reason in choice A is false because there is no comparison to other satellites. It's debatable whether the reason in choice B is true, but the reason the SDO recorded the video is out of place in the middle of an explanation of the optical illusion. So it would be a bad idea to make this addition here. Choice C is true but irrelevant. Again, there's no reason we should explain how the solar atmosphere can affect the Earth in the middle of a story about an optical illusion. That's what choice D has been trying to tell you all along!

16. A) Yes, because it introduces a contrast that is completed in the following sentence.
Choice A gives a true and relevant reason. On one side of the contrast, we have low usage of ZIP codes and slow mail delivery. On the other side, we have rising usage and faster delivery. That's logical and on topic, so it makes sense to add the new sentence. Choice B is false because the new sentence tells us that people didn't use the code, but not the reason. Choices C and D are false because the new information is certainly relevant and it doesn't contradict anything else in the passage.

17. C) Deleted, because it merely repeats an idea stated earlier in the paragraph.
In the first sentence, we learn that employers are required to protect workers from hazards and unhealthy exposures at work. In the underlined sentence, we're told that businesses must provide protections against workplace hazards and health risks. That's the same thing! In the first sentence, we learn that TWH is a way for organizations to "do more." In the underlined sentence, we hear that TWH initiatives are "in addition" to the required stuff. That's also repetitive. This paragraph is already boring enough—nobody wants to read it twice, so it's best to delete the repetitive sentence. Choice A is false because there is no new information. Choice B is false because the paragraph

doesn't say what an employer's *main* responsibility is, and we get no clarification here. Choice D is false because the underlined information, while repetitive, is not irrelevant.

18. C) Deleted, because it blurs the focus of the paragraph by introducing extraneous information. The focus of the discussion is the idea that people want different workplace options to accommodate different working styles. Productivity is off topic, so choice C is true and relevant. Another reason to get rid of the underlined sentence is that it interrupts the contrast set up by the sentences before and after it. *Some people find … Others perform …* is a logical structure that works well and shouldn't be blurred by going off on a tangent about music. Choice A is out because the focus of this paragraph is not about giving advice for choosing a productive working environment. Choice B gives a false reason because the main effect of the underlined sentence is decreased coherence, not increased credibility. As far as choice D, a statement that would truly undermine the claim that some people enjoy listening to music as they work would be something showing that *nobody* enjoys listening to music at work. Because that's not what the underlined sentence says, the reason in choice D is false.

19. B) Kept, because it provides an effective transition to the discussion of Lowe's later pursuits. In choice A, are there really any "common misconceptions" about Thaddeus Lowe? Had *you* ever heard of the guy before reading this fascinating story? Choice C is also false because the idea that Lowe was motivated by scientific curiosity is pretty central to the paragraph—we learn about two of his interests and how he pursued them. Choice D gives a false reason because the underlined sentence doesn't disrupt the logical sequence. It actually fits in perfectly. It provides an effective transition from the balloon discussion to the ice discussion.

20. C) Deleted, because it contains information that interrupts the discussion of recharging fuel cells. The reason given in choice C is true and relevant. The sentences before and after the underlined sentence are about the spent fuel, but the underlined sentence is about generating hydrogen in the first place, so it's definitely an interruption. And that's a good reason to delete it. In choice A, the distinction is off topic, not "important." Choice B is also false because the passage is not about helping readers understand how electric vehicles work. And choice D gives a false reason because the underlined sentence does not contradict the idea that there are challenges related to storing hydrogen and recharging the fuel cells.

Practice Question Set: Figures & Tables　　　　　　page 224

1. B) 2014,
   The first year of major decline is this data point. That's in 2014.

2. B) six thousand
   The number of members bottomed out (reached a minimum) at this data point in 2018. That's just over six thousand active members.

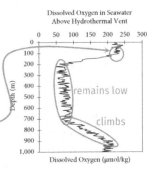

Dissolved Oxygen in Seawater
Above Hydrothermal Vent

3. A) NO CHANGE
    You have to be careful with how you read this figure. It's best to follow the trendline from top to bottom, as if you're descending through the ocean. As you go from top to bottom, values to the left represent lower amounts of dissolved oxygen, and values to the right represent greater dissolved oxygen. For this question, as we move deeper into the ocean, the dissolved oxygen first begins to drop rapidly (move left) at this point, which is at a depth of 100 m.

4. D) remained relatively low
    From a depth of 200 m to 700 m (a 500 m range), the dissolved oxygen remains low. It doesn't climb above 100 µmol/kg again until we go deeper than 700 m, so choice A is wrong. There is some noise in the data, but the levels stay firmly in the range of 50-100 µmol/kg, so *fluctuated wildly* in choice B is too extreme. The levels don't drop below 50 µmol/kg, and they even seem to rise slightly, so choice C is wrong too.

5. D) gains of 5 percent to 32
    This question asks about what Hodges found among *all subjects*, so make sure you're looking only at the rightmost column, which gives the results for all subjects. In that column, there are only positive numbers (gains) listed, and the range is from 5 percent to 32 percent.

Percent Change in Performance on a
Memory Task According to Sleep Patterns
and Activities Prior to the Task

	Subjects who slept less than 7 hours	Subjects who slept 7 or more hours	All subjects
No exercise or meditation (control group)	—	—	—
20 minutes moderate exercise only	–6%	12%	5%
20 minutes meditation only	9%	34%	24%
40 minutes, divided evenly between moderate exercise and meditation	–2%	38%	22%
40 minutes, divided between moderate exercise and meditation according to subject's preference	12%	46%	32%

6. B) were allowed to choose how to divide 40 minutes between meditation and moderate exercise.
    Find 46 percent on the table. It's in the column for subjects who slept 7 or more hours, as the passage says, and the bottom row. The bottom row is for subjects whose activity before the task was "40 minutes, divided between moderate exercise and meditation according to subject's preference," so you need a choice that correctly matches this condition. Choice B paraphrases the information somewhat, but it means the same thing. If subjects "were allowed to choose how to divide" the 40 minutes, then the 40 minutes were divided "according to the subject's preference."

7. C) the forestation process corresponded to the climate transformation.
    Earlier in the passage, we learn Park's hypothesis: the desert must have transformed into a forest over the period from fifteen thousand years ago to five thousand years ago. The graph shows that the region went from very little pine pollen in the sediment to a lot, so it sounds like she was right. Choice A is wrong because the graph is in agreement with her hypothesis. Choice B is wrong because we know that there is a forest there now (pine trees are commonly found in the region) and it looks as if the trees have been there for quite a while now—the pollen levels were already high 6,000 years ago. Choice D is wrong because there is no regularly repeating pattern.

Pine Pollen Content
in Sedimentary Layers

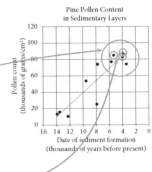

8. D) three of the five
    First, find the data points from less than six thousand years ago (to the right of the "6" line). There are five of them. Next, count how many of those five showed a pollen count of over 80,000 grains per square centimeter. That's three of the points.

9.   D) has changed over time

Check out the trends for the different types of physicians. Oncologists have increased a lot, from 16 to 70, but plastic surgeons have dropped from 42 to 24. The other two categories have changed, but not by much. They haven't all decreased, so choice A is wrong, and they haven't all stayed constant, so choice B is wrong too. Varying in lockstep would mean that they all change in the same way at the same time, and that didn't happen either, so choice C is out. Choice D is the best.

10.   C) oncologists reached a high of 70

Remember to read the entire sentence! The information after the underlined portion makes a big difference in this case. We need a number that's true *in 2020*. That rules out choice B because there were more oncologists than cardiologists in 2020. And it also rules out choice D because there were only 9 occupational medicine folks in 2020. We also need a number that is reached *after years of steady increases*. That rules out choice A because the number of plastic surgeons has been generally decreasing since 1960. Choice C accurately describes what has been happening with the oncologists.

11.   B) only 7 percent of respondents aged 25-40 said the same about their peers.

Not only do you need accurate information from the graph, but you also need to "support the claim made in the preceding sentence." So what is that claim? The previous sentence says there is a clear generational divide in the popularity of subscriptions, so you need to reinforce that idea by showing a difference between the generations. This sentence tells us that a *large* segment of the older generation believes that subscriptions are not popular in their age group. A great way to illustrate a contrast would be to show that a *small* segment of the younger generation believes that subscriptions are not popular in their age group. That's what choice B gives us. Choice A is wrong because, while it is accurate information, it refers to the same older generation—we don't learn about a generational divide. Choice C is inaccurate. The 45 on the tallest bar refers to 45 percent, not 45 services. Choice D is also inaccurate in the same way. 31 is again a percentage, not a number of subscription purchases.

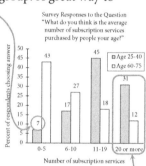

12.   A) NO CHANGE

The last part of the sentence tells us that we need accurate information about the category of subscribing to an average of *20 or more services*. On the graph, that's the rightmost pair of bars. According to the key, the gray bar corresponds to 31 percent of the younger demographic, so that's why choice A is the best. Choices B and D refer to the wrong category (11-19 services). Choice C has the right percentage but the wrong demographic—the white bar refers to the older group.

13.   A) NO CHANGE

You need a choice that accurately describes where the study found population *increases*. Notice that all the squares are at values greater than zero, while all the triangles are at values less than zero. This means the populations all increased in the location instituting dark-sky ordinances, and not at the other location. Choice B is wrong because the populations did not increase in both locations. Choice C is wrong because the populations increased for *all* bird populations in the place with the new laws. Choice D gets the locations backwards.

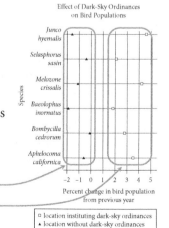

14. C) 3 percent or greater increase

Check out the three populations mentioned in the sentence. They have population increases of 4.6 percent, 4.2 percent, and 3.5 percent, respectively. So choice D is inaccurate because they are not all greater than 4 percent. Choice B is inaccurate because they are increases, not decreases. So why not choice A? Notice that the question asks you to *emphasize* the benefit. It's true that all the numbers are above 1 percent, but that number undersells the size of the effect. The benefit sounds more impressive if you say that all the populations saw an increase of more than 3 percent.

15. D) 79,598

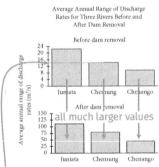

Number of bachelor's degrees conferred by postsecondary institutions in STEM fields of study, 2017–18 academic year

Field of study	Number of bachelor's degrees conferred
Engineering	121,956
Biological and biomedical sciences	118,663
Computer and information sciences	79,598
Physical sciences and science technologies	31,542
Mathematics and statistics	25,256
Engineering technologies	18,727

This answer can simply be read right off the table. The sentence asks for the number of degrees in computer and information sciences. That's the third row of data.

16. A) NO CHANGE

These choices are all a little different, so you have to examine each one. Choice A is correct because it matches the first row of data, and engineering really is the biggest number. Choice B mentions the previous year, but the table only has data for one academic year, so you can't make that statement. Choice C is inaccurate because one STEM field, engineering technologies, had less than 20,000 degrees awarded. Choice D makes a prediction of the future, which is not supported by anything in the table.

17. C) much larger than

Look at each river and compare its values before and after dam removal. Be sure to notice the different axis scales for each graph. For each river, the range is much larger after dam removal. For example, the Juniata river goes from 23 before removal to 114 after. That's definitely not the same or below, so B and D are wrong, and it's much more than just double, so A is wrong as well.

18. B) 14 m³/s

Just read this value right off the graph. We need the Chemung River (the middle bar) and we need before dam removal (the top graph). That's about 14 m³/s.

19. B) in commercial tomatoes is 39 mm²

The sentence is looking for a value for disease severity, so first make sure you're looking at the right bars. Focus on the dark gray ones. After that, you just need an accurate match between the numerical value and the strain. Choice B gets it right.

20. C) disease severity in wild and heirloom tomatoes

There are two ways to get this question right. One is to look at the information in the paragraph's final sentence. It makes the point that more domestication leads to worse disease susceptibility. Since the previous sentence showed that commercial tomatoes have a certain level of disease severity, a good way to strengthen the comparison would be to show that less domesticated tomatoes have *less* disease severity. Perhaps the easier approach is to look at the values given after the underlined portion: 15 mm² and 13 mm². Because plant height is measured in cm and fruit yield is measured in kg, these numbers cannot correspond to those characteristics. That knocks out choices A, B and D. Square millimeters has to be disease severity. Choice C both makes logical sense and presents accurate numbers from the graph, so that's our winner.

1. Verb tense. All the verbs are in different tenses.
Choice B is correct. Because the story happened in 2013, the simple past tense is appropriate.

2. Sentence structure. All the wrong answers have clause or phrase problems.
Choice A is correct. The relative pronoun *who* appropriately connects the clause before the comma with the clause after.

3. Sentence structure. Choice A has too many conjunctions.
Punctuation. Choice C has a bad semicolon.
Transition words. Choice B has an illogical transition word.
Choice D is correct. *Perhaps* is a logical fit because we're talking about a hypothetical situation.

4. Punctuation.
Choice B is correct. The stuff before the colon in choices A and D cannot stand alone. Choice C inserts an illegal comma between the preposition *to* and its object. The other comma in C is also unnecessary.

5. Parallelism. There is a list of three things between the dashes, and each should start with the name of a tool.
Redundancy / concision. The wrong choices are unnecessarily wordy.
Choice D is correct.

6. Pronouns. *He or she* is always wrong. The antecedent is the plural *people*.
Choice B is correct because it uses the plural pronoun *they*. The sentence is not written in the first person, so *we* in choice C is inappropriate.

7. Verb agreement. Choices A and C are in the same tense but have different number. The subject is the plural noun *companies*.
Choice C is correct because it uses the plural verb *operate*.

8. Introductory modifiers. The noun immediately after the comma must be whoever is "working in an area of journalism..." Choice B fails because it's a possessive.
Choice D is correct because it puts the financial reporters next to the modifier.

9. Redundancy / concision.
Choice A is correct. In B, *grown* means the same as *expanded*. In C, *field of research* is redundant because the sentence already said *research field*. In choice D, *dramatically* and *considerably* mean the same thing.

10. Logical comparisons. The proper comparison here is between one animal and other animals, not between one type of camouflage and another.
Choice D is correct. The other choices all refer to camouflage, not an animal.

11. Transition words.
Choice A is correct. There is a contrast between an unfamiliar poet and a widely recognized poet.

12. Parallelism. With the correlative conjunction *not only ... but also*, we need the right words for the conjunction, and we need parallelism between the things joined by the conjunction. The first thing is *the rebirth*. The second thing is *the restoration*. Repeating *led to* (as in choice D) breaks the parallelism.
Word choice. *But also* are the required words when a sentence has *not only*.
Choice B is correct.

About the Author

David Lynch is the founder and lead instructor at StudyLark. With 20 years of tutoring experience and perfect scores on the SAT, ACT, LSAT, GMAT, and GRE tests, David has earned a reputation as a true authority on standardized tests. David has helped tens of thousands of students and written curricula and teaching materials for local and national test preparation organizations. As part of his research-based approach, he has performed a thorough analysis of every test question administered this century.

David earned a B.S. in chemical engineering from Cornell University and an M.S. in agricultural and environmental chemistry from the University of California. When he is not living and breathing test prep, he performs locally with his band. He lives outside Philadelphia with his wife and two daughters.

www.StudyLark.com